THE HAND

BEHIND THE MOUSE

According to aerodynamics,
the bumblebee cannot possibly fly.

—Ub Iwerks

THE HAND
BEHIND THE MOUSE

An Intimate Biography of the Man
Walt Disney Called "The Greatest
Animator in the World"

LESLIE IWERKS and
JOHN KENWORTHY

NEW YORK

Thanks to:

Roy Disney for shining the spotlight on Ub and bringing this book to fruition.
Don Iwerks for his unending support from day one of this long journey.
Bob Broughton for his constant encouragement.
Other friends who have been extremely supportive
and giving of their time, energy, and resources:
Mark Kausler, Don Peri, Joe Adamson, Leonard Maltin, Russell Merritt,
Marvin Iwerks, Fred Lee, The Walt Disney Archives; Dave Smith;
Becky Klein; Robert Tieman, Scott MacQueen, John Iwerks, Betty Iwerks,
Mike Glad, Chuck Jones, Ed Friedman, LeRoy Richardson, Frank Thomas,
Ollie Johnston, John Lasseter, Richard Edlund, Marc and Alice Davis,
John Hench, Virginia Davis McGhee, Eileen Powers George, Tippi Hedren,
Virginia Sommersfield, Bill Cottrell, Friz Freleng, Ruthie Tompson,
Bill Justice, Ken O'Conner, Bob Jackman, Dick Grills, Butch Rigby.
Thank you to the following organizations and research facilities:
The Walt Disney Archives,
Academy Library of Motion Picture Studies,
The Kansas City Central Library.

—L.I.

For Denise and my three boys—Nathan, Dylan and Ian—
may you forever be challenged by the opportunities of the moment
and may you always find the innovation within that will allow all your
bumblebees to fly unfettered into the open sky.

—J.K.

For information address
Disney Editions
114 Fifth Avenue
New York, New York 10011-5690.

Library of Congress Cataloging-in-Publication Data on file.
ISBN 0-7868-5320-4

Printed in the United States of America
First Edition
1 3 5 7 9 10 8 6 4 2

Visit www.disneybooks.com

Contents

Introduction vi

1 Kansas City: Alliances and Education 1

2 Laugh-O-gram 15

3 Ubbe in Cartoonland 26

4 Oswald the Lucky Rabbit 41

5 The Mouse 53

6 Mickey's World 72

7 A New Beginning 85

8 The Greatest Staff 105

9 Classics in Color 121

10 Journeyman .138

11 The Return .145

12 Animating Life 166

13 Ubbeland 178

14 Elephants, Dogs, and the Birds 192

15 Grand Finale 209

Glossary 230

Bibliography 233

Index 239

Introduction

For decades, Ub Iwerks has been the Great Footnote in animation history: the man who helped Walt Disney launch Mickey Mouse and the Silly Symphonies and who then went on to open his own studio, before returning to Disney and working behind the scenes in special effects for the rest of his career.

As this book eloquently proves, there is much more to the story than that.

Truth is in the details, and that is the strength of this volume. To cite just one prominent example, there are facets of Iwerks's relationship with Walt and Roy Disney that have never been revealed before. I thought I knew all there was to know about their notorious split, when the Disney brothers felt abandoned by a trusted colleague, but this book told me much more about the story—as seen from both sides.

Ub has been described by other authors (myself included) in accurate but general terms. This book allows us to know him better, to understand not only his fascination for all things mechanical but his quiet sense of humor, and his inherent modesty. The authors paint a rich portrait of the man, and enable us to understand some crucial career decisions he made at different stages of his life.

For animation aficionados, there is much to be learned about Ub's decade away from Disney: the trials and tribulations of being an independent producer, the creation of Flip the Frog and Willie Whopper, and the details of how Ub came to subcontract work from Warner Brothers, Leon Schlesinger and Columbia's Charles Mintz.

Finally, the authors give us a sense of Iwerks's contributions to Disney films of the 1940s, '50s, and '60s, along with his prominent status at the Burbank studio. The universal respect he commanded from colleagues young and old says a lot about the nature of the man.

The bonus for film buffs is learning about Iwerks's contributions to Alfred Hitchcock's *The Birds*, and to visual effects in general. Few know that Ub was the first to devise the process known as wet-gate printing, to eliminate scratches from film; or that he developed the ultimate formula for making animated rainfall look realistic.

Ub Iwerks was never one to seek the spotlight, but now, at the dawn of the twenty-first century, it's his turn to take center stage. He couldn't have asked for a better team to tell his story than John Kenworthy and his own granddaughter, Leslie Iwerks. Leslie, having produced a feature–length documentary about her grandfather for Walt Disney Pictures in 1999, now shares details that have never before come to light.

Ub might have ducked such attention, but I think the book you hold in your hands would have made him proud.

—Leonard Maltin

chapter 1

Kansas City: Alliances and Education

The interesting background and diverse personal traits that Ub Iwerks possessed were many, but the people who knew him well—including his family—were rarely able to break through the shield that separated his present thoughts from those of the past. By all accounts, he was not a man of nostalgia; he rarely spoke of his own history. He was a visionary, and like most visionaries, his focus was always on the future. For this reason, Ub's personal accounts of his childhood are brief. Still, whether he realized it or not, his family background determined to a large extent who he became and the contributions he made to the world.

Amid the lowland marshes that dot the northwestern coast of Germany, six miles east of the city of Uttum in the province of Ostfriesland lies the village of Abbingwehr. Like much of Ostfriesland—and its western counterpart, Friesland, in neighboring Holland—the area surrounding Abbingwehr is below sea level. The village itself is built upon mounds of earth (called "polders" in the native Frisian language) raised above the marshland. Much of the economy of the region revolves around the limited agriculture that can be supported by its poor soil conditions. The primary source of revenue for Ostfriesland is grazing cattle.

On April 29, 1844, Eert Ubbén Iwwerks was born into this harsh environment. He was the second child of Ubbe Reemt and Maike Iwwerks. Their first child, Grietjke, was born mentally retarded. Eert was raised in Abbingwehr, but on April 7, 1869, at the age of 24, he immigrated to the United States, where he joined family members who had settled in Freeport, Illinois, the prior year. Various members of the Iwwerks clan made homestead claims on South Dakota land in 1881, but Eert did not follow them. He migrated instead to Decorah, Iowa, where he met and courted a young, educated woman by the name of Deborah Mayo Pierce. They were married on August 10, 1880. Eert and his bride moved from Iowa to Kansas City, Missouri, where he would live for the rest of his life.

The couple had two children, Eert Ubben and Lillian Pierce, but shortly after Lillian's birth in 1886, Eert left Deborah to care for the two small children alone. This was only the first of what was to be a series of divorces for Eert.

Four years later he married Carolyn Lehman Miller. Deborah Mae Iwwerks was born in January 1892. Shortly after, Carolyn left Eert and reconciled with her first husband.

In 1899, Eert tried matrimony for a third time. At the age of fifty-seven, he married Laura May Wagner, who was twenty years his junior. Their son, Ubbe Eert Iwwerks, was born on March 24, 1901. Ubbe was born into an era in which innovation and technology would surround him. His childhood would be only slightly more stable than that of his half-brother and half-sisters. Turmoil was common in the Iwwerks household as Eert's restlessness played havoc with family harmony.

During Ubbe's childhood, Eert worked primarily as a barber, but he supplemented the family's income with other ventures. In 1902, he was listed as the Financial Corresponding Secretary for the Kansas City Fancy Poultry Breeders' Association.

For four years, Eert worked as a photographer and maintained his own studio. Young Ubbe was drawn to his father's artistic side. The elder Iwwerks was reported to be a talented painter and inventor. Young Ubbe learned to draw and paint with equal facility. His father's inventions of phonographic systems and recording devices also made an early and lasting impression. It was the dawn of the twentieth century; art and technology were beginning to merge in new and increasingly exciting ways. Eert introduced his son to the astonishing new world of film.

After graduating from Ashland Grammar School, Ubbe enrolled at Northeast High School where he excelled in formal art classes. Before he finished his first year of high school, however, he arrived home one afternoon to find his father had packed up and gone. The sudden departure left Laura May and Ubbe in despair. Very little information exists as to why Eert left the family, but it is surmised he left for another woman. It was reported that at a family reunion in 1925, Eert showed up with a new wife.

The loss of Eert was a devastating blow to both wife and son. Forced to drop out of high school, Ubbe became the sole provider for his mother. He would never speak of or to his father again. In 1915, Ubbe sought steady employment.

Between 1900 and 1910, Kansas City's population had increased by 50 percent. The city began to outgrow its old boundaries, evolving from the livestock town it had been at the turn of the century into a thriving twentieth-century industrial city.

By 1907, an energetic young developer named J. C. Nichols was laying the infrastructure for much of the city's future expansion. City roads, viaducts, bridges, tract homes, railroads, and a new Union Station were built. A wealthy industrialist named Colonel Thomas Swope purchased 1,334 acres of pasture and woodlands to create the city's largest recreational park. Progressive women of Kansas City organized. They fought for milk inspection and playgrounds and the addition of kindergartens and manual training to the Kansas City School system. Progress was everywhere.

By 1915, the city's expanding industrial and financial sectors were opening up many jobs for entry-level workers. Ubbe Iwwerks took first an apprentice position and then a full-time job at the Union Bank Note Company of Kansas City. A year later, he moved to Scotland, Arkansas, to work on a farm.

In September 1919, at the age of eighteen, Ubbe returned to

Kansas City where—against his mother's wishes—he sought his first job in the field of commercial art. Artistic jobs were seldom very well paid, but there was a growing demand for illustrators in advertising. Ubbe applied for a job at the Pesmen-Rubin Commercial Art Studio, a small advertising firm located in the Gray Advertising Building on the corner of 13th and Oak Streets. The firm was looking for young artists to design advertising layouts for local businesses. According to co-owner Louis Pesmen, from the very start Ubbe "was a fantastic lettering man, so Rubin and I hired him immediately." They paid Ubbe $60 a month to do lettering and airbrushing. He excelled at both. Soon he began to embellish relatively uninteresting farm implement catalog designs with cheerful barnyard animal caricatures and backgrounds.

Ubbe had been working for Pesmen-Rubin for a month when a young man named Walter Disney walked into the studio office seeking employment with an impressive portfolio of drawings. The seventeen-year-old Disney was hired immediately.

Young Walter had just returned from France, where he drove a Red Cross ambulance at the end of World War I. Although he had taken some fine art classes, he soon realized that commercial art was a different undertaking altogether. "When you go to art school, you work for perfection," Disney later recalled, "but in a commercial art shop you cut things out, and paste things over, and scratch around with a razor blade. I'd never done any of those things in art school. Those are timesaving tricks."

Working on several projects together, Ubbe shared some tricks of the trade with Walter. In short order, the two became fast friends. Ubbe was amused that Walter always used his own name to practice lettering. Most artists used the alphabet for practice, but Walter would try different approaches in designing his own name: Walter Disney, W. E. Disney, Walt Disney, Walter Elias Disney. Walter asked Ubbe which he preferred. "Walt Disney," Ubbe replied. Walt it was.

In December 1919, Walt Disney lost his job at Pesmen-Rubin. He found work as a mailman. A month later, after the Christmas rush,

Pesmen-Rubin reduced its staff again and Ubbe was laid off. The layoff was a devastating blow to the young artists, especially to Iwwerks, who was still supporting his increasingly difficult and demanding mother.

In January 1920, Iwwerks and Disney were still struggling to find work as artists. Short on prospects, they decided to go into business for themselves. The two friends pooled their meager resources together and created Iwwerks-Disney Commercial Artists. They initially wanted to call their venture Disney-Iwwerks, but agreed that it sounded too much like an eyeglass company.

Walt took a portfolio of samples to Al Carter, a Kansas City restaurant owner who had originated the "Sizzling Steak." Carter, a former neighbor of Walt's, now owned the *Restaurant News* newspaper. "My partner and I would like to handle your artwork," Disney told him.

"Sorry," Carter replied, "I don't have enough work to keep anybody busy."

"Just give us desk space and we'll do any artwork you have for free," Disney responded. "It won't cost you a penny and you'll be able to say the *Restaurant News* has an art department." Walt was a born salesman.

Carter looked through the artwork Walt had brought. He especially liked a caricature of Gloria Swanson that Walt had drawn. He agreed to provide Iwwerks-Disney Commercial Artists with a workroom—actually the spare office bathroom—in exchange for illustrations in his newspaper.

Iwwerks-Disney's first paying client was the *Leather Workers Journal*. The father of Walt Pfeiffer, a childhood friend of Disney's, was an officer with the leatherworkers labor union. Disney made a business call upon the elder Pfeiffer and agreed to create mastheads for the journal.

Another early project was creating the cover for an oil company's promotional prospectus, for which Ubbe drew an oil well that gushed $20 bills. In the first month, Iwwerks-Disney earned a respectable, if not earth-shattering, $135.

The excitement of success was short-lived, however. On January 29, 1920, Ubbe saw an advertisement in the Kansas City Star newspaper:

ARTIST
Cartoon and Wash Drawings
First Class Man Wanted
Steady, Kansas City Slide Company
1015 Central

The partners discussed the opportunity. They decided that Walt would apply for the position and Ubbe would stay and manage Iwwerks-Disney Commercial Artists. Walt impressed the head of the Kansas City Slide Company, A. Vern Cauger, who offered him a position for $40 per week.

Unfortunately, Ubbe was unable to sustain a steady income. His business acumen and sales abilities paled in comparison to his talents as an artist.

Meanwhile, the Kansas City Slide Company was expanding to larger, more accommodating facilities at 2449 Charlotte in downtown Kansas City. The name was changed to the Kansas City Film Ad Company. The new name reflected a growing enterprise for Cauger's artists, the creation of neatly lettered title cards for silent movies. Many local businesses found that advertising their products at the movies was a new and exciting marketing tool and Cauger capitalized on the popular trend with his "Film Ads."

In March of 1920, Ubbe initiated bankruptcy proceedings to put an official end to Iwwerks-Disney Commercial Artists. Walt Disney, knowing of Ubbe's plight, asked Vern Cauger if he'd be interested in hiring his friend. The expansion of the business meant that Cauger now had room on his staff for a young man with Ubbe's obvious talents.

When Ubbe joined the team, he was excited by the hustle and bustle of an active, successful graphics company. The Kansas City Film Ad Company also gave Ubbe his first exposure to the mysterious new world of animation production. The hum of projectors, the whir of

35mm film rewinding onto spindles, and the clicking of stop-motion cameras together made an exciting music. Experimentation was in the air.

Artists at the Kansas City Film Ad Company had just begun to embellish their titles with crudely animated cutout figures. Paper dolls with gawky, jointed arms and legs were filmed in stop-motion. The figures were pinned in one position, filmed, moved slightly, and filmed again. The animation was jerky at best.

Walt and Ubbe spent extra hours altering the paper cutouts to make them more flexible and able to move more fluidly on the screen. They devised a method of hiding the visible joints, thus vastly improving the appearance of the puppets.

At the Kansas City Public Library, they found several books on animation, the very first of their kind. They read them all. *How Motion Pictures Are Made,* published in 1918, contained a chapter called "The Making of an Animated Cartoon." *How to Draw for the Movies* by John Robert McCrory was published in Kansas City the same year. *Motion Picture Magazine* included an article by Bert Green that revealed the inner workings of the Moser Studio in 1919 and the 1920 *A Course in Motion Picture Photography* provided additional technical insight. But the most valuable books to Ubbe and Walt were Eadward Muybridge's classic books of photographs of human and animal motion and Edwin G. Lutz's *Animated Cartoons: How They Are Made, Their Origin and Development.* Muybridge had photographed people and animals running, walking, jumping, hopping. The photographs were taken a fraction of a second apart, giving a detailed representation of the cycles of living motion.

Muybridge's book had been used by biology students and art students alike to study in painstaking detail how human and animal forms move through space. It was an ideal primer for young animators. Walt and Ubbe made photostats of many sequences and kept them at their desks for reference.

E. G. Lutz, on the other hand, was to animation what Henry Ford was to the automobile industry. *Animated Cartoons* illustrated labor-saving devices to create a kind of assembly-line production method. The means often included cut-and-slash techniques (first developed by Raoul Barre), limited animation, and cycles. It was also filled with technical tips on how to animate perspective runs, peg registration, in-betweening, and even studio organization. Lutz wrote:

> Presuming then, that the scenario has been written, the chief animator first of all decides on the portraiture of the characters. He will proceed to make sketches of them as they look not only in front and profile views, but also as they appear from the back and three-quarters views. It is customary that these sketches—his models, and really the dramatis personae, be of the size they will have in the majority of the scenes.

Walt and Ubbe drank in the commonsense advice and adapted it to the projects they were working on. Together they devised ways to test and perfect new techniques.

Jimmy Lowerre, cameraman for the Kansas City Film Ad Company, showed them how to film in stop-motion. The process required two people. The cameraman turned the camera crank one revolution for each frame of film, maintaining a consistent speed throughout. The other person changed the drawings on the table beneath the camera.

Not satisfied with the two-person process, Ubbe began to study the camera and Lutz's book eagerly. Lutz explained:

> A motion picture camera of the most approved pattern is an exceedingly complicated and finely adjusted instrument. Its principle of operation can be understood easily if it is remembered that it is practically a snap-shot camera with the addition of a mechanism that turns a revolving shutter and moves a length of film across the exposure field, holds it there for an interval while the photographic impression is made, and then moves it away to continue the process until the desired length of film has been taken. This movement, driven by a hand-crank, is the same as that of a projector.

Tinkering with the camera during his off-hours, Ubbe came up with a solution to the problems of the manual-cranking process. He devised a motor drive with a telegraph-key switch that would automatically turn the crank on the camera, creating a consistent exposure. This allowed one person to perform the entire task while seated in front of the animation table. Ubbe had just streamlined a key part of A. Vern Cauger's production line. For Ubbe, this was just the beginning.

One of the key similarities between Iwwerks and Disney during these developmental years was their joint enthusiasm and appreciation for technology and tinkering. Disney, from the outset, was fascinated by how things worked and how machinery could be used for artistic purposes. Ubbe and Walt's similar Midwestern sense of humor, artistic talent, fascination with technology, and excitement about popular art fueled their inspiration in the animation field. They spent their spare time haunting movie theaters, reading humor magazines and attending popular vaudeville entertainments. They studied any available movie—live-action or animation—that they could afford to see. Ubbe studied the rubber-limbed characters of Paul Terry's Farmer Al Falfa series. Walt watched Charlie Chaplin create humor through character. Their schools were the theaters of Kansas City; their teachers were their fellow artists.

On one such educational excursion, Ubbe saw a cartoon that would change his life forever. The film was *Gertie the Dinosaur* by Winsor McCay. McCay had been a newspaper cartoonist for the *New York Herald*. His earlier animated efforts included the cartoons *Little Nemo in Slumberland*, which was based on his comic strip of the same name, and *Story of a Mosquito*, which was just that.

Gertie is a re-creation of McCay's classic vaudeville routine, which features a live-action McCay (actually life size on the big screen) talking to the audience and interacting with a cantankerous cartoon brontosaurus named Gertie.

The animated Gertie appears to follow each of McCay's commands dutifully. When he orders her to raise her foot, she complies. She even dances upon her two prodigious hind legs like a reptilian hula dancer. At one point, McCay tosses a live-action pumpkin to

Gertie, who gulps it down. She quenches her thirst by drinking a cartoon lake dry. The film closes with Gertie picking up the now animated McCay in her mouth.

Gertie the Dinosaur remains a revolutionary and remarkable film, even today, for its ability to generate emotional pathos from the simple animated line. The concept of combining live action and animation would become one of Ubbe's greatest fascinations.

Gertie, in fact, was not a true combination of live action and animation, but a smoothly executed synthesis of excellent staging and clever editing. At the J. R. Bray Studio in New York, animator Earl Hurd—who had patented the labor-saving cel animation process— took McCay's implied innovation of combining live action and animation and did it for real.

Bobby Bumps, an adaptation of R. F. Outcault's Buster Brown comic strip, was drawn on screen by the live-action hand of Hurd. In short pants and cap, Bobby was an all-American boy with an all-American dog, Fido. The addition of Earl Hurd's hand in the live-action sequences bordered on the revolutionary.

Also in New York, two brothers, Max and Dave Fleischer, innovated even further. Ko-ko the Clown, star of their *Out of the Inkwell* series, would begin each cartoon in a manner similar to Bobby Bumps. Ko-ko would come to life by being drawn out of an inkwell onto Max Fleischer's drawing table. Ko-ko's cartoon form would then interact seamlessly with the live-action Fleischer. Unlike the godlike hand of Earl Hurd, Fleischer acted as both on-screen creator and antagonist for the sympathetic clown. He interacted with his creation. Ko-ko rarely stayed in the live-action world long, however, for it was too costly and time consuming. He would spend the majority of each episode in the more comfortable environs of an animated world.

Aside from the combination of live action and animation, the Fleischer brothers patented the rotoscoping techniques used in *Out of the Inkwell*. Max Fleischer would initiate the process by filming brother Dave, costumed as Ko-ko. Dave acted the various scenes on film, whereupon they would then be projected back onto the drawing board frame by frame, allowing the animators to model the motion. The rotoscoping process allowed them to achieve fluid human movement, yet maintained the freedom to add requisite cartoony touches. While other cartoon characters plodded about aimlessly—or remained static on screen—Ko-ko lived and seemingly breathed.

The Fleischers' rotoscoping technique and Ubbe and Walt's process of flipping photocopies of pages from Muybridge's book were two separate methods of resolving the issue of creating realistic movement. Both methods allowed the animators to focus on developing memorable characters.

Krazy Kat and Felix the Cat cartoons frequently played in Kansas City theaters. Ubbe and Walt saw them all. Due to low budgets and a premium on speed, the Krazy Kat animators were forced to use repeated action and shortcuts at the expense of storytelling. The fastest of the Krazy Kat artists was animator William C. Nolan. Bill Nolan at one point was reputed to be able to complete as many as six hundred drawings a day—a phenomenal rate.

Felix the Cat was by far the more successful of the two jet-black felines. Felix was the creation of animator Otto Messmer who, along with producer-director Pat Sullivan, defined Felix's character as a mischievous, always creative roustabout. A unique feature of Felix the Cat is that he set the standard for animated figures (cats in particular) in the use, reuse, and misuse of their own body parts. Felix often utilized his tail in anthropomorphic ways. His tail became a prop that was not all that far removed from Chaplin's cane or Harpo Marx's coat.

Ubbe and Walt continued to practice and study the art of animation with a near religious fervor. Their experimentation, coupled with Ubbe's innate technical brilliance, allowed them to try the same things that they had seen McCay, Hurd, and the Fleischers do so magnificently. Walt came up with the idea of creating short animated advertisements mixed with topical local humor of the day. His hope was to sell the ads to the local Newman Theater to be shown with the regular "News and Views" program that incorporated newsreels, vaudeville acts, and comedy shorts. After successfully convincing Cauger at the Film Ad Company to lend him a company movie camera, Walt set up shop with his older brother Roy in the garage of the Disney family home at 3028 Bellefontaine. Moonlighting, Walt, Roy, and Ubbe began work on a demo reel they hoped would sell the idea.

Walt Disney, cartoonist, makes his first on-screen appearance in the demo reel. In visor and vest, and with pipe clenched firmly between his teeth, Disney is seen intently working at his drawing board. The camera cuts to Disney's hand feverishly drawing a cartoon figure.

It was not easy to achieve the illusion, since Walt's hand would not fit between the camera and the drawing paper while remaining in focus. To solve this problem, Ubbe borrowed a trick previously used by animators Earl Hurd and Max Fleischer, which was to take a photograph of Walt's hand and use the print to simulate the lightning-fast artist at work. The photograph of Walt's hand was flat and could be photographed at the same level and resolution as the drawings.

Before long, the three-hundred-foot comedy reel was completed. Walt took the finished product to Milton Feld, the manager of the Frank Newman Theater chain in downtown Kansas City (Feld later went on to great acclaim as a circus promoter). Impressed by the freshness of the cartoon, Feld and Newman ordered a series of short joke films from the Kansas City Film Ad Service. He paid thirty cents a foot for one film each week. It wasn't a large sum, but it was encouragement nonetheless. The series of films were to be called the "Newman Laugh-O-grams." A fresh mix of local humor and advertising, Kansas City audiences enjoyed the novelty of the silent cartoons.

One Newman Laugh-O-gram features an animated birthday cake for the Newman Theater out of which pop various motion-picture stars. Another cartoon features a little professor chiding theatergoers not to talk aloud with the titles. If they persist, a Rube Goldberg–like invention kicks the patrons out of their seats.

Walt and Ubbe's next project was a series of short films illuminating the plight of those reliant upon Kansas City's inefficient public transportation system. In one film, a flower design on a young woman's stockings begins to grow as she waits for a street car. By the time the car arrives, the unfortunate lass is surrounded by flowers. In another, a young man's youthful appearance metamorphoses into that of an old man with a flowing white beard before his street car finally arrives.

Still another series of Newman Laugh-O-grams pokes fun at Kansas City's serious pothole problem. Entire vehicles vanish into potholes never to be seen again. In another notable cartoon, a title card titillatingly reads, "Kansas City girls are rolling their own now." It went on to explain, "Ladies stockings come so high now, they have to roll them down at the top." At the bottom of the screen the advertiser is recognized: "As seen at Petticoat Lane." The lightning hand draws a shapely leg to demonstrate the thigh-high hosiery rolled down at the top. On either side of the stockings, the hand draws a female figure clad only in a filigreed petticoat. It turns out that the stockings the audience has been admiring are actually worn by mannequins on display in the Petticoat Lane shop window. Signs announce that there are specials on both the petticoats and hose.

The Kansas City girls in the petticoats—unlike most cartoon caricatures—were rendered realistically. Often Walt and Ubbe would use local models. One of their favorite models was a beautiful young woman from Texas named Lucille LeSueur. Aside from modeling, LeSueur danced in local theatrical productions under the stage name of Billie Cassin. One day when Ubbe needed a model to sit for him for a commercial project, he contacted the modeling agency to request LeSueur. Ubbe was saddened to learn that LeSueur had left Kansas City to try to make it big in New York City.

Ubbe later learned that she had done just that. Lovely Lucille LeSueur from Kansas City, Missouri, had been discovered while dancing on Broadway. She was signed to dance in MGM musicals and eventually stepped forward out of the chorus line to land leading roles in motion pictures. When she did, she did so under yet another pseudonym. Lucille LeSueur, a.k.a. Billie Cassin, would legally change her name to Joan Crawford.

The political scene in Kansas City had stars of its own. Boss politics had been a part of the fabric of Kansas City since the turn of the century. With eighteen years as an alderman, Boss James Pendergast controlled the city through its media, primarily William Rockhill Nelson's *Kansas City Star* and its radio station affiliates. The scandalous politicos of city government provided ample material for Walt and Ubbe to satirize.

One politically charged Laugh-O-gram focused on the corruption that was perceived to be rampant within the Kansas City police department. In "Kansas City Spring Clean Up," a line of identically rendered policemen march woodenly into a police station. Great commotion occurs within the station—all off camera. Flying clothing and the repeated words, "Your *[sic]* fired!" are the only clues that mayhem reigns within the station. Eventually, the policemen march back again in a single line, this time with bandages and bruises marking the offstage brawl. A police sergeant reaches around the open door of the station and hangs up a sign, COPS WANTED!

Walt and Ubbe were justifiably proud of these efforts. Walt felt that they could now create a legitimate animated series not unlike the Fleischer brothers' work in New York. In their off-hours, they began to work on an animated fairy tale. Walt suggested the series to Vern Cauger, head of the Kansas City Film Ad Service. Cauger showed little interest in the new series; he was pleased with his advertisement business just the way it was. If Walt wanted to succeed with a new fairy-tale series, he would have to go into business for himself. Walt and Ubbe had been down this path before with very limited success, but they decided to try again. Their relentless enthusiasm ensured that their next project could be their best. Optimists to the core, they believed that success was just around the corner.

chapter 2

Laugh-O-gram

Walt Disney was so certain of the new venture's success, he quit his job at the Kansas City Film Ad Service (which had changed its name to United Film Ad Service). On May 23, 1922, he incorporated his new company, Laugh-O-gram Films, with an initial investment of $15,000. The money came from a loyal group of friends and supporters who contributed between $250 and $500, believing in the imminent success of the enterprising young Disney. Among these early supporters were a local doctor named John Cowles and his wife, Minnie, who provided a large portion of the initial investment.

Disney officially set up shop at 1127 East 31st Street on the second floor of the McConahay office building in Kansas City. Disney was eventually able to hire a small staff. Joining Walt were Hugh Harman, Rudolph Ising, Carman "Max" Maxwell, Otto Walliman, Lorey Tague, Aletha Reynolds, Walt Pfeiffer, Red Lyon, office manager Adolph Kloepper, and salesman Leslie Mace. Notable among those not present, however, was Ubbe Iwwerks.

Ubbe realized that cartoons were transforming before him. The subject and story matter that Disney was proposing would move the Laugh-O-gram concept out of the novelty-act arena into a fully realized use of the medium of film. Walt Disney was maturing into a charismatic leader and visionary whose powers of persuasion were not lost on Ubbe. Had it not been for his financial commitments to his mother, he would have preferred to join Walt, but this time he had to be sure. He returned to the Film Ad Service, where a steady income was assured.

Walt's skeleton crew began production on an updated version of *Little Red Riding Hood*. During this time, the fledgling animators learned that telling a story differed greatly from the process of spinning gags. On Disney's watch, the artists honed their craft and began to perfect their art form. While *Little Red Riding Hood* was underway, Walt and crew began drafting out the ideas for *Four Musicians of Bremen* and *Jack and the Beanstalk*.

Hoping to sell the cartoons as a series, salesman Leslie Mace traveled to New York in September 1922 with the newly completed *Little Red Riding Hood* under his arm. Mace eventually talked Pictorial Clubs into distributing the fairy-tale series. On September 16, 1922, Pictorial Clubs agreed to buy Laugh-O-gram's first six cartoons for an astounding $11,000. Excited about the new order, Disney agreed to a mere $100 deposit for the series, with the rest due upon delivery of the finished product. It was not the most sound, up-front business transaction, but production began in earnest nonetheless.

The news of distribution was all Ubbe needed to be convinced that Laugh-O-gram Films, Inc. was finally on solid ground. He left the Kansas City Film Ad Service to rejoin Walt in November 1922. In legal documents, Ubbe Iwwerks described his duties at the Studio as including "work, labor, and service in drawing, etching, printing, and manufacture of diagrammatic or cartoon moving picture films and prints."

Colleague Rudy Ising remembers Ubbe's contributions: "Ubbe was really a lettering man. He didn't do much animation to start with, but he'd do all the titles. . . . Oh, he was a hell of a good lettering man, always with a brush. He did everything with a brush—he didn't animate with a brush, but he could have. That is where he got that beautiful swing that he had, he was great with a brush."

Animation in the early 1920s, in comparison to what it evolved into by the 1930s, was rudimentary at best. Most artists were studying from the Lutz book as well as copying from the competition. The industry was literally laying its own groundwork with each new and innovative step. Ising explains one of those innovations, the model sheet: "Very often you'd trace the character off a model sheet. And that model sheet was photographed and it was three different sizes: for close-up, medium shot, or long shot. Because the camera didn't move, you had to draw a close-up and you used the bigger heads then." Tracing, copying, and reversing cycles were common devices.

Laugh-O-gram characters were stereotypical. The villains can be recognized by their black masks and unshaven faces. As they are introduced on screen, they are identically rendered and completely interchangeable.

In the Laugh-O-grams, nearly all elements in the film are anthropomorphic. When faced with a barrage of cannon fire, a house ducks, jumps, and gets out of the way. A cat climbs out of a chimney, quickly detaches his tail and makes like Babe Ruth swatting cannonballs back at the villains. A cannonball flies too close for comfort. It carries the cat away upon it. In a gravity-defying feat, he will ride the ball for much of the remainder of the film.

The cat, a successor to Felix and Krazy Kat, knows no Newtonian strictures of objects in motion. The cat and the cannonball sail through a building and around trees. He finds that if he pulls off his tail and uses it for a rudder, then he can control the direction in which the ball sails.

Exaggerated character action in the Laugh-O-gram films is illustrated by comic-strip conventions such as eye dashes, speech bubbles, or, more commonly, beads of sweat that explode from the heads of characters who are startled, angered, happy, or otherwise motivated. Stars and squiggles indicate pain. Speed lines represent movement. Exclamation points and ampersands indicate the unprintable being spoken.

Detachable appendages were commonplace for cartoon animals in the 1920s. Fellow felines Felix and Krazy Kat often used their ingenuity to find any device or mechanism to escape their predicaments. Often times this extended to using body parts, mechanical props, or even car parts.

Puss in Boots and *Cinderella* were among the first Laugh-O-grams. Modernizing timeless fables for modern-day audiences was Laugh-O-gram's trademark. Several films of the fairy-tale series *Jack and the Beanstalk* and *The Four Musicians of Bremen,* among others, were notable in that either Walt or Ubbe or both would revisit the tales later in their careers. One film, *Jack the Giant Killer,* was especially remarkable, in that both Walt and Ubbe would revisit the tale separately later in their storied careers long after the Laugh-O-gram version had disappeared from public memory. Walt would later film his version as the *Brave Little Tailor.* Ubbe would call his 1934 version *The Valiant Tailor.* All versions were based on a Celtic fairy tale, *Jack the Giant Killer,* which tells the ironic story of an unassuming young man who is mistakenly identified as a hero and has further heroism thrust upon him.

Laugh-O-gram had to work hard for its successes. By this time the Laugh-O-grams' gang liked to believe they were a serious entity to contend with in animation, but the truth was they were still just a blip on the radar screen. As part of the initial funding for Laugh-O-gram, Walt Disney purchased a used Universal camera for the hefty sum of $300 (more than twice his monthly salary at the time). This would give the fledgling company the ability to produce the films they envisioned. According to an advertisement in the *Kansas City Star,* Laugh-O-gram had "added the feature of photographing youngsters to its regular business of making animated cartoons." Aside from baby pictures, Walt took outside jobs as a cameraman covering local Kansas City news events for national newsreel organizations including Selznick, Pathé, and Universal.

Often the animation staff would get together during off-hours to experiment with Walt's new camera. The local hangout, Swope Park, became their stage. Photographs from the time show the Laugh-O-gram staff posing in a wide variety of comic situations. Standing high in trees, hanging off cliffs, and sprawled across the park grounds, each snapshot recorded the free-spirited fun of an enterprising young group. Several reels of live-action film from the Disney family archives contain outtakes of the madcap crew laughing and waving to the camera while sitting inside an old log cabin. Publicity stills from the time show the "actors" engaged in a mock fight atop the Laugh-O-gram roof. Walt is shown holding Ubbe over the edge of the building with the butt of a gun raised above his head. One false move and it was lights out for Ubbe. There is no doubt by their on-screen enthusiasm that they were truly enjoying being "filmmakers." Ultimately, many of these live-action efforts found their way into short comedic films dubbed Lafflets.

In one Lafflet, Ubbe is seen walking up to a lump of clay. In an adaptation of the lightning-artist technique, he works feverishly on the clay to sculpt a bust of Warren G. Harding. Ubbe then walks away, leaving the bust of Harding smoking. Rudolph Ising explains that the scene was shot in reverse. "I think we did a slow crank on that [to speed up the animation on screen]." Each new film tested and perfected some aspect of animation or effect.

In all, the group made at least eight Lafflets, including films with the intriguing titles *Golf in Slow Motion, Descha's Tryst with the Moon, Esthetic Camping, Reuben's Big Day, Rescued, A Star Pitcher, A Pirate for a Day,* as well as *The Woodland Potter.* Many of the Lafflets were attached to the Laugh-O-gram reels when they were shipped to the distributors' Pictorial Clubs.

A Pirate for a Day was an especially interesting outing for the young filmmakers, since its footage occupied three reels of film as opposed to the more common single reel. It was not quite feature length, but it was significantly longer than typical short subjects, a serious effort from a budding studio. By all appearances it seemed that Laugh-O-gram was on its way.

Not so fast.

In 1923, after shipping the completed Laugh-O-gram prints to their distributor, Walt learned that Pictorial Clubs had declared bankruptcy. Laugh-O-gram was left high and dry. The initial $100 deposit would be the only money to reach Kansas City from the $11,000 promised by Pictorial Clubs. Once again, Ubbe and Walt faced financial ruin.

During this desperate time, Walt Disney never lost hope in himself or in his endeavors. Business Manager Adolph Kloepper recalled, "He was always optimistic about his ability and about the value of his ideas and about the possibilities of cartoons." Disney scrambled to find outside projects to generate revenue. One of the outside projects for the studio was a film called *Tommy Tucker's Tooth*. A local dentist, Dr. Thomas McCrum of Kansas City, commissioned Laugh-O-gram to create the film, which illustrated the importance of dental hygiene. Laugh-O-gram received a much-needed $500 for this effort.

Unfortunately, this was not nearly enough to forestall the wolves at the Laugh-O-gram door. Disney and Iwwerks found that their credit had run dry. They defaulted on payments to such creditors as E. I. DuPont de Nemours (for animation cels), Chas. M. Stebbins Picture Supply Co. (used tripod, 2 cranks, and legs), the Intercollegiate Press (imprinting of 2,000 business cards), *Motion Picture News, The New York Times, Kansas City Journal, Exhibitors Trade Review, Film Daily,* Schutte Lumber, the Old Mill Carbon and Ribbon Co., and virtually all of the employees and themselves. Ubbe and Walt may have found themselves penniless, but their inspiration was far from bankrupt. As it often had, Kansas City itself provided the impetus for their next endeavor.

In the early 1920s, Kansas City was evolving into a melting pot for the cultural avant garde. Aside from fledgling animators, Kansas City—and Missouri, in general—was a hotbed for young jazz artists. In St. Louis and Sedalia, as well as Kansas City, a new style of jazz music was being mastered by ragtime musicians, including Scott Joplin.

In Kansas City, the Jenkins Music Company popularized ragtime music by publishing sheet music written by some of the local talent. In 1922, the Jenkins Music Company was promoting its latest "star" attraction, the Coon-Sanders Original Nighthawks Band. With Carleton Coon on drums and Joe L. Sanders on piano, the Original Nighthawks had established themselves on the Kansas City scene through live concerts broadcast six times a week from the Plantation Grill in the Muehlbach Hotel. The broadcasts on radio station WDAF featured the catchy gimmick of having listeners telegraph their song requests to the Kansas City Star (which owned WDAF). Fleet-footed couriers would race the requests down the street to the hotel where Joe Sanders would read the telegrams on the air.

Sanders was as renowned for his cheery on-air personality as he was for his legendary exploits on the baseball field. He had once struck out all twenty-seven batters he faced in a minor-league baseball game. The "Old Left Hander," as he was dubbed, charmed Kansas City audiences with his easygoing banter.

A competent composer, Sanders penned minor hits with "Little Orphan Annie," "Blue Moonlight," "She Loves Me Just the Same," and "Beloved." A 1922 Sanders composition entitled *Martha, Just a Plain Old-Fashioned Name* found its way to the attention of Walt Disney and Ubbe Iwwerks. Several local artists including George Goldman, "The Man Behind the Voice," and the McLaughlin Sisters, "America's Greatest Dancing Duo," performed the song in their acts. To capitalize on the song's success, Carl Stalling—the seventeen-year-old movie theater organist for the Isis Theater in Kansas City—approached his acquaintance Walt Disney to film a live-action song reel to complement Stalling's rendition of the popular tune. Disney had recently provided two such song reels to Stalling: *The End of the Perfect Day* and Victor Herbert's *A Kiss in the Dark*.

Walt was familiar with most of the movie theater organists in the region. He knew that an accompanist's performance could make or break a silent film. He would routinely slip a dollar bill to the keyboardist to ensure their best efforts for his own cartoons on screen.

Stalling did not need such prodding. He was acknowledged as Kansas City's finest organist, with a huge repertoire of songs, and singled out in advertisements for the Isis Theater. In order to supplement his income, Disney agreed to supply Stalling with the song reel.

Walt's concept—a precursor of modern music videos—was dubbed the Song-O-Reel to reflect the Laugh-O-gram company name.

The *Martha* Song-O-Reel, shot as live action, featured the unlikely (and painfully shy) Ubbe Iwwerks cavorting playfully with a bevy of beautiful Missouri girls in Swope Park. Sanders's lyrics provided the rough storyline for Ubbe's leading-man debut.

> There's a quaint old-fashioned girl that everybody knows,
> Radiant as the poppy, lovely as the rose.
> Martha, just a plain old-fashioned name like Mary or
> Molly or Rose.
> She's just a plain old-fashioned girlie and everybody knows.

Ubbe also drew the elaborately designed title card for *Martha* that reflected the elegant, nostalgic feel of the song. "Old fashioned girlies" were standard in the Laugh-O-gram cartoons of the time. Many of the films were unabashed romances, though definitely of a juvenile sort.

While trying to keep his head above water, Walt Disney kept his watchful eye upon the competition. In New York, the Fleischer Brothers continued to turn out innovative *Out of the Inkwell* cartoons. Walt suggested turning the Fleischer formula around for a new series. Instead of using a cartoon character in a live-action environment, he suggested to Ubbe that they would use a live-action girl in a cartoon environment. It was now Ubbe's task to figure out how.

For the starring role, Walt remembered a little girl he had seen in advertisements for Warnecker Bread named Virginia Davis. "He was at the theater to see how his films—the Laugh-O-gram—looked and [he] saw me," Virginia Davis recalls. "*Alice's Cartoonland [sic]* was something he had been thinking of doing. I guess when he saw me he thought, Here was a little girl who could do it. I think that's where it all started."

At the age of four, Davis was already a veteran performer. "He [Walt Disney] contacted my mother and pitched this idea about how great it would be for her little girl. Mother was open to suggestions, so she said okay. I remember going to the office, Laugh-O-gram's, and Ub was photographing it at the time. I remember him and several of the other young men. They were all young then, as we all were."

As Disney had suggested, the film would be entitled *Alice's Wonderland*. The technique that Ubbe and Walt created for the Alice comedy was very much born out of experimentation and seat-of-the-pants improvisation. But it was Ubbe's growing ability to find the technical means to see things through that made this cartoon their best effort yet. Bob Broughton, technical assistant to Ub Iwerks in the 1950s, sums up the revolutionary process: "They would shoot this little girl against a white screen and keep her in a certain position. Then they would plan the animation so that the animation did not come in contact with her. After they shot the girl, they would get a print made and then they would bi-pack that print—which had just the picture of the girl, and clear film where the white was—and bi-pack that in the camera. Then they would shoot the animation frame by frame, and so help me, it worked."

With the idea fully conceptualized, on May 14, 1923, Walt Disney sent a letter to Margaret J. Winkler, the influential distributor of the *Felix the Cat* and *Out of the Inkwell* series, in hopes of pre-selling her on the series:

> We have just discovered something new and clever in ani-
> mated cartoons! The first subject of this distinctly different
> series is now in production, and will require a few weeks
> more for completion. It is a new idea that will appeal to all
> classes, and is bound to be a winner, because it is a clever
> combination of live characters and cartoons, not like Out of
> the Inkwell *or* Earl Hurd's *but of an entirely different
> nature, using a cast of live child actors who carry on their
> action cartoon scenes with cartoon characters.*

A letter in response from Winkler a short time later expressed her interest in seeing the film when it was completed. With this initial bite, Walt and Ubbe continued on in making the demo as best they could.

During the autumn of 1923, as they neared the completion of the film, Walt Disney's luck turned from bad to worse. Money had reached an all-time low. Unable to pay his rent, he was forced to move in with Ubbe and his mother for a couple of weeks. Walt contacted all of his past investors, but no one was interested in throwing good money after bad. Not even Minnie Cowles or Dr. McCrum would come to his rescue this time.

By this time, Ubbe had worked many weeks without pay to keep the production afloat. The prospect of ever collecting on the $1,003 back wages owed to him by Laugh-O-gram seemed remote, as did getting back money he had invested from his personal savings. With no stones left to turn, Laugh-O-gram had no choice but to declare bankruptcy.

Bankruptcy in the 1920s was more shameful than it is today. One would expect a young Disney to have been devastated by the loss of such a significant investment, but letters to family and acquaintances showed no trace of shame or embarrassment, just continued optimism.

Within months, Walt's brother Roy convinced him to move to California. Roy Disney had spent the last few years moving from hospital to hospital in the southwest recovering from a bout of tuberculosis. After hospital stays in Santa Fe and Tucson, Roy was then recuperating in a Veterans' hospital in western Los Angeles. Walt saved up the $40 he needed for the trip and boarded the train for Hollywood.

Author Russ Merritt notes that even this decision was rooted in Walt's naïveté. "You'll notice as Ub and Walt feel their way through the animation business, they can only survive by being supremely naïve about the prospects of getting distribution and finding money. They are consistently being fleeced, consistently being bamboozled, and nothing stops them. The very decision to go to Hollywood rather than New York is an example of that naïveté. But it's that carefree spirit of Ub and Disney combined with this limitless passion and disregard for issues of respectability, security, or the sensible things people care about that drives them."

After the Laugh-O-gram dissolution, Ubbe returned to steady employment at Kansas City Film Ad, which was renamed yet again, becoming United Film Ad Service. For a short while, Ubbe would lose touch with Walt.

Ubbe spent the better part of 1923 developing his skills at Film Ad, from printing and layout to advanced stop-motion techniques. Several photos of the time show Ubbe hunched behind a stop-motion camera, wearing a printers' smock that covered his tie, vest, and long-sleeved white shirt.

An adventurer at heart, Ubbe purchased a motorcycle to scoot around the back roads and city streets of Kansas City. He still maintained friendships with the remaining Laugh-O-gram gang including Hugh Harman, Rudy Ising, and Carman Maxwell. The trio of Harman, Ising, and Maxwell had since formed their own company called Arabian Nights. Having acquired the old Laugh-O-gram equipment, they too attempted to produce a trial animated film, but their efforts did not pay off. Animation production in Kansas City was becoming an increasingly difficult prospect and only the best would survive.

Despite this turbulence of Ubbe's youth, Laura May was proud her son had grown up to be a talented and ambitious young man. In 1922, the two relocated to a new home at 2008 Chelsea Avenue, in a suburb just outside downtown. With Walt gone and Ubbe's finances stabilized, Laura May could relax, knowing Ubbe had finally settled down. The comfort wouldn't last long. Having recently been promoted to head of the Art department, Ubbe was just catching his breath financially from the Laugh-O-gram debacle when he received a letter from Walt.

chapter 3

Ubbe in Cartoonland

Walt Disney corresponded with Ubbe from California, where he had set up Disney Brothers' Cartoon Studios with his brother Roy, in a storefront studio near Vermont Avenue. When Walt arrived in California, he avoided continuing his career in animation. He was determined to become a feature-film director. But after knocking on doors and crashing movie sets, his efforts proved unsuccessful. Finally, he leaned upon his only true asset and last resort, *Alice's Wonderland*.

He drafted another letter to Margaret J. Winkler, who had already expressed interest in the cartoon and shipped the print off to New York. Walt didn't know what to expect. Known for her aggressive promotion and marketing skills, Winkler was certainly the apple of any aspiring animator's eye. Walt was elated when Winkler responded with a telegram, the key words popping off the page: "BELIEVE SERIES CAN BE PUT OVER. . . WILL PAY FIFTEEN HUNDRED EACH NEGATIVE."

Winkler offered the ecstatic twenty-one-year-old Disney a six-picture deal plus an option for six more. She added a stipulation indicating that the agreement was contingent upon the quality being as good as the first, and upon Virginia Davis's reprising the role of Alice. Walt attempted to sell Davis's parents on the idea of the Alice series. Of great concern to the Davises at this time was the health of their talented little daughter. "I'd had double pneumonia and almost died," Davis recalls of the traumatic time. "The doctor told my mother that I would be better off in a drier climate. So I think when this all came up, it was another incentive that brought us to California." Virginia Davis's father, Jeff, was employed as a traveling salesman. Her mother was a housewife. California was viable for both. The Davises began their journey from Kansas City to Hollywood by train.

Ginny Davis started right away in *Alice's Day at Sea*, the first film under the new contract. With her thick curls and winning smile, Davis resembled a miniature Mary Pickford. She was also a fine young actress.

The first six Alice short subjects were completed by Walt with assistance from Roy on camera and a handful of hired help. With each new film, the quality improved slightly, but even with the joint Disney effort it proved to be a rocky start.

Early in the series, a major shift in the relations between Walt Disney and his distributors occurred when Charles Mintz, a former Warner Brothers booking agent, married Margaret Winkler and took over the day-to-day duties of dealing with the Alice comedies. Critical comments about the timing, the gags, and the combination of live action with animation became increasingly common. Mintz did not share the native optimism of his bride nor her geniality in dealing with the Disney Brothers.

In his correspondence with Disney, Mintz did not mince words. One such missive bluntly stated, "The first seven pictures were an absolute total loss to us and you can further take my word for it when I tell you that we have not made one single dollar on any picture that we have gotten from you." He went on to admonish the young Disney, "you should wholeheartedly be ashamed of yourself." Walt Disney knew that he and Roy would have to make changes if they wanted the Disney Brothers Studio to survive. They needed the one artist who could put the cartoons on solid ground.

When Ubbe received Walt's enthusiastic and typically persuasive invitation in May of 1924 to come out and join them in California, he knew the inherent risks. If anyone understood Walt's smooth-talking ways, overzealous drive, and financial naïveté, it was Ubbe. At age twenty-two, they had already gone through two bankruptcy proceedings and lost thousands of dollars of their investors' money, not to mention Ubbe's own personal losses. How was this venture going to be any different? Even though he would have to take a pay cut from from $50 a week at United Film Service to $40 a week at Disney Brothers. Studio, something told Ubbe that things would be different. Within days, Walt received an acceptance letter from his former partner confirming his arrival. The strength of draughtsmanship and skill that Ubbe could provide were exactly what Walt and Roy needed to secure the continuance of the series, not to mention the excitement of having their old friend back. Walt, ever the salesman, wrote Ubbe on June 1, 1924, expressing great relief that he had committed himself to coming out.

> Dear Friend Ubbe,
>
> I'll say I was surprised to hear from you and also glad to hear from you. Everything is going fine with us and I am glad you have made up your mind to come out. Boy, you will never regret it—this is the place for you—a real country to work and play in—no kidding—don't change your mind— remember what ol' Horace Greeley said: "Go west young man—go west!"
>
> We have just finished our sixth comedy for M. J. Winkler and are starting tomorrow on the seventh of the first series of twelve. Miss Winkler is well pleased with them and has given us some high praise—she is leaving New York for here June 1st, and I believe we will be able to start a twice a month schedule, instead of our monthly schedule.
>
> I can give you a job as artist-cartoonist and etc. with the Disney Productions, most of the work would be cartooning. Answer at once and let me know what you want to start and I will write more details. At the present time I have one fellow helping me on the animating, three girls that do the inking, etc. while Roy handles the business end. I have a regular cast of kids that I use in the picture and little Virginia is the star.
>
> Write and tell me how soon you want to come out—if you can leave before the first of the month all the better—of course you would sell all of your furniture and also your car?

Wouldn't you? I believe it would be best if you did. Anyways, write and let me know all the details. Give my regards to everyone at the Film Ad and the boys at the Arabian Nights, and also to your mother. As ever your old friend,

Walt—

Don't hesitate—Do it now—
P.S. I wouldn't live in Kansas City now if you gave me the place. Yep. You bet. Hooray for Hollywood!

Unable to make it alone without the support of her industrious son, Ubbe's mother, Laura May Iwwerks, reluctantly agreed to make the trip to California with him. When Virginia Davis's family took the train to California, they had left their automobile behind. Jeff Davis arranged for Ubbe to drive the seven-passenger Cadillac out west.

Ubbe documented the trip from Kansas City to Los Angeles in a series of photographs. In picture after picture, his dour-faced mother posed against the barren backdrop of the early twentieth-century West. As they traveled through dry, desolate lands that the dustbowl would soon lay waste, mother and son saw the great amber fields of wheat metamorphose gently into the greenery and the majesty of the Rocky Mountains. Mile upon mile of dusty roads passed beneath their wheels. As they at last rolled out of the hot desert into the temperate flat lands of Southern California, they were greeted by a landscape unlike any that they had ever experienced before.

Stretched out before them were acres upon acres of California orange, lemon, and avocado groves that led right out to the Pacific Ocean. The newly built HOLLYWOODLAND sign commissioned by mogul Mack Sennett sat austerely in the hills above the broad, shaded streets of eucalyptus and pepper trees. The "Big Red Car" (an electric trolley) linking Hollywood with Santa Monica and downtown Los Angeles, wound its way past the Mack Sennett, Vitagraph, and Nestor studios. By the early 1920s, Hollywood had become the new motion-picture production center and the town was abuzz with the excitement of the movies. Ubbe had arrived!

Excited that his old friend had finally joined them, Walt Disney wrote to his benefactor, Doctor McCrum in Kansas City, "Ubbe has been with us now for over a week and we are certainly making use of him. . . . He has bought a big Cole Eight roadster. After driving a big car, he couldn't go back to a small one." Soon after settling into a rental house, Ubbe was reunited with Walt and Roy at the Disney Brothers Studio.

From the outset, Ubbe was the highest-paid artist on the staff (including Walt) and became the top animator. From this point on, Walt would no longer animate. A short time later, fellow Laugh-O-gram animators Hugh Harman and Rudy Ising closed down their Arabian Nights Studio to make the trek to join Walt, Roy, and Ubbe.

One of the first changes that occurred upon Ubbe's arrival in California was a name change. Many had found the uniqueness of his name a subject of great interest and even humor. He had heard both his first and last names pronounced in every manner possible. In 1924, he shortened the name "Ubbe Iwwerks" to the more easily pro-nounced and spelled "Ub Iwerks." Walt nonetheless always referred to his friend as "Ubbey." (Even though he had changed his name legally to "Ub Iwerks" in 1926, there were still frequent references to him in studio documents as "Ubbe Iwwerks." In fact, on poster designs for the later *Trolley Troubles* series, Ub even signed his name, "Ub Iwwerks.")

Aside from a new name, Ub brought the studio renewed energy and new techniques. Abandoning the stiff and rudimentary methods of animation he had previously learned, Ub would begin to evolve his own straight-ahead style of drawing, which did not rely on model sheets or extremes. A key aspect of the Lutz orthodoxy was pose-to-pose animation, in which, for any action, a character was drawn in its starting and ending positions (or "extremes") and intermediate poses were filled in later. Model sheets were used to trace over the original figure, allowing the animator to simply alter the parts of the body that needed variation. Ub instead professed a new method. He felt he could coax more expressive feeling from a drawing if he used model sheets as rough guides rather than being chained to them. By trusting in his own creativity and sense of movement, he threw out all structure to make way for his own free-flowing impulses.

Russell Merritt and J. B. Kaufman in *Walt in Wonderland* assert that "If Iwerks had made no other contribution to the Studio, he would deserve to be remembered for this one. It marked the beginning of the smooth, flowing 'Disney style' of animation; and one can see it developing, slowly but surely, as the Alice series progresses."

The first film Ub animated upon arriving at the studio was *Alice the Peacemaker,* which adroitly demonstrated his fluid new animation style. During an era in which animators would hold a pose for up to fifteen seconds, Ub's animation of a cat and a mouse fighting in a kitchen never comes to a complete rest for nearly two minutes. The characters are in constant motion as they try to outwit one another with increasingly ingenious maneuvers, their bodies and tails jumping, twirling, curlicue-ing in one continuous cycle of movement. From drawing to drawing Ub would adjust speed, emotion, and body characteristics as he went along. He often created new gags on the spur of the moment as he saw fit. The films began to garner interest from the industry. With the exception of the Fleischer Brothers Studio in New York, where the artists were equally as frenetic, no other studios were interested in adopting Ub's more adventurous, more athletic type of animation technique. Only animators with Ub's raw confidence, foresight, and native talents could pull it off. As a result of Ub's innovations, the quality of the Alice films markedly improved.

Much of the cleverness of the Alice comedies could be directly attributed to the novelty of the live-action Alice interacting with her animated counterparts. Virginia Davis recalls the process of filming the live-action portions: "We'd film in a vacant lot. Walt would drape a white tarpaulin over the back of a billboard and along the ground, and I'd have to work in pantomime. They would add the animation later. It was such fun. Kids in the neighborhood would act as extras, and Walt paid them fifty cents apiece." Because film stock was expensive, each scene was usually shot in a single take.

Ruthie Tompson was a young girl living two doors from Walt's uncle Robert on Kingswell. She recalls her early fascination with the budding studio. "I met Walt, Roy, Ub, Jack Cutting, Les Clark, and others while their studio was on Kingswell Avenue. I was nosey and saw girls painting. I walked in and everyone was really nice. They were great with us kids, very patient, letting us look around. I knew Roy best. I used to sit on the bench by him when he was shooting. I stopped in often on my way home from grammar school. Going into the 'animation lab' was a wonderful experience—watching the drawings being made and later traced onto celluloid with pens, and then painted. What kid wouldn't be fascinated!"

The early relationships she witnessed as a girl certainly set the stage for the future. "I think Walt and Ub were much alike in their purpose," Tompson continues. "Ub had more artistic and general all-around talent. Walt appreciated talent in others and had a knack for picking good talent to work for him. He probably would have gone off the deep end if it hadn't been for 'brother Roy' to manage the affairs. Ub wasn't that lucky. He needed Walt and Walt needed him and that's why he rejoined the Disney Brothers. A lucky day for Disney's I'd say!"

By 1925 the studio was in full force. Virtually cornering the market in Hollywood as cartoon producers, this small operation consisted of a dirt lot, simple wooden sets, a camera, and some drawing tables. Job specialization was unknown, gags were abundant, and everyone did everything. Ub in particular was instrumental in figuring out the intricacies of combining the footage of Alice with his animation.

Author Donald Crafton, in *Before Mickey*, elaborates further: "The girl was filmed first as she gesticulated with her invisible (in fact nonexistent) acting partner. Ub Iwerks then supplied the animators with sketches he made from the rushes."

Assistant animator/cameraman Rudy Ising recalls that the technique of combining the live film of Alice with Ub's animation was a fairly complex and involved process. The completed live-action film would be placed inside a camera that had been adapted to serve as a crude projection device. The film would then be projected frame by frame onto an animator's desk, where the animator would trace the outline of Alice onto a sheet of paper. "From that tracing we had to make what they called a traveling matte," Ising recalls. "They were filled in in black on the white paper. And we shot that and got a negative made, around her, and then the white part of her was matted out. And then when it was printed, it was double-printed, just in reverse. You used the traveling matte with the animation negative, and you used the reverse when you double-printed her in."

While Alice was the nominal star of the series, it was the resourceful cat, Julius, who captured much of the audience's interest. Early in the series, before her new husband took over, Margaret Winkler had made reference to the idea of using a feline co-star when she wrote Disney, "I might suggest that in your cartoon stuff you use a cat wherever possible and don't be afraid to let him do ridiculous things." Walt and Ub had listened dutifully. Like Felix and Krazy Kat before him, Julius made resourceful use of whatever availed him (usually his own tail) and was frequently involved in doing "ridiculous things." Because of the difficulties and expense of combining the live action with the animation, in some films Ub almost exclusively used animated footage featuring Julius. Margaret Winkler would have been happy. Charles Mintz on the other hand was less than thrilled at any efforts to undercut the main selling feature of the series.

Alice the Peacemaker utilized a shortcut style, in which a photographic cutout of Alice was used beneath the camera in a manner similar to Walt Disney's lightning-artist hand used in the Newman Laugh-O-grams. The photograph of Alice running was then moved slightly for each frame. In effect, this stop-motion technique, combined with the animation surrounding it, saved the time and expense of shooting live action and the expense of using the traveling-matte technique to create the marriage of the animation with the live action. It was also a fairly unsubtle, obvious technique.

A more subtle device was used for the prison escape film *Alice the Jailbird*. In this short subject, Alice was sometimes not shot in live action at all but actually animated by Ub for brief periods of time.

Any grand movements on Alice's part were performed by the drawn version. An animated Alice crawls out of a hole. An instant later, the animated figure jump-cuts into a live-action Alice. The transition is virtually unnoticeable.

By his fifth California cartoon, *Alice Cans the Cannibals,* Ub had hit his stride. Walt explained his comedic intentions to Charles Mintz. "We have endeavored to have nothing but gags, and the whole story is one gag after another." *Moving Picture World* likewise reviewed the film positively, "Each one of these Walt Disney cartoons . . . appears to be more imaginative and clever than the preceding, and this one is a corker."

Throughout his fledgling career, Ub had been fond of creating visual puns. *Alice in the Jungle* features some clever gags that pushed the envelope of invention in other ways. In this film, he outdoes himself. A pair of juvenile elephants prances to an inviting swimming hole. The trunk of the young elephant boy turns into a suitcase trunk, which contains a pair of swimming trunks. One iteration of the *trunk* pun would have been funny, two rounds take it to the level of absolute corn.

Another set of gags in *Alice in the Jungle* illustrates the extreme liberties the animators were willing to take with the medium. When Julius is trapped in the middle of a lagoon in danger of becoming lunch for a trio of chomping alligators, he spies a log near the shore on which he might find safety. Familiar dashed sight lines flash from Julius's eyes to the log. Julius grabs the sight line and walks hand over hand to the log. Once finished with his journey, he snaps the sight lines from the background and tosses them aside.

When Alice is trapped by lions, and calls for assistance in *Alice in the Jungle,* the word *HELP* floats to Julius and then turns from a word into a boot that summarily kicks the surprised cat in the fanny. A similar scene occurs in *Alice Stage Struck* when Julius makes a bear literally eat his words. In the world of animation, anything was possible. Ub realized even at this early point in the evolution of animation that believability was far more significant to the art form than reality.

The menagerie of supporting characters that Ub created included an oversized creature named Pete who would frequently play the heavy in the Alice comedies. Pete appeared first in the 1925 comedy *Alice Solves the Puzzle* as the nefarious One-Eyed Pete. As a bootlegger, Pete (also known as Bootleg Pete) terrorizes Virginia Davis's Alice by stealing her crossword puzzle and chasing her into a lighthouse. Julius had to appear at the last second to save his friend from Pete's comically melodramatic grasp.

For the resilient Pete, it was far from a fatal defeat. Over the course of a career that would eventually span more than seventy years, Pete would repeatedly take such defeats in stride. Through many changes of role, at least two changes of species (bear, wolf, cat), and numerous changes of name (Tough Pete, Putrid Pete, Peg Leg Pete, even Pete the Bear, among others), he would continue to be an adversary, enemy, and even bumbling friend to some of the greatest of Disney's cartoon stars.

Pete's more recent incarnations have included a domestic role as Goofy's long-suffering neighbor in Walt Disney Television's *Goof Troop* and *The Goofy Movie* and as the monster in Mickey Mouse's sci-fi send-up *The Runaway Brain*.

Little Virginia Davis's Disney career would prove far less enduring. After she had finished filming the first fourteen Alice comedies, Virginia was offered a new contract that stipulated only eighteen working days for the entire year. Davis's mother found those conditions unacceptable. Charles Mintz wrote the Davises from New York. "[Mintz] threatened to replace me if I wouldn't appear under the new terms of the contract," Virginia Davis recalls. "He wrote that he still wanted me, but under his terms. All of the time he had someone else, perhaps a relative, in mind, and Mother would not accept his terms."

Mintz made good on his threat. A child actress named Dawn O'Day played Alice in the next film, *Alice's Egg Plant*. It was to be her only appearance.

Overall the quality of *Alice's Egg Plant* is excellent, with a better-than-average story line and Ub's steady animation. The animators complained, however, about the density of the celluloid they used for production. In some scenes, inconsistencies of density caused several of the chickens to appear to change color value. After enough complaining from the Disneys, the Du Pont Chemical Company (apparently forgetting their earlier litigation against Laugh-O-grams during the Kansas City bankruptcy proceedings) attempted to improve the process by thinning the cels' thickness to a much thinner grade of celluloid. This thinning greatly enhanced the quality of the image and allowed for consistent exposure.

After her role as a failed strike breaker in *Alice's Egg Plant,* Dawn O'Day was relieved of her Alice duties. She was followed in the series by Margie Gay, a spunky tyke with a Clara Bow haircut and a questionable ability to jump up and down on command.

With the change to Margie Gay, Alice's part in the films was relegated to even more of a spectator's role. It is not known whether this was a result of pressure for more gags, the cost efficiency of doing less live action, or Gay's lack of theatrical experience.

Not that they did not try to promote little Margie. The staff posed dutifully for publicity photos with their newest starlet. The animators, conscious of the latest clothing styles in trendy Hollywood, tucked their pants into their socks to give the appearance that they were wearing fashionable knickers.

Knickerbocker pants were not the only concession to style for the young animators. In 1925, they held a mustache-growing contest. In the end, most of the lads shaved, but Walt and Ub retained theirs. In fact, they kept them for the rest of their lives. Disney's mustache gave the young man a more mature, respectable, and commanding appearance. Ub's pencil-thin mustache—similar to that of swashbuckling silent screen star Douglas Fairbanks—gave the shy Ub an air of intrigue and mystery. Ub and Walt had frequently been inspired by the dashing Fairbanks, liberally borrowing story lines and cinematographic techniques from Fairbanks' films.

Alice Picks the Champ used the Fairbanksian device of distorted shadows to heighten the drama of a climactic prize fight between

Julius and Tough Pete. Russell Merritt and J. B. Kaufman in *Walt in Wonderland* remark on the similarities: "One suspects that here Disney was recalling the startling use of shadows in the climactic dueling scene of Fairbanks' *Robin Hood*." In both films, the dueling characters are dwarfed by their grotesque, exaggerated shadows. The stark quality of the black shadows seemed to imbue the violence of the fighting with deepened emotion. Ub took the stylization even further by using the shadows to blur the identity of the combatants. The audience remains fully involved in the rigors of the fight without ever knowing who is getting the upper hand. Fairbanks may have been the inspiration, but it was Iwerks who supplied the payoff.

Julius the Cat particularly seemed to take his inspiration from Fairbanks in dueling scenes in such films as *Alice on the Farm, Alice's Spanish Guitar* (which features a whip no less!), and *Alice Foils the Pirates*. With his swashbuckling grandeur, Julius began to take an even more upfront role in the Alice comedies.

Alice Chops the Suey is essentially an animated film featuring Julius with only a brief cameo appearance by Alice. Throughout the film, Julius defies the rules that normal folks live by. Even Sir Isaac Newton's law of inertia (which states that an object in motion will remain in motion until acted upon by a force) is set on its ear as Julius frequently appears to be an object in motion entirely devoid of friction or fatigue—nothing slows the action of Ub's kinetic drawings.

Not only do Ub's characters break immutable rules of physics, but in the process they often satisfy Ub's innate interest in mechanical contraptions by turning into machines themselves. At times, Ub instinctively uses these transformations in the manner of the Greek playwrights as a deus ex machina device that comes at the last second to neatly wrap up an irresolvable conflict. In *Alice Chops the Suey*, Julius turns his tail into a helicopter propeller to precisely that end.

The gags in *Alice Chops the Suey*, like those of most of the Alice comedies, stem from rural settings and situations that fit with the animators' Midwestern background. For New York City animators such as the Fleischer Brothers, the settings were often interior and urban.

Even though *Alice Chops the Suey* begins in Chinatown, the action quickly moves to a chase sequence that takes place entirely in a rural countryside—complete with a pig in a pond! "We never did like the New York film ideas," explains animator Rudy Ising. "If you look at the films, you'll see that we really developed a whole different type of humor than back there. Back there [New York], some of it was kind of distasteful."

Not that the Disney animators always adhered to their own dictum. *Alice's Orphan* contains a particularly distasteful scene in terms of contemporary mores and acceptability. A lively scene of Julius the Cat happily ice-skating is literally shattered when a female cat falls into a hole in the ice. Julius, being the good cat that he is, heroically rescues the poor lass. When he now sees his rescuee up close, Julius is shocked to find that she is snaggletooth ugly. He kicks her back into the hole in the ice, then closes up the hole so that she cannot get out.

Such moments of animation cruelty were proven comedy techniques. In *Alice's Orphan*, Ub surpasses his own slapstick tendencies. At times during the Alice comedies, Ub had used violent episodes as comedic devices. Characters were beaned by boulders, stabbed by knives, blasted with cannons, and generally pummeled into oblivion, but in *Alice's Orphan*, the violence takes a decidedly domestic turn. Trying to lull the orphan baby to sleep, Julius—frustrated by the effort—resorts to bopping the babe with a hammer.

While the ending of *Alice's Orphan* would no doubt raise some concerns at the Humane Society and the MPAA, they are no more violent than the films of the Keystone Kops or Charlie Chaplin's Little Tramp. Although many hands were involved in the creation of the cartoon, there is little doubt as to which animator was responsible for the slapstick comedy and dark humor. Years later, Ub would re-create many of the scenes from *Alice's Orphan* at his own studio in the Flip the Frog cartoon *Little Orphan Willie*.

Throughout the Alice comedies, Walt Disney maintained a running dialog with Charles Mintz concerning the quality of the films. Some of the discussions bordered on invective. When Walt complained that payments were not being remitted quickly enough to accomodate production cashflow, Mintz responded with such condescending phrases as, "Haven't you a single spark of appreciativeness in your whole soul?" "If you think this is a fair agreement, you have another think coming," and "I think you will concede that I probably know a little more about what the market wants than you do."

Mintz was not pleased with the continued shift of emphasis from the live-action Alice to the animated Julius. On February 13, 1926, he wrote to Disney, complaining that *Alice's Mysterious Mystery* was "short both on live action and on the entire footage." He wanted to get his money's worth. For Walt Disney, it made more financial sense to utilize his animation ace in the hole, Ub. Because of Ub's incredible drawing facility and his straight-ahead style of animating, Walt found that he was far better served by eliminating the live-action Alice—which required a lot of time-consuming planning and processing—and simply cutting Ub loose on the animation. Ub did not always have an idea when he sat down of where his drawings would take him, but he jumped in with a reckless enthusiasm nonetheless. Somehow, from the hidden depths of his creative instincts, bizarre images and gags would emerge upon the page in violent fits and starts.

Protective of his lead animator and his unique style of animation, Walt strove to remain diplomatic in his relations with Mintz. He wrote back. "I agree with you in regard to the live action and will assure you that I will do everything I can to work for the betterment of the pictures." In reality, it was already too late.

By late 1926, it had become apparent to both Disney and Mintz that despite all of their efforts, the Alice comedy series was nearing the end of its course. Disney began discussing with Mintz the idea of starting a new series—this time, fully animated. Liking the idea, Mintz began searching for distribution.

In the meantime, production continued on the Alice series with yet a fourth actress, Lois Hardwicke, taking the lead role. Hardwicke was an established actress who brought professionalism—if not an abundance of charisma—to the part, but Walt and Ub were already well beyond any thoughts of success with Alice, Julius, or the combination of the two.

The combination of live action and animation had been a neat parlor trick for the young artists. Over the last five years, it had helped launch their careers and established them in the industry. After producing more than fifty Alice cartoons in a scant four years, they realized that the technique was simply not all that novel anymore.

When Universal announced the decision to launch its own cartoon series, Mintz got Ub and the Disney Brothers in on the ground floor.

"I am negotiating with a national organization," Mintz wrote, "and they seem to think that there are too many cats on the market." Carl Laemmle, the head of Universal Studios, suggested to Mintz that his animators design for him a new lead character—a rabbit.

chapter 4

Oswald the Lucky Rabbit

While the character of Oswald the Lucky Rabbit was in development, Walt Disney sought outside resources to supplement the meager income of the Alice comedies. As he had done in Kansas City, Disney subcontracted with other companies to bolster the cash flow. One of these projects involved animating titles for a film called *The Silent Flyer*. The titles of *The Silent Flyer* were to be produced by Leon Schlesinger's Pacific Title and Art Studio. Schlesinger subcontracted with the Disney Studio to provide the animated titles for producer Nat Levine's first serial film for Mascot Pictures.

Over the next few years, Leon Schlesinger would head up Disney's chief cartoon competitor, the cartoon division of Warner Brothers Studios. The films of Bugs Bunny and Porky Pig would go head-to-head with those of Mickey Mouse and Goofy. The manic bluster of Donald Duck would be countered by the even more frenetic antics of Daffy Duck (whose trademark lisp was modeled after Schlesinger's own voice). Through the years, the two studios would battle harshly for animators, theaters, and audiences. However, at the time, the joint effort of Schlesinger and Disney was mutually beneficial.

Of equal benefit to Disney was the influx of cash from a sequel to the dental hygiene film *Tommy Tucker's Tooth*, which had been produced at the Laugh-O-gram Studio for Dr. Thomas McCrum. The new film, called *Clara Cleans Her Teeth*, featured Walt Disney's niece Marjorie Sewell in the title role. Like its predecessor, the film was intent on showing the horrors of neglecting proper dental care. Poor Clara is teased mercilessly by schoolmates who refer to her as Snaggletooth Susan. Even more disturbing is a frightening dream that haunts Clara. In the nightmare, for which Ub designed a surreal combination of live action and animation, dental paraphernalia spook Clara into practicing good dental hygiene.

These excursions into commercial work for hire were stopgap measures to keep the studio afloat while they worked on designing the new cartoon rabbit, Oswald. Carl Laemmle, the head of Universal Pictures, had been credited with coming up with the idea of using a cartoon rabbit. Long before Bugs Bunny or Crusader Rabbit hopped upon the drawing boards of Warner Brothers and Jay Ward Productions respectively, Oswald the Lucky Rabbit would set the standard for cartoon rabbits. In an era when cats and clowns and human characters ruled the animated screen, the mere fact that Oswald was a rabbit made him a novelty.

The name for the rabbit has been credited to P. D. Cochrane of the Universal publicity department who, on March 4, 1927, represented the studio in signing the contract with Charles Mintz of Winkler Productions. In a press statement accompanying the agreement, it was announced that the Oswald series "will be released under the brand name of Snappy Comedies." In some initial announcements, the lead character's name was erroneously given as Oscar instead of Oswald.

Oswald would be a distinct departure for the young team of animators. Unlike Julius the Cat from the Alice comedies, this new character was much less angular, featuring instead round, rubbery features that were every bit as pliable and useful as anything found at rival Paul Terry's studio at the time. Like Julius, Oswald was able to detach and use his appendages to his advantage, most notably his long, supple ears. Russell Merritt continues this theme:

> but now there are somatic consequences. When you tweak his
> nose, pull his ears, he hurts. He can cry. He can laugh. He
> can become a manic depressive. You're getting away from the

*slapstick gag into more of these personality gags, and as you
do that, some of Ub's quirky personality traits start coming
to the surface. This sense of anarchy rules as it never had in
the Alice cartoons.*

Another difference between the Oswald cartoons and the Alice
comedies was that in many of the Oswald cartoons, romance would
play a key dramatic role. This may have been a natural result of Walt's
recent marriage to Lillian Bounds, a charming girl from the ink-and-
paint department, or Roy's recent marriage to spunky Edna Francis.

Oswald provided the young animators a great character around
which to wrap romantic fables. Most often the object of Oswald's
attention was a female rabbit named Fanny. At other times, Ozzie
lavished affection upon a saucy lady cat. Despite their long work hours
and seemingly singleminded intent, the young animators found the
time and inclination to come of age. Hollywood in the mid-1920s was
a hotbed of flappers and scoundrels, alcohol, and scandal. Yet amid
this celluloid Babylon, amid Tinseltown's inherently seductive
debauchery, Ub Iwerks somehow retained his native Midwestern values. Ub was notoriously shy with women, a fact not lost on his fellow
animators.

A story, often told, relates how Ub was the butt of a practical joke
by Walt Disney when the latter arranged for a date between the tongue-
tied Ub and a pretty coworker named Margaret Metzinger. Disney had
intimated that *he* was going to meet the willing Metzinger, but instead
sent Ub, who was unaware of the subterfuge. As the flustered pair discovered the prank, Disney supposedly watched from afar, relishing the
discomfort of his friend and his unwitting female companion.

Not every date ended as disastrously for Ub. Ed Wehe, a friend of
Ub's who worked at the Santa Fe Railroad in Los Angeles, set up a
date between Ub and another pretty coworker. Mildred Sarah
Henderson, like Ub, was a recent migrant from the Midwest. Mildred
hailed from Topeka, Kansas, and had recently been hired by the Santa
Fe Railroad to work in the financial department as a comptometer
operator, posting financial data.

This date proved to be a far more successful venture for Ub. After a yearlong courtship, which included weekend trips to Santa Barbara with Walt and Lillian, Ub and Mildred were wed on January 5, 1927, in a private ceremony in Los Angeles. While Ub was gone on a well-earned week-long honeymoon, several new employees were hired to fill his temporary absence and to increase the animation staff. Hugh Harman recommended hiring Friz Freleng from the United Ad Service in Kansas City. For a slight increase in pay and the chance to work with his old friends, Freleng readily agreed to join the Disney staff.

The first Oswald the Lucky Rabbit cartoon, *Poor Papa,* continued the trend that had begun in the Alice comedies of embracing subject matter that bordered on the distasteful. In the film, Oswald the Lucky Rabbit as the title character is set upon by a veritable air force of storks dropping babies down upon his humble home. In a play upon rabbits' proverbially prodigious procreative skills, the babies just keep on coming.

Oswald, like many a new father, becomes frustrated and agitated at the onslaught of infants. Unlike many a new father, he brandishes a shotgun and begins shooting the babies out of the sky. The embattled storks respond by using the babies as weapons. This nasty little scene surpasses Julius's abuse of little Oscar in *Alice's Orphan* in the lack-of-taste department.

Oddly, when the finished film was shown to Charles Mintz, the subject matter was seemingly the only aspect of the film that did *not* offend the producer. Mintz's response to *Poor Papa* was blistering.

> 1. *Approximately 100 feet of the opening is jerky in action due to poor animation.*
>
> 2. *There is too much repetition of action. Scenes are dragged out to such an extent that the cartoon is materially slowed down.*
>
> 3. *The Oswald shown in this picture is far from being a funny character. Sometimes there are hints that something is going on underneath, but it is buried too deep to bother*

about. He's just flat. He has no outstanding trait. Nothing would eventually become characteristic insofar as Oswald is concerned.

4. The picture is merely a succession of unrelated gags, there being not even a thread of story throughout its length.

5. Why is Oswald so old, sloppy and fat? Audiences like their characters young, trim, and smart. This one is practically decrepit.

To others, Walt Disney staunchly defended the work of his friend, Ub, of which he declared, "I am willing to put him alongside any man in the business today." Nonetheless, he declared that he and his animators intended to turn the rabbit into "a younger character—peppy, alert, saucy, and venturesome, keeping him also trim and snappy."

Rather than try to fix the debacle that was *Poor Papa*, Ub and his fellow artists cut their losses and moved on. Ub was given the task of figuring out how to solve the myriad problems. The resultant Oswald cartoon, *Trolley Troubles*, had been inspired by a short film from 1917 starring comic genius Harold Lloyd. *Luke's Trolley Troubles* featured a pre-glasses Lloyd as a frenetic bumpkin, Lonesome Luke. Lloyd's rube was not unlike rural oaf Oswald.

Lloyd was only one of many screen stars then enjoying the extreme popularity of motion picture entertainment. More than 14,500 movie houses across the nation showed more than four hundred movies each year. Movies became America's favorite form of entertainment, ever changing, always developing into something new and even more exciting.

Trolley Troubles premiered in Los Angeles at the Criterion Theater along with Metro Goldwyn Mayer's *Flesh and the Devil* on the Fourth of July, 1927. Eleven days later, it played the Roxy Theater in New York City along with 20th Century Fox's *Singed*. In both locations, Ozzie's debut garnered generally good reviews. The *Film Daily*, noting the obvious influence of cartoonist Fontaine Fox's popular Toonerville Trolley comic strip, reviewed *Trolley Troubles* positively, "As conductor on a 'Toonerville' trolley, Oswald is a riot."

Walt Disney was less certain of Oswald's success. After *Trolley Troubles* was completed, he wrote to Charles Mintz. "We are changing the rabbit still more from the way he looks in this picture." To accomplish this metamorphosis, Ub removed Oswald's suspenders and overalls. He was redrawn slightly thinner in an attempt to make the rabbit agile, younger, and yes, "snappier."

To remedy the jerkiness of which Charles Mintz had complained in *Poor Papa,* Ub constructed a new, smoother-operating drive on the animation camera to ensure that the entire film would be exposed uniformly from beginning to end. Ub knew that the limits of the machinery and not his animation were to blame for the jerkiness of the film. He had already added a new, smoother switching mechanism; now he created a drive to go with it.

Walt Disney explained Ub's solution to Mintz. "I am also installing a new motor drive on the camera to eliminate a certain unevenness in the photography that has been noticeable in the past," Disney wrote. "I believe this will give much cleaner and better stuff in the future." While Disney often used the pronoun "I" to mean the Disney Studio, more often than not, it referred directly to Ub. Ub never appeared interested in publicity per se, and in fact would shun it in later years, but the impression that Walt Disney did everything himself was not lost on Ub, who in fact *could* do practically everything himself.

The first outing for the newly revamped Oswald was the film *Oh Teacher*. At one point in the cartoon, Oswald's girlfriend cries for help. The word *HELP* drifts over to Ozzie and kicks him in the pants to get his attention. Once alerted, Oswald mounts the word, which carries him like a bucking horse to chase after the villain. When Oswald later draws a line in the dirt challenging the villain to cross it, the villain nonchalantly takes the line and tosses it away. Likewise, when Ozzie is in dire straits and needs luck, he simply unscrews his foot— it *is* a rabbit's foot after all.

A similar rabbit's foot scene had occurred in *Trolley Troubles*. Friz Freleng, who was assigned the scene to animate, was confused as to how to accomplish the feat. "What do I do, do I show a bone?" he asked. Walt suggested a subtle approach.

Like the films that preceded it, *Oh Teacher* was met with a positive critical and public response. The same would hold true of each of the cartoons that followed. Ub and Walt were on a roll.

The Mechanical Cow, which came next, overflowed with Iwerks gags. The title character was a bovine robot. Decades before robots and computers would become commonplace, mechanical representations of human or animal life intrigued the public.

Several Alice comedies, for example, had used mechanical animals. In particular, mechanized horses were used to race against the organic kind in *Alice Wins the Derby* and in *Alice's Brown Derby.* With their detachable limbs, both Julius and Oswald were in some manner mechanized. Julius's tail had metamorphosed into ladders, hand-cranks, baseball bats, helicopter blades, and unicycles. Oswald's ears did much the same, though in a manner that was more motivated by the story line and less by spontaneous or random acts of comedy.

Merritt and Kaufman report this particular predilection of Ub's in *Walt in Wonderland*: "Certainly the robot animal crystallized Iwerks's well-known enthusiasm for mechanical engineering, eccentric character movement, and bravura straight-ahead animation pyrotechnics." *The Mechanical Cow* fulfilled all three requirements.

Another stock Iwerks device was the androgynous appearance of his female characters. Befitting the chauvinistic times that were represented in silent film serials such as *The Perils of Pauline,* Ub's female characters were often victims passively awaiting their heroic menfolk to rescue them from the clutches of some horrific terrorist.

Great Guns, which followed on the heels of *The Mechanical Cow,* was a war vehicle for the lucky rabbit that featured an uncharacteristically strong female lead and a maturity of theme and treatment not in evidence before. It was a film entirely unlike anything either Ub or Walt had ever done.

Ub's secondary characters had often resembled the contemporaneous illustrations that Harrison Cady drew for the *Bedtime Story* series of books by Thornton Burgess. Pete the policebear in *Great Guns* particularly resembled Cady's Buster Bear character from the popular children's series. Other characters—particularly giraffes, hippos, and elephants—were all derivations of characters from Paul Terry's *Aesop's Fables* cartoon series. The mouse character that Hugh Harman provided as Oswald's comic foil was clearly inspired by the hordes of mice that ran through Terry's films.

Great Guns received similarly positive reviews as its predecessors. *Motion Picture News* called *Great Guns* "chock-full of humor." *Moving Picture World* was also effusive: "The animation is good and the clever way in which Disney makes his creations simulate the gestures and expressions of human beings adds to the enjoyment."

Ubbe's Beach Story was the working title for the 1927 Oswald short *All Wet.* More often than not, Ub would work from stories created by Walt Disney, embellishing them with his own special touch. For this cartoon, however, Ub was credited not merely for animating the film but also for creating the story itself.

Aside from *All Wet,* Iwerks received similar story and animation credits for *The Banker's Daughter,* which he conceived together with Friz Freleng. In *The Banker's Daughter,* Oswald is a limousine driver trying to win the favor of his boss's daughter. When he flirts too assiduously for the father's liking, Ozzie is fired. The unlucky—for the time being—rabbit is only able to redeem himself when the villainous Peg Leg Pete robs the bank. Ozzie returns to the good graces of the banker and his daughter by tracking down the villain and bringing the money back to the bank. Ub continued to imbue Oswald with the "rubber-hose" style of animation—loose limbs and flexible movements remained his trademark.

At this point in his career, Ub was taking great interest in all aspects of the animation process. He tried his hand at a variety of the disciplines surrounding cartoon film production. In Ub's eyes, one of the more overlooked aspects of production during these experimental years was the quality and condition of the studio paint room. During production of the Oswald series, Ub purchased three stone mills from

Charles Ross & Sons to grind the paint pigment. A catalog advertisement for the stone mills explained some of the functionality of the devices:

> The feeder pot, which is removable, is made of steel and has a holding capacity of about one and a half gallons, and is intended for mixing one gallon at a time. The Mill is water cooled and is furnished complete with a one half horsepower motor direct coupled to the drive shaft of the Mill.

Ub consulted with paint experts and created a palette of paint formulas that were used from the Oswald series in the 1920s through the mid-1980s, when they were scrapped in favor of off-the-shelf paints.

Although he was immersing himself in the mechanisms of animation, Ub still found time to pursue his myriad outside interests. Among these was a deep interest in aviation. The 1920s saw the rise of aeronautic experimentation. Since the end of World War I, innovation in aviation technology enabled adventurous pilots (such as barnstormers and air racers like Jimmy Doolittle and Charles Lindbergh) to set many speed and distance records. On September 28, 1924, three army planes circumnavigated the globe in a flight time of 363 hours, a new record; in May 1927, Lindbergh landed at Le Bourget Field in Paris after his historic 3,600-mile flight from New York. *The Ocean Hop* was Ub's own animated attempt to wrap a tale around the theme of a transatlantic race from New York to Paris. Among the group of pilots gathered to fly their anthropomorphic airplanes is the nefarious Peg Leg Pete. Oswald, the dark horse, pulls beside Pete, who laughs mightily at Ozzie's tiny aeroplane. Oswald and his plane both thumb their noses back at Pete. They are confident that in spite of daunting odds, they will eventually win the race, which of course they do, earning appreciative but unappreciated kisses from the French diplomats in attendance.

Kisses on the cheek and good critical reviews aside, Oswald the Lucky Rabbit enjoyed a popularity with the viewing public that far exceeded the Alice comedies' modest success. Ub and Disney had by this time evolved into mature filmmakers, each taking roles in the studio that emphasized their individual strengths as artist and as businessman.

Ozzie had evolved into an appealing rabbit. He was capable of appearing in any number of situations, all of which made him marketable by the Universal promotional machine. Even before his first on-screen appearance, products bearing Oswald's likeness hit the streets.

Actually, the likeness was not all that much *like* Ub's rendering of Oswald at all. Universal, confident of the new character's prospective success, licensed Ozzie to Vogan Candy for an Oswald chocolate frappe bar. Unfortunately, the rabbit depicted on the packaging did not resemble Oswald, but was simply a rabbit (and a rather homely rabbit at that). Pins for the Philadelphia Badge Company and stencil sets for Universal Tag and Novelty Company followed.

Oswald the Lucky Rabbit was a financial success. Since the series had been produced under a one-year contract, Roy and Walt Disney prepared to renegotiate the contract with Charles Mintz and Universal.

In late 1927, Ub began to become suspicious of Mintz's brother-in-law, George Winkler, who seemed to be spending an inordinate amount of time at the studio visiting with the animation staff. Ub thought this uncharacteristic behavior strange and confronted Winkler. When Winkler presented Iwerks with an offer to break away from Disney to form a new studio, Ub's suspicions were confirmed. Winkler was trying to steal animators away from Disney to form a new animation enterprise—the Charles Mintz Studio. According to Winkler's claims to Ub, in fact, he had already done so.

Though Ub tried to warn him, Walt Disney was on his way to New York to negotiate a better deal for the *Oswald the Lucky Rabbit* series and would not believe that his men would betray him. Because of Oswald's success at the box office, Walt thought that he could get an increase from $2,200 to $2,500 for each cartoon. He was in for a rude awakening.

Charles Mintz offered Disney $1,800 per cartoon, a far smaller amount than he had been receiving. Walt was stunned. He had expected that the success of Oswald would give him *more* bargaining power, but found the opposite to be true. He asked Mintz to explain. Mintz told him that Oswald the Lucky Rabbit was the property of Universal Pictures and that not only did he feel he could produce the series more cheaply on his own, he had also already signed away all of Disney's key animators.

Walt could not believe what he was hearing. His world was falling apart. He called Roy back in California. Roy confirmed that Mintz had signed practically the entire staff. Only Ub Iwerks and two apprentice artists refused to sign.

Charles Mintz attempted to entice Walt to join his new staff, but Walt was not interested. He vainly tried to negotiate a deal to wrest back control. He wrote Roy, "Charlie is very determined to get absolute control of everything and will do everything in his power to gain his end." Eventually Walt was forced to concede defeat. In his own naïveté, he had simply signed a bad contract. Mintz was acting within his rights in the animation business of the 1920s. Control of a series and a character rested with the distributor, not the producer.

When Mintz told Disney that he had signed away his animators, Disney warned his former producer to watch his back. "These boys will do the same thing to you, Charlie. If they do it to me, they'll do it to you. Now watch out for them." Walt Disney's words belied a bitterness that would fester and grow with each defection of his valued staff. Walt's prediction came true a short time later, when Oswald was taken from Mintz to be animated directly by and for the Universal Studios cartoon department. As the nominal creator of Oswald, Universal owned all copyright claim to the Lucky (and much traveled) Rabbit. Immediately, Laemmle began searching for a veteran animation director to head this new cartoon venture. Producer Sam Van Roenkel suggested that Walter Lantz, who animated Col. Heeza Liar for the J. R. Bray Studios, would be an ideal choice. Lantz had frequently joined Van Roenkel and Laemmle at Thursday night poker games.

"He's been in the business longer than Disney has," Van Roenkel reasoned.

Laemmle replied, "He's been lucky for me in poker, he should be lucky for me in producing cartoons."

Lantz would later joke, "He [Laemmle] won me in a poker game." Unfortunately, Oswald would prove to be only marginally more lucky for Lantz than he was for Disney. It would be with Andy Panda, Chilly Willy, and Woody Woodpecker that Walter Lantz would achieve his greatest successes.

As far as Ub Iwerks was concerned, Lantz could darn well have the rabbit. Ub had something else up his sleeve.

chapter 5

The Mouse

Oswald the Lucky Rabbit was gone. Owned by Charles Mintz, he was roughly handed to Carl Laemmle and Walter Lantz, which left Walt Disney feeling decidedly unlucky. Disney was without a lead character, without a staff, without financing, and seemingly without hope. What remained for Walt was Ub Iwerks. In the final analysis, that would be enough, but it certainly didn't seem that way at the time.

In the spring of 1928, Walt confirmed to Ub and Roy the disheartening news about Ozzie. With characteristic optimism, he suggested that Ub start drawing up new character ideas. At first, Ub tried sketches of frogs and dogs and cats, but none appealed to him. There were already too many cartoon cats, he thought. The frog looked promising, but it needed work. A female cow and a male horse were good, but they seemed more like humorous supporting characters than stars. As Clarabelle Cow and Horace Horsecollar, Ub later used them for just those kinds of roles. No, right now, he needed a character that would make an immediate impact upon the screen.

Ub sought inspiration anywhere he could find it. He rifled through stacks of magazines. He looked in *Life* and *Judge*. A panel of cartoon animals by Meeker caught his attention. A mouse! There hadn't been any animated mice in leading roles. The only mouse in cartoons was Krazy Kat's pathetic love interest, Ignatz.

The circle had always been a basic design element at the

animator's disposal. As Ub's pencil traced these elemental circles upon the page, an old publicity photo from the Alice days came to mind. In 1925, Hugh Harman had drawn some sketches of mice around a photograph of Walt. With minor alterations to the nose of Harman's mice, Ub took the basic design elements of Oswald and transformed his circles into a new character. The Mouse was born.

Ub knew that Walt Disney was fond of mice. Once, when they were still working in Kansas City, Walt had befriended a mouse that regularly climbed onto his drawing board. Walt eventually gained the mouse's trust and was able to feed it small morsels by hand. Walt named his little friend Mortimer. When he came back discouraged from New York and saw Ub's designs, he suggested that they name this new mouse Mortimer, too.

Walt's wife, Lillian, thought that Mortimer was a sissy name. As an alternative, she suggested Mickey. Mickey Mouse. It seemed to fit better with the sassy character that Ub had created. Together, Walt and Ub set about to create the first cartoon.

Every dashing man needs an ingenue for whom to fight. Ub created a female mouse to be Mickey's counterpart. The name of this female lead required less introspection or deep thought. Walt named her Minnie Mouse in honor of the benefactor of the Laugh-O-grams Studio: Minnie Cowles. Despite the financial settlement against Laugh-O-grams, Minnie Cowles had maintained friendly contact with Walt, Roy, and Ub throughout the years. Walt honored her loyalty.

Names weren't the major concern for Ub and Walt. It was character and personality that mattered to them. As far as Mickey Mouse's character was concerned, Ub needed little prodding. He already had a model for the Mouse. Years later, he recalled that

> *Mickey was based on the character of Douglas Fairbanks, Sr. He was the superhero of his day, always winning, gallant, and swashbuckling. Mickey's action was in that vein. He was never intended to be a sissy, he was always an adventurous character. I thought of him in that respect, and*

I had him do naturally the sort of thing Doug Fairbanks would do. Some people got the idea that in Plane Crazy, *Mickey was patterned after Lindbergh. Well, Lindy flew the Atlantic, but he was no Doug Fairbanks. He was a hero to boys because of airplanes and what he had accomplished flying the Atlantic. But Mickey wasn't Lindy—he was Doug Fairbanks.*

With the character of Mickey Mouse firmly in mind and the airplane theme for a story line already established, Ub had now only to animate the darned thing. Because the defecting animators had two weeks of work remaining on the last Oswald cartoon to be done at the Disney Studio, Ub and Walt kept their new project completely under wraps. In their fragile situation, they could ill afford any breach of confidentiality that would doom their new series. Locking himself in his office, Ub worked frantically to complete the first Mickey Mouse cartoon.

Ub had reason to be on edge. Financially and emotionally, he had risked everything he owned on the studio's future success. At home, he and his wife, Mildred, were not only dealing with the responsibilities of raising their new baby son, Don, but they were also coping with the continued presence of Ub's mother, Laura May. Laura May had not responded well to Ub's marriage to Mildred and suffered from bouts of depression and jealousy that culminated in an apparent suicide attempt. She had since moved in with the family and was under the direct care of Mildred. With his financial and family pressures mounting, Ub had to give this effort everything he could.

Ub began production using very few crowd scenes and lavishing his attention instead on the two stars, Mickey and Minnie. Where he could, Ub used cycles and repeats as time saving measures. In this way, he churned out more than seven hundred drawings a day on *Plane Crazy*—a feat that eclipsed Krazy Kat animator Bill Nolan's record six hundred drawings a day. "I really extended myself," Ub says of his competition with Nolan. In fact, Bill Nolan very nearly became a Disney employee. Walt wrote of the situation to Roy. "Bill seems to think he and Ubbe would make a good team." Bill Nolan eventually chose to join the *Oswald the Lucky Rabbit* animators instead. One can only speculate on the impact Nolan would have had on the Disney Studio. Whether Nolan's output would have influenced or been influenced by Ub's will never be known. It stands to reason, though, that with those two prolific artists aboard, there would certainly have been a lot of it.

Ub had a style and technique all his own. He drew in a unique straight-ahead fashion that emphasized a series of poses rather than the flowing continuity of in-between drawings. The effect was not dissimilar to the techniques used by pantomimists in accenting the extremes of their body positions. It was visual punctuation.

Whenever any of the defectors would come into his office, Ub would quickly put a drawing of Oswald over the top of the Mouse. Surreptitiously, Ub completed drawing upon drawing upon drawing. Relentlessly, passionately, the first Mickey Mouse cartoon seemed to leap from his pencil. Each day, Walt and Roy would take stacks of Ub's completed drawings and—under the guise of going to get some work done on one of their cars—would take them to Walt's home garage where Roy's wife, Edna, and Walt's wife, Lillian, along with Hazel Sewell, Walt's sister-in-law, would ink and paint the drawings onto cels. Roy E. Disney recalls: "That was really, I gather, pretty much the company: Walt and Lilly, Mother and Dad [Roy and Edna], and Ub. You know, right at first, that was about it."

At night when all the Oswald animators had left for the day, Walt would bring the cels back to the studio, where the loyal cameraman, Mike Marcus, would photograph them. By morning, the bleary-eyed crew would clean up the studio to give every appearance of business as usual.

In just two frenetic weeks, the first Mickey Mouse short was completed. Every frame of the film was animated by Ub Iwerks: storyboards, extremes, in-betweens, backgrounds, *everything!* The creation of *Plane Crazy* was a Herculean feat unequaled in all of animation history, but it would have been a hollow accomplishment for the studio had it not been for the fact that the quality of the film was also incredibly high.

Ub was repaid for his effort with a byline on the title card which read "A Walt Disney Comedy. Drawn by UB Iwerks." The Mickey Mouse series would be the last time that any artist would share the title screen with Walt.

We first meet Mickey Mouse as he admires a picture of aviator Charles Lindbergh in a magazine. Mickey roughs his hair up and smiles like his hero, Lucky Lindy. He smoothes his hair back down to his usual Douglas Fairbanks self again.

Mickey Mouse is a barnyard pilot. He interacts briefly and sometimes cruelly with a barnyard filled with animals. First he contorts a long dachshund into a staircase for boarding the airplane. Then the versatile dachshund climbs into the interior of the plane. It bites the propeller shaft. The ground crew—that is, a pig outside the craft—winds the propeller, twisting the dachshund's supple body like a rubber band. A crowd of barnyard well-wishers cheer madly for their hero, Mickey. He takes a horseshoe aboard for good luck. He's going to need it.

Despite the chaos of its creation, *Plane Crazy* is filled with personality, charm, and action. Animator Ollie Johnston points out that it is possible to believe that Mickey is actually thinking about what he is doing. This internal motivation was revolutionary in a cartoon industry that had long thrived on illogical gags and blackout comedy. "I don't know if anyone had done any kind of acting like that before," Johnston says, referring to Ub's role in instilling Mickey with believable humanity.

Aloft in his aeroplane, Mickey Mouse puckers up for a kiss. Independent Minnie will have none of it. He reaches over and tickles her under the chin. Rebuked, Mickey, in a decidedly inappropriate gesture, forces himself upon the unwilling lass. She slaps him hard across the face.

Mickey and Minnie's byplay was effective because it "had the acting in it that the audience could identify with," Ollie Johnston suggests. "They identify with it not just because it's Mickey and Minnie, but because the two characters are interacting. Just like it could be something that happened to the people watching." It was Ub's ability to project such emotional complexities that showed through in the Mouse. In many ways, Ub Iwerks was one of the first Stanislavskian animators, concentrating as much on internal motivation as on the external characteristics of his cartoon stars.

Mickey certainly seemed to have motivation behind his actions. You could tell what he was thinking—and it was not exactly nice. Funny, yes. Endearing, of course. Nice?— hardly. Roy Disney comments on Mickey's actions: "He was feistier earlier. I think in those early cartoons, he was quite a different guy from what I think most people now think Mickey is." The early Mickey had a cruel streak as long as his malleable tail.

Mickey's tail was not the only part of his body that could be altered according to the dynamics of the situation. When Mickey startles himself by pulling the steering wheel out of the plane, his ears fly from his head in shock, thus continuing the legacy of detachable appendages that had been used extensively in the films of Oswald.

Without a steering wheel, Mickey loses control of the plane. The plane nosedives, spiraling straight down to the ground, with trees and foreground objects whirling past realistically. Seen from Mickey's point of view, the spinning ground careens in and out of view with a realism that suggests our heroes are truly going to crash. Ub's mastery of the perspective involved is total.

However, according to Frank Thomas, one of Disney's famed "Nine Old Men," Ub had originally conceived of a different ending for *Plane Crazy* that featured a live-action set through which Mickey's plummeting airplane would crash:

> It was coming in a spiral, turning around as it came toward
> the ground. . . . So, [Ub] made a little tower of houses and

trees and things for the plane to crash into. Combining kind
of a live-action device along with his cartoons. But when the
picture came out, what he had done didn't look too well, I
guess, because they had all those things that were used in
Batman later on—the words WHAM, BAM, *or* WOW, *or*
CRASH—*things like that would be animated against a*
black background. That was the crashing of the airplane.

During the summer of 1928, Disney's last Oswald the Lucky
Rabbit cartoon, *Hot Dog*, was completed. With *Hot Dog* in the can,
the Oswald animators had finished their obligations to Disney and
Disney had fulfilled his obligations to Mintz. Ub was finally able to
come out of seclusion to work in the open.

Plane Crazy was screened with a piano accompaniment and a full
house on May 15, 1928, as a sneak preview at a movie house on
Hollywood Boulevard. The audience reaction to the new character was
positive, if not overwhelmingly so. Ub recalls that it "got quite a few
laughs." It was enough of a reaction to bolster the animators' spirits
and to keep them going. They knew they were onto something.

The loyalists had little time to consider their achievement. In
accordance with his modus operandi for the rest of his career, on May
29, 1928, Walt gathered his men around him in a semicircle and
acted out the next cartoon. He mimed, mugged, and even squeaked
for Mickey in a high-pitched voice that set the animators rolling with
laughter. Along with Walt and Ub at this time were newcomers Les
Clark and Wilfred Jackson.

Jackson, a young former art student from the Otis Art Institute,
had been with Disney for only a week when the Oswald animators
made their exit. During that week, he had observed the Oswald
animators laughing and chatting, but on Saturday, he was amazed
that they took their seat cushions, visors, and personal items home.
"They're a strange bunch," Jackson thought, "they have fun together
all week, but they don't trust each other enough to leave their personal
belongings at the studio." On the following Monday, Jackson discovered that Ub, Clark, and Johnny Cannon were the only ones left from

the animation staff. Les Clark and Johnny Cannon were veterans of the Oswald series. The defection of the others thrust them into the spotlight. They made the most of the opportunity.

The story Walt described for his staff at the story session was a rollicking South American tale they called *The Gallopin' Gaucho*. Where *Plane Crazy* had been inspired by Charles Lindbergh's transatlantic flight, *The Gallopin' Gaucho* had been inspired by Mickey's true role model, Douglas Fairbanks, Sr. In the 1927 silent film, *The Gaucho*, Fairbanks played the title role with typical gusto and aplomb. The swashbuckler starred opposite the always vivacious Lupe Velez.

Mickey Mouse picked up where Doug Fairbanks left off. Minnie reprised the Mexican spitfire role.

In *The Gallopin' Gaucho*, Ub altered Mickey's appearance slightly. The Mouse, barefoot in *Plane Crazy*, gained shoes. His eyes, which had previously been outlined by ovals with black pupils inside, now were simply defined by the black oval pupils. In some sequences, though, Ub's initial design was used. His personality remained raucous.

While Ub was beginning to work on animating *The Gallopin' Gaucho*, Walt Disney made a trip to New York with a print of *Plane Crazy*. He enlisted the help of film dealer E. J. Denison to try to sell the series to New York film distributors. Walt was asking $3,000 per cartoon, but Denison could find no takers. Everywhere they went, they heard the same thing, "Cartoons are dead!" At the time, animation was seen as a dying novelty, not as a legitimate and lasting genre. Much of the cartoon output during this era was of substandard quality and had rightfully earned its low opinion. Disney was desperate to find some new way to generate interest in his cartoon series and to prove the naysayers wrong.

Ever since the premiere of *The Jazz Singer* on October 6, 1927, Walt had foreseen the use of sound in cartoons. Ironically, Carl Laemmle had predicted synchronized sound in 1908, although he did little about it on his own. Laemmle declared that sound was "the greatest improvement in the moving-picture business. If you believe I am a good prophet, order a Synchroscope [early motion-picture sound-recording system] now, for I tell you that talking pictures are the coming craze in all America." Crude technology for synchronizing sound with motion pictures had already been invented, but the innovation lacked the proper impetus needed to drive its proliferation into movie theatres. With the growing popularity of recorded jazz music, the concept finally had the impetus it needed.

In the year that passed after its release, *The Jazz Singer* had indeed revolutionized the motion-picture industry forever. In the process, it set America literally on its ear. Laemmle was right. Everyone was talking about Al Jolson and his immortal cry, "You ain't heard nothin' yet!" Practically overnight, silent film stars' careers were in jeopardy as all the studios clamored to make talking pictures.

Walt had heard rumors that other animation studios were jumping on the sound bandwagon with their own sound cartoons. Aesop's Fables and the Fleischer Brothers supposedly each had sound projects in the works. Not to be outdone, Walt looked for a suitable vehicle to use for *his* sound production.

The options available for sound at this early date were limited. One of the techniques then being used was to make phonograph recordings of the cartoon soundtrack. This technique had been proven too unwieldy in practice. Because it required that the record and the film be started simultaneously, it was simply too easy to lose synchronization. Also, records were easily broken or lost in transit.

An improved technique of recording directly on the film called Vitaphone was introduced. A thin optical strip ran along the edge of the film. This sound strip—or "soundtrack" as it was commonly called—appealed to Walt. "Roy, what do you think about trying sound?" Walt asked his brother. "You know they've got the track right on the film now, so you can't get out of sync." Roy reluctantly agreed that they should try a cartoon using the soundtrack technique. It was up to Walt and Ub to find the right vehicle for such an event.

Walt had long been fond of the silent film clowns. He had often found inspiration in the short films of Charlie Chaplin, Buster Keaton, and Harold Lloyd when he was in need of comic situations in which to place his cartoon creations.

In 1928, Buster Keaton starred in *Steamboat Bill, Jr.*, a tale of a young man laboring aboard a steamship. Walt Disney conceived of a story for Mickey Mouse derived partially from this film and partially from another Keaton vehicle, *The Navigator*. Disney called the result *Steamboat Willie*.

An early script for *Willie* written by Walt with accompanying thumbnail sketches by Ub illustrates how even at this early stage, they had already begun to think of cartoons in terms of sound as well as visual imagery.

> *Scene # 2.*
>
> *Close-up of Mickey in cabin of wheelhouse, keeping time to last two measures of verse of "Steamboat Bill." With gesture he starts whistling [sic] the chorus in perfect time to music... his body keeping time with every other beat while his shoulders and feet keep time with each beat. At the end of every two measures he twirls wheel which makes a ratchet sound as it spins. He takes in breath at proper time according to music. When he finishes last measure he reaches up and pulls on whistle cord above his head. (Use FIFE to imitate his whistle.)*

The finished script for *Steamboat Willie*, which was filled with scenes of a musical menagerie, appeared to be an inspired first choice for Disney's use of the new sound innovation. Ub would later refer to this event as the "sound renaissance of 1928." Renaissance or not, it was a mammoth and expensive undertaking at the time.

The animation was planned with meticulous detail. Les Clark remembers, "We worked with an exposure sheet on which every line was a single frame of action. We could break down the sound effects so that every eight frames we'd have an accent, or every sixteen frames, or every twelve frames. And on that twelfth drawing, say, we'd accent whatever was happening—a hit on the head or a footstep or whatever it would be, to synchronize to the sound effect or the music."

Since apprentice animator Wilfred Jackson had a working

knowledge of how a metronome worked, he was enlisted to draw up bar sheets to assist in the synchronization of the music and sound effects. One of the fundamental problems that Jackson and Iwerks faced was the anomaly of film speed.

Sound film ran at twenty-four frames per second whereas silent film ran at eighteen frames per second (fps). The animators had been used to the eighteen-fps standard. Because Ub animated straight-ahead, he had to adjust his thinking to the twenty-four-fps standard for sound. If he did not compensate for the variance in projection speed, his usually fluid animation would look jerky and rushed when it was projected on the sound projector.

Ub wanted to give it a dry run first. Unfortunately, Disney had no formal projection room at that time in which to preview films. If they wanted to review a film, they had to see it in the so-called sweat box, a claustrophobic, closet-like room for testing completed film footage. Obviously a sweat box would be an inappropriate venue for a showing in front of guests. Everyone understood that this was a momentous occasion. Walt invited the animators' wives and girl-friends to a special showing at the studio. They gathered in an empty room. The excited animators strung a bedsheet across an open door to use for a screen. Ub rigged a projector to project through a window so that the motor noise would not detract from the sound effects that the audience was about to hear.

Roy ran the projector. The others gathered around a microphone behind the bedsheet screen. Ub had built a crude speaker out of an old crystal radio set. While watching *Steamboat Willie* from this vantage point, Wilfred Jackson played the melody of "Steamboat Bill" on his harmonica in rhythm with the action on the screen. Les Clark pro-vided percussion. Ub played washboard and sliding whistles. Johnny Cannon imitated various barnyard animals. Walt performed the squeaks and whistles of Mickey Mouse himself. He also provided the voices of Minnie Mouse and a parrot who cried out "Man Overboard! Man Overboard!"

The wives and girlfriends were unimpressed. Mildred Iwerks

remembers talking in the lobby about recipes and babies when Walt ran out and exclaimed: "You're out here talking about babies and we're in here making history."

"What did they expect?" Lillian replied. "We had absolutely no idea what was going on. And in any case, it sounded terrible."

Walt and Ub could not have been happier. Their passion ignited, they instinctively knew that history was being made. They ran the film again and again. Each time, one of the animators would step in front to take in the full effect. "It was terrible," Walt recalled, "but it was wonderful! And it was something new!"

Ub's reaction was similarly effusive. "It was wonderful; there was no precedent of any kind. I've never been so thrilled in my life. Nothing since has ever equaled it. That evening proved that an idea could be made to work."

In spite of the animators' joy, *Steamboat Willie* remained essentially a silent film. The finished footage, while planned for sound, had already been completed by Ub as a well-timed silent. The sound that was to be recorded would have to be post-synchronized to match existing actions and beats. Knowing that this process would tax the limits of their meager resources, they nonetheless decided to forge on. Sound was a make-or-break proposition for the studio, but one in which they both wholeheartedly believed. "Walt," John Hench recalled, "was absolutely obsessed with the whole idea of getting on with something. He had kind of a sense of destiny and I think Ub was optimistic about what could be done to force the communicable quality of the cartoon." For Walt and Ub, the dangers involved were mitigated by their united belief that *Willie* was well worth the risk.

Walt took a print of *Steamboat Willie* to New York City to record a soundtrack. On the way, he stopped off in Kansas City to see his old friend Carl Stalling. They talked of sound and what it would mean for the cartoon business. Walt showed Stalling the bar sheets that Wilfred Jackson had created for *Steamboat Willie*. Stalling looked at the crude score. "This man's no musician," he joked. He offered to help.

Walt gave Stalling copies of *Plane Crazy* and *The Gallopin'
Gaucho*. Carl began to compose musical scores for the two silent films
at his home in Kansas City. He also agreed to join Disney in New
York if need be to participate in the recording sessions for *Steamboat
Willie*.

Upon arriving in New York, Disney made the rounds of the sound
recording studios. He made a disappointing visit to Fox to discuss its
Movietone system. They were uninterested. He then went to RCA
Photophone. RCA was at first mildly interested in the film. They
agreed to record the soundtrack. Thrilled by the prospect, but knowing
that his financial future was at stake, Walt wanted to see a sample first.

On September 1, 1928, Van Beuren premiered a cartoon entitled
Dinner Time. Walt Disney was present for the preview. He wrote back
to Roy and Ub.

> *MY GOSH—TERRIBLE—A lot of racket and nothing
> else. I was terribly disappointed. I really expected to see some-
> thing half-way decent. BUT HONESTLY—it was nothing
> but one of the rottenest fables I believe that I ever saw, and I
> should know because I have seen almost all of them. It merely
> had an orchestra playing and adding some noises. The talking
> part does not mean a thing. It doesn't even match. We sure
> have nothing to worry about from these quarters.*

Apparently, Walt attributed the shortcomings in the preview to
Van Beuren and *not* to RCA. He maintained his interest in the
Photophone process. RCA Photophone, for its part, although inter-
ested in *Willie*, quickly priced itself out of the running by padding
their $600 fee with royalty charges, music taxes, and orchestra fees.
"I have dropped them from my mind entirely," Walt sadly wrote.

Patrick A. Powers was a businessman of a different ilk. Powers
was a New York City entrepreneur who operated on the edges of
many worlds. His forte was taking existing innovations, making
slight changes in the design, and using them as his own inventions
while deftly avoiding patent infringement.

Powers was born in Ireland in 1869, and started his career in

Buffalo, New York, as a distributing representative for the Edison Phonograph Company, as well as Victor. He was credited with having brought worldwide recognition to Victor's trademark, "His Master's Voice." Powers' career as an industry leader started in 1912 when, in association with Carl Laemmle, RH Cochrane, Charles Bauman, David Horsley, and W. H. Swanson, he formed Universal Film Manufacturing Company, the forerunner of the present Universal International. Powers later sold his interests to Laemmle and Cochrane and subsequently created the Film Booking Offices (FBO), which ultimately was absorbed by RKO. With the coming of sound pictures, he helped develop the Cinephone sound system. Not unlike Movietone or Photophone, the Cinephone process involved a similar optical soundtrack recording/playback system. Cinephone was one of the earliest sound devices, having been active in the first experiments of sound-on-film.

Powers sold Disney on the process, claiming that promoting Cinephone—and not Mickey Mouse—was the sole reason for his interest in *Steamboat Willie*. He claimed to have no designs on the Mouse at all. After the heartbreak of losing Oswald, this was exactly what Walt wanted to hear. Disney signed an agreement with Powers wherein the Disney Studio would pay $26,000 a year for use of the Cinephone process. Roy Disney thought this to be an exorbitant sum, but Walt considered it fair. "What the hell," he said, "I needed the equipment."

Roy E. Disney recalls his father Roy's role in matters such as this. "Dad was always the one who got it at arm's length. Immediately he'd say, 'Wait a minute, let's think about this. It's going to cost more money!' But clearly, once it happened, and once Walt said, 'Look, it makes sense to do this,' I think Dad was susceptible to Walt in the same way everybody else who worked for Walt was—he was an awfully good salesman."

Pat Powers took the greenhorn Disney under his oh-so-experienced wing. He introduced Walt to New York City–based actors, producers, and assorted motion-picture personnel. Among the more impressive of these to the impressionable Disney was Carl Edouarde, the charismatic leader of the pit orchestra at the famous Broadway Strand Theater in New York. Edouarde agreed to record the soundtrack for *Steamboat Willie*—at a cost.

Despite the cost, Disney could barely contain his enthusiasm for Edouarde and the recording session. On September 14, 1928, he wrote Ub and Roy from New York:

We are using a seventeen-piece orchestra and three of the best trap drummers and effect men in town. They get ten dollars an hour for this work. It will take three hours to do it, plus the time the effect men put in today.

Edouarde believed that he could synchronize the orchestra to match the actions of the film as it was projected. He found this to be much more difficult than he had imagined. Despite projecting the film on a wall of the studio, the musicians—and Edouarde himself— were entirely unable to discern or maintain the meter of the music required. The images seemed only to distract and confuse the flustered conductor.

In spite of all the efforts, the first day's recording session had been a total bust. Walt wrote Ub from New York. "Personally I am sick of this picture *Steamboat Willie*. Everytime I see it, the lousy print spoils everything. Maybe it will be different looking at the picture with sound. I sure hope so."

Walt was growing more frustrated with the New York musicians' attitudes. He wrote to Ub again on September 20, "Boy, the unions are sure tough on movie recording. They are doing all they can to discourage the 'Sound Film' craze." Nevertheless, Disney retained his optimism for Mickey Mouse and his undiminished belief in the inevitable success of the sound cartoon.

With money quickly being frittered away in the unproductive first recording session, Walt was forced to wire his brother, Roy, to sell his Moon Cabriolet roadster to generate some operating capital for the company. The Cabriolet, with its red and green running lights, was Walt's pride and joy. Somehow, however, he sensed that this was to be his defining moment and that all the chips had to be left on the table.

The Cabriolet was sold to finance a second recording session. Walt admonished his brother, "I think this is Old Man Opportunity rapping at our door. Let's not let the jingle of a few pennies drown out his knock."

Ub arranged for another print to be made and delivered to Walt in New York. This print contained none of the distracting flashes that had marred the first print. For this film, Iwerks devised a system of bouncing balls that rhythmically indicated where beats should strike. This time, the film was not projected for the musicians to follow but instead was projected directly onto the sheet music on Carl Edouarde's conductor stand. Edouarde followed the bouncing ball and the musicians followed Edouarde.

This bouncing-ball technique of Ub's combined with a smaller, more manageable studio orchestra assured that the second recording session was deemed an artistic if not exactly a financial success.

When Carl Stalling arrived in New York on October 26, 1928, with the finished compositions for *Plane Crazy* and *The Gallopin' Gaucho* in hand, he found that *Steamboat Willie* was done and in the can. Stalling and Disney immediately set about recording the soundtracks for the first two Mickeys at Pat Powers' studio.

In spite of the challenges that *Steamboat Willie* had faced to this point, Walt Disney realized that the concept of sound was sound indeed. He wrote Ub to begin work on a fourth Mickey Mouse cartoon, *The Barn Dance*. Even though he was bone weary of working on *Steamboat Willie*, Walt knew that from start to finish it was a great film.

Steamboat Willie begins with a whistling Mickey at the wheel. As Walt's script had suggested, he whistles several bars of the tune "Steamboat Bill." Pete enters to grab little Mickey by his stomach. He stretches it like a rubber band. As with the earlier Mickey Mouse offerings, Pete is once again a menacing giant, terrorizing the tiny Mickey. From there, all similarities to Mickey's first two silent films cease.

The individual drawings of the opening sequence reveal that Ub's drawings of Mickey were frequently little more than a combination of circles loosely attached with rubber-hose appendages. There is no attempt at realizing any verisimilitude of anatomy in the figures. Muscles, organs, and joints are ignored completely, replaced with geometry in motion. Animator-historian Mark Kausler explains, "When you look at his drawings, they're very, very loose. They're almost like little toothpick sketches, and in some cases, he would draw one side of an arm and not complete the other side." Even in these static drawings, the implication of motion is evident. Seldom do the drawings achieve any sort of aesthetic pose or tableau. It is only when viewed consecutively as animation that their impact is fully realized.

The exceptions to this are the circles that comprise Mickey's head and ears. In every drawing, the head is posed in an expressive three-quarter or profile view. The ears are always viewed as if seen from the front. Regardless of the view, the three major circles are perfectly visible. Secondary circles are reflected in the eye cavities and jowls.

These circles reflected Ub's instinctive sensitivity to unity of design. Babies respond innately to round objects. Universally, the circle represents a form of perfection and harmony.

When Mickey goes ashore to retrieve a menagerie of animals waiting on a pier, he at first attempts to lift an emaciated cow with a crane, but the beast is simply too skinny to fit the harness. Mickey solves this problem by shoving an entire pitchfork full of hay down its throat, swelling its belly to fit the harness. This scene was animator Les Clark's only contribution to *Steamboat Willie*.

For his part in *Steamboat Willie*, Wilfred Jackson had been assigned to animate a cycle of Minnie Mouse running along the riverbank. In the scene, Minnie first appears making a mad dash for the ship in three-quarter view. She has inadvertently been left ashore. She runs along the shoreline trying to catch up with the departing steamboat. "Yoo-hoo!" she cries. Mickey maneuvers a crane toward shore. He catches Minnie's panties with a boat hook and successfully pulls her into the boat.

Meanwhile the animals aboard ship are making themselves right at home. Each of their actions elicits a distinctive corresponding sound, demonstrating the innovation of the new medium. A hungry goat swallows the sheet music to "Turkey in the Straw." Immediately thereafter, it swallows a guitar. Minnie cranks the goat's tail like a Victrola. Musical notes fly out of the goat's mouth to the tune of "Turkey in the Straw."

Mickey joins in the merrymaking by adding his own musical accompaniment. He puts his foot on a cat's neck while he roughly pulls its tail and then squeezes the belly of a goose like a bagpipe. Pigs in a row suckling at their mama are Mickey's next musical victims. He pulls the piglets' tails one after another, eliciting a different squeal from each.

A xylophone made of cow's teeth (with the cow still attached) is the next instrument of choice for Mickey. He even gets in some nifty flourishes before he realizes that he is being watched—Pete is watching Mickey's antics with great scrutiny. Mickey looks out at the audience sheepishly. He whistles low. He knows that he has been caught shirking his duties.

Steamboat Willie debuted on November 18, 1928, at the Colony Theater in New York City. After all Walt's struggles to record the sound, after all of Ub's heroics in completing the animation, after all Roy's fundraising feats, after the defections and the bad feelings and the exhaustion—all of the efforts expended in getting the cartoon to the screen—they were rewarded with an astonishing success. At the premiere, Stalling and Disney sat in the back row of the theater relishing every chortle and chuckle.

Following the audience reaction at the Colony, the reviews the next day were merely icing on the cake. The raves were loud and long. *The New York Times* cried "an ingenious piece of work with a good deal of fun." The reviewer at *Exhibitor's Herald* claimed that *Steamboat Willie* "knocked me out of my seat." Other reviews were similarly effusive: "Recommended unreservedly"; "left them applauding."

Mickey Mouse was the overnight success that had taken Ub Iwerks and Walt Disney over a decade to achieve. After all their travails, they had finally made it. On opposite sides of the United States, the two old friends enjoyed their greatest success together. With the spotlight now burning brightly on the small studio in the Los Feliz area of Los Angeles, the energy within its walls was practically impossible to contain.

For Ub Iwerks, these were among the best times of his life. He later recalled those halcyon days. "Making films in those days was lots of fun. It really was. We'd hate to go home at night, and we couldn't wait to get to the office in the morning. We had lots of vitality, and we had to work it off. . . . We all loved what we were doing and our enthusiasm got onto the screen."

chapter **6**

Mickey's World

The enthusiasm generated by Mickey Mouse continued to build. *Film Daily* called *Steamboat Willie* "a real tidbit of diversion." To *Variety,* it was "a high order of cartoon ingenuity." *The New York Times* thought the film "an ingenious piece of work." It was indeed.

A few short years later, *The New York Times Magazine* would proclaim that "Mickey Mouse is the best-known and most popular international figure of his day."

A few well-proportioned circles, a pair of buttoned shorts, and an unmistakable charisma had combined to create an international wunderkind. Established entertainment stars also moved quickly to jump upon the Mickey Mouse bandwagon. Douglas Fairbanks, Mickey Mouse's true alter ego, took a reel of Mickey Mouse cartoons to the Polynesian islands as a means of breaking the ice with the natives. Ub's design of Mickey transcended language boundaries and cultural distinctions. In any land, under any name, Mickey was accepted lovingly. He was called Topolino in Italy, Micky Maus in Germany, Μικκι Μαους in Greece.

A teenage Bob Clampett—years before his own successes in animation at Warner Brothers and at his own studio animating Beany and Cecil—designed a Mickey Mouse doll with his aunt. The enterprising duo sold the concept to Walt and Roy Disney, thus creating one of the first pieces of Mickey Mouse merchandise. Walt was photographed at the studio surrounded by the stuffed dolls. Mickey

Mouse Clubs sprang up spontaneously in theaters around the country more than twenty-five years before the Disney television show of the same name.

Walter Lantz, who in 1929 was continuing to animate Oswald the Lucky Rabbit for Universal, recalls the impact of *Steamboat Willie* and the sound revolution in cartoons:

> Sound and music opened an entirely new field for animated cartoons. They became in demand again in theaters. It was much easier to watch, and this fascinated audiences because they'd never seen anything like it before.

Because Ub had begun work on *The Barn Dance* before Carl Stalling arrived from New York, like its predecessor, *Steamboat Willie*, it too had to be post-synchronized. The first Disney film to feature Stalling's presynchronized music was the fifth offering, *The Opry House*. *Willie*'s use of sound transformed Mickey Mouse from an extremely charming silent cartoon character into an out-and-out cultural phenomenon, unparalleled in the history of entertainment. Before Frank Sinatra crooned his way to superstardom, before Elvis or the Beatles caused mass hysteria, before *Star Wars* or *Titanic* broke all box office records, there was Mickey Mouse and *Steamboat Willie*. It is virtually impossible to overstate the importance of Walt and Ub's creation upon the motion-picture industry.

For *The Opry House*, Ub drew horizontal lines on the film that rose and fell to the rhythm of Wilfred Jackson's bar-sheet timing. As a result, Carl Stalling was able to match his music perfectly to the actions of the characters onscreen. *The Opry House* begins with Mickey Mouse sweeping the porch of a rustic theater advertising a "Big Vaudville Show *[sic]*" featuring "Yankee Doodle Girls." As the melody of Yankee Doodle plays, Mickey marches in step with the song. The lively broom joins in with Mickey in a gravity-defying dance that, while physically impossible, would become a part of Ub's cartoon oeuvre from that moment on. The impossible had never stopped Ub before.

As Mickey rides the broom merrily across the porch, an obese pig saunters up on a horse. Unable to fit through the door, the pig struggles mightily. Mickey gives a few well-intentioned shoves to assist the swine, but his efforts are to no avail. Only when the pig's girth is punctured like a balloon does the pig—now quite thin—fit through the door.

Inside, an animal pit orchestra plays snippets of several classical tunes. A goat violinist breaks his violin, and resorts to bowing his long goatee instead. A pig percussionist pulls cats' tails in sequence. The squeals elicited change in pitch, depending on the relative size of the cats. Teeth are played like castanets. A tuba-playing dog blows soap bubbles from the bell of his horn until it is flushed like a water closet. For Ub, sound and sound effects had replaced movement as the impetus for gags.

As he had done in *Plane Crazy,* Ub gives Mickey an opportunity to perform an impersonation of a famous person—in this case, the classical pianist, Paderewski. Mickey sweeps his Paderewski-ish hair back dramatically and sits down at a piano to play. The piano bends and responds to Mickey's every touch. When the Mouse needs a high note, he simply spits a bit of chewing tobacco upon the required keys. As he becomes more and more passionate in his playing, Mickey rises from the piano stool and begins punching the keys with his fists. The piano, being fully anthropomorphic, fights back valiantly, kicking the overzealous Mickey from the stage. The piano ends the concert by playing itself while it dances joyously with the piano stool. When Mickey Mouse returns to the stage, an asbestos fire curtain falls upon him, thus ending the not-so-grand ol' opry.

Like *Steamboat Willie, The Opry House* did not tell a cohesive story so much as offer a series of humorous vignettes based on a specific locale. It is interesting to note that in his very first season of utilizing sound, Ub had already found a device that he would repeat often throughout his career, a unique woodblock effect that mimicked the footsteps of the characters as they walked or danced.

When Carl Stalling was scoring this first series of Mickey Mouse cartoons for Disney, he and Walt would often get into great arguments about the musical score. Stalling would frequently lobby for a more predominant role for his music. Walt argued instead for the music to more closely fit the action he had planned. One day in 1929, Walt gave in. "Look," he told Stalling, "let's work it out this way. We'll make two series." He suggested that the visuals of the second series would be drawn to fit the mood and rhythm of Stalling's music, which would take precedence.

At first, Disney thought that Stalling meant to do a series similar to the Song-O-Reels they had done back in Kansas City. That, however, was not Stalling's intent at all. Instead, he proposed using inanimate objects sprung to life. For a first endeavor, he suggested the idea of a dancing skeleton. "*The Skeleton Dance* goes way back to my kid days," Stalling recalls. "When I was eight or ten years old, I saw an ad in *The American Boy* magazine of a dancing skeleton, and I got my dad to give me a quarter so I could send for it." Stalling had always remembered enjoying the toy and imagining what it would be like to see real skeletons dancing. The idea was given to Ub, who, as usual, ran with it.

On February 29, 1929, while in New York City on a trip to pre-sell the new series, Walt had written a letter to Ub in California, "I am glad the spook dance is progressing so nicely—give her Hell, Ubbe—make it funny and I am sure we will be able to place it in a good way. I have them all worked up and raring to see it—so we can't disappoint them—we have a wonderful score to it. The music sounds like a little symphony."

Carl Stalling had indeed written a miniature symphony. He used a bit of Edvard Grieg's *March of the Dwarfs* for dramatic effect, but a portion of the music was an original minor-key fox-trot. Ub's drawings perfectly fit the syncopation of Stalling's rhythms.

Stalling suggested using the name *Symphony* coupled with a humorous word as the title for the series. Walt asked, "Carl, how would 'Silly Symphony' sound to you?" Stalling thought it an inspired choice. With *The Skeleton Dance*, the Silly Symphonies were born.

As he often did, Ub went to the local library for inspiration. He returned with several books. In one of these books, Ub had found pictures drawn by the English cartoonist Rowlandson of skeletons dancing humorously. In other books, he discovered photographs of skeleton dances as depicted upon the walls of Etruscan tombs. From these scant sources Ub concocted the macabre imagery of skeletons arising from their tombs and dancing about a graveyard.

Too jazzy to be truly scary, *The Skeleton Dance* featured some of the most inspired animation of its day—or any day. The sight of the skeletons arising from their graves, not to wreak havoc upon the citizenry or to cause some horrendous ruckus, but for the sole purpose of putting their bony thumbs upon their heads and turning fey pirouettes, was a whimsical and novel concept that was executed well. Ub placed an imaginary camera in places we as an audience had never gone before. Skeletons jumped out toward us and through us. We traveled inside their rib cages and back out again. Boundaries of perspective disappeared as Ub pushed on through to discover an almost psychological level of filmmaking.

Years later, Ub humbly recalled his role in creating this milestone of animation history:

> In February 1929, I did The Skeleton Dance. *It was a different type of film from the Mickeys. I did all the animation, but I did it rough, in line form. Other guys put in the rib cages and teeth and eyes and bones.*

This was to be Ub's modus operandi over the years. He would supply the rough drawings to young apprentices who would do "clean-up" work on the drawings to complete them.

One of these apprentices, Les Clark, was even given a chance to animate a scene alone, his first opportunity for such an honor. He created a whimsical scene of a pair of skeletons playing the spines of other skeleton dancers like calcified xylophones. Once again, the rest of the animation was entirely Ub's.

Ub's manner of animating *The Skeleton Dance* began to become a bone of contention for Walt and for Ub. Walt wanted Ub to make better use of his time by drawing only extreme poses and employing apprentices to draw all the in-betweens. Disney thought it a horrible waste of Ub's considerable talent for him to do his own in-betweens.

Ub disagreed on principle. Ub preferred drawing straight-ahead without pausing the action for static poses. He reasoned that if he did only the extremes, he would lose the control over the kineticism of his art. His work would become static, uninteresting. The Ub Iwerks style was constant, motivated motion. Ub admired the Fleischer Brothers' concept of moving holds, but he took it even further to an almost balletic level. According to animator Mark Kausler, Ub "created more of a dance. The characters move their arms . . . and they move across and around in perspective. He really figured out how to give a dance-like rhythmic quality to his animation."

Over the years, from Alice to Oswald to Mickey, Ub sat one-on-one with his characters, breathing life into each line. Ollie Johnston reasons that "[Ub] would have to visualize that stuff—a lot of animators can't visualize. Some of us are in-between guys. Milt Kahl could see the drawing on his paper and just draw the lines around it. I have a feeling Ub was like that, otherwise he couldn't have turned out that kind of work. If you had to fool around and try to draw them, you could never have moved them around like that."

Walt Disney, on the other hand, favored holding poses for dramatic emphasis. Sometimes when all the animators would go home at night, Walt would go to Ub's animation desk and re-time the exposure sheets that Ub had drawn up. The same drawings would be used, but the camera instructions were rewritten to emphasize Walt's preferred style.

When Ub arrived in the morning, the rearrangement of his previous day's work—coupled with rather cold demands from Walt—began to sting. Mark Kausler explains Ub's frustration:

> Walt would be constantly rewriting Ub's exposure sheets to change the timing to something he wanted, and it was different from what Ub imagined when he was animating it. Timing is very sacred to an animator because it's such an integral part. It's not just drawings. It's drawings as applied to film time. The rate of exposure is very important to get the effects

across that an animator wants. The fact that somebody was changing it—Walt was fooling around, changing it—probably disturbed him fundamentally because it was breaking that connection between drawing and film timing.

Ub was furious at this tinkering with his timing. He confronted Walt on the issue. "Don't you ever touch my drawings!" he demanded. "These are my drawings and this is how I solve the problems, keep your hands off them!" Ub won the immediate battle on *The Skeleton Dance*, but the issue was far from resolved. Both men knew that they would revisit this argument time and again. The differences in their production methods—producer versus artist—were not easily squelched. Walt was becoming aware of the industrial automation techniques employed by automakers such as Henry Ford and the necessity of producing films quickly. Ub was thinking only in terms of the methods that worked best for him.

In spite of this growing tension, Ub completed *The Skeleton Dance* almost single-handedly. Less heroic but more sophisticated than *Plane Crazy,* less monumental but more technically brilliant than *Steamboat Willie, The Skeleton Dance* was the work of an artist at the pinnacle of his craft. It was the work that advanced both Ub and the Disney Studio to the next level of excellence.

Walt Disney proclaimed, "With each picture we produce we are experimenting." This experimentation extended to the choice of subject matter as well as to the mechanics of animation, sound, and effects. Not everyone was pleased with the direction this experimentation was taking.

When *The Skeleton Dance* was finished, Disney sent a print to New York for Pat Powers to use as a sample reel to sell the new series to prospective customers. Powers replied tersely, "They don't want this. MORE MICE."

The response from a press screening in Los Angeles was equally pessimistic. "Can't recommend it," the theater manager said. "Too gruesome." Audiences disagreed. They loved it.

Chuck Jones recalls, "Charlie Chaplin said Disney had the finest sense of what the public would buy rather than what the audience wanted—well, we didn't know what we wanted—but they knew what Walt wrote and what Ub animated was remarkable."

Their second Silly Symphony, *Hell's Bells*, like *The Skeleton Dance*, was more gruesome fare. For a man depicted by many as mild mannered, almost saintlike, many of Ub Iwerks's creations had an extremely dark, almost occult bent that gave them a decided edginess in comparison to typical Disney fare. *Hell's Bells* featured a spider protagonist, one of Ub's favorite characters. As with most of Ub's spiders, this demon bore six legs instead of the biologically correct eight. As animated flames leapt at the inferno walls, evil imps and dark bats filled the screen with nonstop eccentric action.

The music that Carl Stalling chose to accompany *Hell's Bells* was the very same haunting melody that would later resurface some thirty years later as the distinctive theme song for Alfred Hitchcock's similarly macabre classic television anthology series, *Alfred Hitchcock Presents*. In both cases, it was the perfect musical accompaniment for mayhem.

Walt Disney would later state, "I can't think of the pictorial story without thinking of the complementary music that will fulfill it." He went on to explain the formation of the Silly Symphony series and how it complemented the Mickey Mouse cartoons. "The whole idea of the Symphonies was to give me another street to work on, you know. Getting away from a set pattern of a character. Each Symphony, the idea would be a different story based on music with comedy and things."

Despite the diversion of the new series, the popularity of Mickey Mouse remained at a fever pitch throughout 1929. To capitalize on the Mouse's success, Disney released the Silly Symphonies under the title "Mickey Mouse Presents a Walt Disney Silly Symphony."

Fluffy articles continued to be written around the world hailing the new superstar and his young creators. Many times the articles singled out Ub as the sole inspiration and creative brainchild behind the Mouse, as in an article from the French magazine, *Pour Vous*:

"Mickey the mouse plays music in Hong Kong and Berlin, Paris and New York. He has become the adored mascot of all the world. And the man who created him, Ub Iwerks, the American draughtsman, became famous with him."

This newfound fame placed Ub in an awkward position within the Disney organizational hierarchy, creating a strain upon the delicate relationship between Ub and Walt. Disney had always generously granted Ub full drawing credit in the title cards of the cartoons, an honor that most other animation studios did not bestow in any manner. Now Ub's visibility was diverting the marketing focus away from Walt.

Throughout his career, Walt Disney understood that he was and should be the single focal point for his enterprise. Roy Disney recognized the irrefutable business sense of this and further suggested that the name of the studio be changed from the Disney Brothers Studio to the Walt Disney Studio. It stands to reason that if Walt would not position his brother Roy—who was instrumental in every success the studio had ever earned—to share the limelight, he certainly would not be comfortable with one of his animators basking in that glow, not even Ub. Years later, animator Ken Anderson was told this in no uncertain terms. Bob Thomas relates a telling anecdote in his book, *Walt Disney: An American Original*:

> Walt approached the young Anderson early in his career to tell him, "You're new here, and I want you to understand one thing: there's just one thing we're selling here, and that's the name 'Walt Disney.' If you can buy that and be happy to work for it, you're my man. But if you've got any ideas of selling the name 'Ken Anderson,' it's best for you to leave right now."

Near the end of his career, Walt admitted, "*I'm* not Walt Disney anymore. All of *this* is Walt Disney." *This* meant the whole Walt Disney enterprise: movies, theme parks, television, merchandising—the works.

Even the famous signature logo that to this day signifies all things

Disney was manufactured to promote the name "Walt Disney." It has been rumored—and is indeed highly likely—that the logo, based on Walt Disney's actual signature, like Mickey Mouse, was first drawn by Ub Iwerks and later modified by other Disney artists. Regardless of how it was created or the artists whose hands graced its delicate curves, it remains every bit Walt Disney's signature.

It seemed that everyone wanted the phenomenal Mouse. "Because I had done the animation," Ub recalled, "I got a letter one day from somebody at King Features Syndicate asking me to do a Mickey Mouse newspaper comic strip. I turned the letter over to Walt—that wasn't my business. He made the deal, and I did the drawings for a few strips. Actually, with all the animation work, I had no time for comics, I had too much else to do."

Because of these demands on his time, Ub merely roughed out the art for the first eighteen strips. Win Smith, who Ub described as "quite good with a pen," did the inking. The story line of the first series, entitled "Lost on a Desert Island," was adapted from the cartoons *Plane Crazy* and *The Castaway* (which had not yet been released). Even though he passed the strip on to Win Smith, who later relinquished it to Floyd Gottfredson, Ub Iwerks would receive credit in a byline that would continue to run for almost a year. The byline read "By Walt Disney and Ub Iwerks."

The first comic strip came out on January 13, 1930. The first few were gag-a-day strips that even without Ub's full attention retained his unique brand of humor and artistic nuance. A typical scene would involve castaway Mickey Mouse following mysterious footprints along a deserted beach only to discover that they were created by a pelican nonsensically wearing human boots. The gags, like the cartoons, featured Ub's trademark punctuation marks and sweat bubbles accentuating the action within.

As both the Mickey Mouse and Silly Symphony series faced immediate and growing success, the brewing tensions between Ub and Walt were becoming more and more evident. The difficulties were perhaps exacerbated by the promise offered by the Silly Symphony series.

Because there were no readily identifiable characters, the audience held no preconceptions. Ub Iwerks was given a blank canvas upon which to unleash his restless imagination. In the Sillies, Ub was not restricted by subject matter, story constraints, or convention itself. His mind was free to be as spontaneous, as innovative, as predisposed to attempt the impossible. Ub's only restrictions were Walt Disney's opinions.

With the stress to keep up with the demand for new cartoons, Walt transferred that pressure onto Ub in chilling letters that clearly reveal the duality of his emotions toward his longtime friend. When he was in New York City working on the soundtracks for the Mickeys, Disney wrote telling instructions back to Ub in California. At the same time that he was exalting Ub's native talents, Walt Disney—as he was known to do—could browbeat Ub in a very personal and condescending way. "Listen, Ub. Show some of your old SPEED. Work like hell, BOY. It is our one BIG CHANCE to make a real killing. Forget a lot of the fancy curves and pretty-looking drawings and devote your time to the ACTION. You can do it—I know you can . . . GIVE HER HELL . . . Don't tell me it can't be done. It has got to be done . . . So quit acting nervous and fidgety. Forget everything . . . get that DAMN picture back here in time."

As Walt became more insistent and critical, Ub became more distant and unwilling. His strengths and intentions were being undermined and his motivation declined. If Ub resisted the urge to vent his frustration in public arenas, privately he never got used to the insults. For a time, he tolerated them as best he could, but by the end of 1929, it had all become too much for him. His work ethic, which had never diminished, even during his most trying times, began to wane. For a time, the Symphonies provided Ub with the challenge he needed to cloak his emotions, but now even those were losing their luster for him.

Musical director Carl Stalling suggested creating a new subset to the Silly Symphonies that revolved around the seasons. Ub was assigned to direct these. With Ub's absence on the Mickey Mouse series, newcomer Burt Gillett took over the animation duties. Gillett was a talented director in his own right, but his version of Mickey retained little of Ub's anarchy. Gillett—at Walt's urging—civilized Mickey.

Ub began to work on the newest Silly Symphonies. The *Summer* entry in the series takes place in a by now all-too-familiar forest glade. A long caterpillar crawls out of an ear of corn. He is joined by three others, who begin to dance, accompanied by Ub's woodblock effect. The three are clones of one another. They bounce from left to right and from right to left along a single plane. Ub's animation on this new series reverts back to an earlier, simpler, less developed style.

Over the years, because time was always short, Ub had become quite adept at using "cheats" and shortcuts in his animation. He reasoned that if one character looked good doing some action, three doing the same thing looked astounding! Most cycles were repeated at least once in this manner. If a character danced across the stage in one direction, Ub would simply reverse the drawings and have the character dance back in the opposite direction.

In *Summer,* he utilized all of his shortcuts to excess. A scene wherein butterflies dance in a one-dimensional ballet is followed by one in which a ladybug plays a dragonfly like a xylophone, taking advantage of one of the standard animation sound effects, the sweeping, swishing swipe of an arm along a xylophonic path.

For Ub, the increasing pressures from Walt were taking their toll. Mildred would see her husband's mood change daily and she was often frustrated seeing him stifle his emotions. Ub tolerated Walt's demands, but by the end of 1929, he found it just too difficult. Mildred recalls the tension she witnessed during a discomforting evening at a Hollywood party. As Walt, Lillian, Ub, and Mildred were engaged in conversation, a young boy approached Walt Disney asking him to draw his famous character and autograph it. Turning to Ub, Walt said, "Why don't you draw Mickey and I'll sign it." Astonished, Ub fired back, "Draw your own—Mickey!" and stormed out. The public credit Walt took, coupled with the criticism he gave, became all too insulting for Ub. Perhaps in Ub's mind was the thought that if Walt knew it all, he certainly didn't need *him* anymore. To industry insiders, Ub had often been viewed as the strongest talent at the Disney Studio. Now with his own reputation and skills to ground him, Ub considered going it on his own. *Autumn,* the next Silly Symphony to go into production, would be one of the least inspired of Ub's efforts. As forest animals dance in syncopated rhythm from the pages of his drawing board, thoughts of independence floated in his head.

chapter 7

A New Beginning

Nineteen twenty-nine was a year of crashes. On Wall Street, in an atmosphere of panic and widespread distrust, the stock market plummeted, setting off the Great Depression. At the Disney Studios tensions continued to surface that would shatter the fragile harmony of the friendship between the Disney brothers and Ub.

It was against this backdrop that Pat Powers had an associate privately approach Ub with an offer that would give him the artistic freedom he coveted. Combined with the prospects of distribution by MGM, a $300 weekly salary, strong financial backing from Powers (although Powers's personal participation remained unknown to Ub for a time) and the ability to be his own boss, it was simply an offer that Ub could not and did not refuse.

He began immediately to surreptitiously recruit animators for the Ub Iwerks Studio, privately telling his coworkers of his plans. They took interest. Old friend Rollin "Ham" Hamilton, who had defected with Oswald, was among the first to sign on. Recruiting within the Disney Studio itself was more problematic. Merle Gilson, currently working on the Mickey Mouse series, quietly agreed to jump ship and join Ub as well.

Floyd Gottfredson, a young in-betweener who had been working with Dave Hand, Norm Ferguson, and Wilfred Jackson on the Silly Symphony series for less than a month, was surprised when Ub handed him some drawings saying, "Do these for me, will ya'?"

"I couldn't believe it," Gottfredson recalled. "Here was the great Ub Iwerks asking me to do in-betweens! So I flipped through the things and down in the middle of them was a note asking me to meet him for lunch. So I went off with him and he told me that he'd been watching me and he was impressed with my work and would like to have me come to work for him. This was the first I knew he was setting up his own studio. I was quite flattered."

Ub offered Gottfredson $25 a week, a considerable raise from his Disney wages. Gottfredson accepted. "I knew by then that Ub was *the* man in the animation business, and he told me that he would be able to teach me a lot of things that would be beneficial to me."

On January 21, 1930, Ub told Roy Disney that he was leaving to form his own studio. Roy was astonished and made an unsuccessful attempt to talk Ub out of it. The financial stability and creative independence Powers offered held too strong an allure. Roy immediately telegrammed Walt in New York.

> *Ubbe resigns effective soon as possible. Wants to leave at completion [of] this picture. Will hold him long as possible. Gives his reasons personal differences with you, admits other connections. Declines to say where or what. Will attempt settlement of his interest. Will get full release from all possible claims. Will consult attorney on same. Our talk was limited. He has not yet given any views on what he expects. I will deal with for settlement on two basis*(sic): *preferably outright amount or agreement of sharing interest on profits of pictures to date.*
>
> *Suggest stop all publicity immediately on Ubbe's name. Feel that sooner we have definite release from him the better.*

On the first day of the shocking news, Roy Disney had already fully assessed the situation well and was in the process of damage control.

The next day, Roy and Gunther Lessing, Disney's legal counsel, drew up an agreement that released Ub from his contract and transferred all his "right, title, or interest" back to the Disneys in exchange for a cash settlement of $2,920.

Unbeknownst to Ub, at that very moment, Pat Powers was meeting with Walt Disney in New York City. Though the purpose of the meeting was ostensibly to renegotiate a new contract, Powers took the opportunity to pit the fortunes of the Disney Studio against those of the Iwerks Studio. He tried to leverage a deal with Walt. Disney hadn't received the telegram yet and was stunned to hear that Ub was leaving.

"Pick up the phone," Powers told him, "and call out there. Your brother knows about it. Call."

"Don't be upset," Powers continued. "You haven't lost him. You can still have him. All I want is a deal."

"No," Walt responded bitterly. "I wouldn't want him. If he feels that way, I could never work with him." The decision was final—no deals.

Roy wrote Walt in New York: "Not trying to excuse Ub, but just trying to size it up all the way around, I believe Ub at the start meant O.K., and I am sure that right now, even though he won't admit it, he regrets very much the outcome." A later telegram from Roy stated bitterly that he wished Ub would go to New York "to make his pictures." The further Ub was removed from the Disneys and California, the better.

Roy told Carl Stalling of Ub's defection. "When Ub left, I thought something was wrong," Stalling remembered. "When Roy Disney told me that Ub was leaving, I told him, 'Well, I guess I'll be leaving, too.' It was not very pleasant to think about, because we were all good friends. But we were getting worried. Walt paid only half salary for a year or two and I had a home and expenses."

Stalling feared that Ub's departure would deal a death blow to Disney, which was still operating in the red because of the high cost of the sound process. He felt, as many did, that Ub was the pillar around which Disney had built his cartoon world. Now that Ub was leaving, Stalling foresaw that world crumbling down. He immediately signed a contract with Van Beuren's Aesop Fables. He left within days of Ub's announcement.

Others at the Disney Studio did not share Stalling's pessimism. Burt Gillett and Wilfred Jackson pulled Floyd Gottfredson aside. "No, you're absolutely wrong about Ub," they told him, "and you shouldn't have done this. While Ub is a great animator, Walt is really the brains and the creative man here—he's the man who's going to build this place into something really big."

Gottfredson began to get cold feet and went to Roy Disney. Roy called Ub. "Look, Ub, this Gottfredson is the last straw. You've been trying to get our key men around here, trying to get anybody that you can while Walt's back in New York looking for animators. We've just had enough of this, and it's got to stop."

Ub released Gottfredson from his contract. The tension between Ub, Walt, and Roy had reached its peak. "Walt was devastated when Ub left the studio," remarks Disney archivist Dave Smith. "Ub was such an accomplished animator. He was really the father of the animators at Disney—they all looked up to him, they all went to him when they had questions, and losing that key person at the studio caused Walt to have a lot of worries about what was going to happen in the future." Walt's reaction surprised Ub, until he learned of the connection with Pat Powers. On January 25, 1930, Roy Disney sent a letter off to Walt in New York. "I had quite a talk with Ub this morning, a very calm, quiet attitude on both sides. I told him frankly that the worst feature of this whole affair was the fact that a fellow as close to us as he had been should turn on us at a time like this. . . . Also I told him that from a financial angle we would benefit greatly by his withdrawal but that we were deeply shocked and hurt at being treated as we have been by two fellows (Ub and Carl Stalling) in whom we heretofore had every confidence and trust. Ub wilted and said that up to this time he had said nothing, thinking that whatever he said would not be believed anyhow. I said, 'For pity's sake say something and at least try to keep us from having such a nasty, mean opinion of you as circumstances and conditions are forcing us to have as long as you keep your mouth shut.'

"So he started out from the first and told me how the whole thing

developed. Before the conversation ended he said he was going to write to you and took your address. He said he did not want you to feel hard against him—that he would never have gone into this had he had any idea it would turn out as it has, that the whole thing was misrepresented to him entirely different as having no connection with us or affecting us in the least. He said he did not even know until two days before he received his contract that P. A. Powers was behind it..."
An associate of Powers who failed to represent himself as such handled all the negotiations. Ub told Roy that when he was first approached by this fellow he was experiencing considerable friction with Walt. In an interview with author Lawrence Watkins in the 1960s, Ub simply said "he had made up his mind to step out and since the henchman had represented it to be outside parties entirely with a national releasing outfit, he thought it was perfectly just and right."

In February 1930, Ub decided to leave the mouse he had once designed and the studio he had helped to build. At the age of twenty-eight he had a new studio to call his own.

IWERKS, CELEBRATED CARTOONIST OF THE
SCREEN, PRODUCES NEW AND FUNNIER
SERIES WITH SOUND

Ub Iwerks now devotes his energy, originality, and skill to the task of surpassing all that he has done heretofore. He starts in where he left off with other subjects in this field. He has added new ideas and has taken advantage of his own new improvements in production methods.
Press Sheet—1930, Ub Iwerks Studio

The Ub Iwerks Studio was divided into three rooms: a camera room, an ink-and-paint room, and an animation room, where Merle Gilson, Rollin Hamilton, and new recruit Ben Clopton set up shop alongside Ub. They began to try out character ideas.

Ub settled on the idea of a series featuring a frog as a central character. Frogs had frequently been a part of Ub's repertoire. He had included a model sheet of a frog as a suggestion for a replacement character when Mintz took Oswald. A recent *Silly Symphony,*

Summer had featured a bouyant scene of frogs leaping across a bucolic lily pond.

An announcement in *Exhibitors Herald-World* explained the appeal. "It is pointed out by cartoonist Iwerks that a frog more nearly represents a human being than anything else in all nature. A frog may be the epitome of laziness or lightning-like action as may suit his erratic impulses. . ."

As a name for his new creation, Ub favored "Flip the Frog." Charlie Giegerich, who worked for Pat Powers, had different ideas. "The name of 'Tony Frog' would indicate a snappy sort of individual and, consisting of two words, it more readily fits on theater marquees."

Ub opted instead for alliteration. Bobby Bumps, Ko-ko the Clown, Betty Boop, and Mickey Mouse were all popular cartoon characters with alliterative names. Giegerich responded, "I personally have difficulty in pronouncing the words 'Flip the Frog' without lapsing into a lisp. Try it out on a number of people and see how many can pronounce the sentence without stumbling." The tongue twister test proved inconclusive. Flip the Frog it was.

On March 4, 1930, Ub placed a help-wanted advertisement in the *Los Angeles Times*. The ad sought aspiring artists who wanted "to learn the cartoon film business." The next day, a Monday, more than fifty applicants waited in a line that extended around the block for a chance to fill one or two positions at the Ub Iwerks Studio.

One by one, each applicant took a drawing test and showed his portfolio of artwork to Ub, who was personally conducting each interview. Fred Kopietz, a young artist fresh from Chouinard Art School, was hired to paint backgrounds. Another young artist, Jim Pabian, was so excited at the prospect of applying at the Iwerks Studio that he had forgotten his portfolio. When he got to the front of the line, he told Ub what had happened and showed a glowing letter of recommendation. Ub smiled and asked Pabian to take the drawing test, which consisted of tracing a character onto a piece of celluloid.

Pabian had been watching as one by one the applicants ahead of him would get a case of nerves and were rejected because their lines were too shaky. "I didn't wait to bolster my courage," Pabian recalls. "So with a bravado I forced upon myself, I grabbed the pen, dipped it into ink, and quickly traced the drawing onto the cel. When it was done, Mr. Iwerks told me to take a chair in the adjoining room and wait until he was through with the remaining few applicants."

When Ub returned, he offered Pabian $25 a week to be an inker. It was more than twice what Pabian had expected. He was so ecstatic that he improvised a little cheer, which he repeated until Ub insisted that he stop: "Iwerks, you works—we all works for Iwerks!"

With the key positions filled, Iwerks began to fill entry-level positions at the studio. Fred Kopietz recommended a classmate from Chouinard Art School named Chuck Jones for a position as a cel washer. "When I told my friends I was a cel washer," Jones recalls, "they thought I worked in a prison or jail washing cells after the drunks had finished with them." After each cel had been inked, painted, and photographed, it was carefully washed, dried, and reused. In the Depression-era 1930s, cel washing was an essential way of reusing resources and saving crucial operating cash. Each piece of celluloid cost seven cents, and with thousands of cels used for each film, the money saved through reusing the cels could be spent on technological advances and innovations.

Chuck Jones recalls his first impressions of Ub. "He seemed to always be thinking of something else. Of course, he would have nothing to do with me being a lousy cel washer and in-betweener, but he was nice, he was always friendly . . . but as far as my contact with him I had zero, but I got a lot of information of course from Grim Natwick, and Grim admired him as an animator very much, and Grim was one of the great ones."

Much of Ub's mind during this time was preoccupied with the new idea of color in cartoons. Ideally, he would have insisted on using the new state-of-the-art three-color Technicolor process (process #4) then in development, but he knew that Walt Disney had already signed an exclusive two-year agreement for the use of three-color Technicolor in cartoons.

Ub was forced to use the inferior—yet still revolutionary in animation—two-color Technicolor process (process #3) for Flip the Frog's pilot film, *Fiddlesticks*. Two-color Technicolor utilized a red-and-green subtractive process to create a limited but functional palette that nonetheless served adequately for the simple forest scenes and animal life depicted in *Fiddlesticks*. With a minimum of fanfare, in his first solo outing, Ub Iwerks had made the colossal leap from black-and-white into color. It would be two long years before Disney would receive international acclaim (and an Oscar) for producing the first three-color Technicolor cartoon, *Flowers and Trees*. Ub had the technical genius to beat Disney to the punch, but he lacked the marketing skill necessary to promote his innovations to the public.

Ub's use of color went largely unnoticed. Perhaps the reason for the indifference was that the woodland scene depicted in *Fiddlesticks* too strongly recalled some of Ub's earlier efforts with the Silly Symphonies. The technology was a breakthrough, but the story felt like a retread of past successes. Like countless beavers, squirrels, and birds before him, Flip the Frog danced gleefully across a series of lily pads to the accompaniment of a syncopated wood block. An eclectic band of insect musicians provided perfectly synchronized musical backing. A spider played drums. A penguin—seriously out of his realm—served as maitre d'. The incongruity of the insect orchestra was cute enough, but the audience had seen all this before.

It was apparent from the start that although he was fluidly drawn, Flip was a far from overpowering character. In this first film, he did not speak at all, but mercilessly mugged, squeaked, and cavorted with a two-dimensional, rubber-limbed abandon that recalled the influence of Paul Terry. From his webbed hands and feet to his bulbous eyes, he was every inch a frog. Ub had suggested in a press announcement that Flip the Frog "would live up to his name in action and sound." That he did.

The only concession to fantasy was a natty-looking bow tie, a few buttons down his chest, and a predilection for the old soft shoe. A cut-off stump provided a rustic stage on which Flip could perform the elaborate gravity-defying dance that Ub had perfected for Mickey Mouse and the dancing broom in *The Opry House*.

At the conclusion of the dance, a very Mickeyish mouse joins Flip on stage. The mouse plays fiddle while Flip accompanies him on piano. The faux Mickey is so emotionally moved by his own violin playing that he suddenly bursts into tears. A similar scene occurs in Disney's Mickey Mouse cartoon, *Fiddlin' Around*. Because the two films were made at the same time, it is difficult to discern which influenced which, but it is obvious that both studios were openly borrowing inspiration from each other.

This is no more evident than in the coloring used on the mouse in *Fiddlesticks*. Iwerks's Mickey Mouse clone wore distinctly red-colored shorts a full two years before Mickey Mouse appeared in a similar outfit in his first color cartoon, 1935's *The Band Concert*. Even out on his own, it was possible that Ub was still influencing the direction that Mickey Mouse was taking.

In fact, the Disney brothers, aware that Ub's prodigious talent could offer them strong competition in the marketplace, watched every move that their old friend, now adversary, made. In a letter to Walt on April 26, 1930, Roy Disney wrote: "I hear considerable about Flip the Frog. Powers isn't even trying to sell it now. He is waiting for a good picture. They were all very disappointed with the first."

Not that the Disney Studio came through Ub's leaving unscathed. Animator-historian Mark Kausler surmises:

> [Disney] just didn't have the strength of draughtsmanship. It took them a long time to recover that, to once again get up to where they thought they should be. And I think that was a big impact that Ub made by leaving. He took a lot of the strongest draughtsmanship with him out of the Disney films. The style that people associated with the early Mickey was gone and Walt was probably very disturbed at that too because he had relied so heavily on one man. I don't think he ever did that again.

Despite the fact that *Fiddlesticks* was one of the most expensive cartoons ever made at that point, and although it exploited audiences' desires for more and more sound-effects gags—in color no less!—Flip the Frog did not generate much critical or audience interest.

Ub launched his second Flip cartoon, *Puddle Pranks*, into production before *Fiddlesticks* was released. The result in the theaters was very much the same as *Fiddlesticks*. While interested in distributing the new series, Metro-Goldwyn-Mayer insisted that Flip be redesigned to become more round and boylike. As much as Ub was trying to break away from the circular construction that he had popularized with Mickey Mouse, the appeal in the design was proving to be universal. Ub went back to the drawing board with one objective in mind—to create a more appealing character.

Flip's initial changes were subtle and mostly involved his apparel and other superficial characteristics. Ub gave him pants, gloves, shoes, and a hat. He grew a chin and his eyes moved from the top of his head to a lower location on his face. Also, for the first time, he was given a voice with which to speak, not merely squeak.

Ub's personal style was stamped more on these early Flip the Frog cartoons because he was acting as both key animator and director. Walls, furniture, and most anything with a straight line became slightly curved. There was an inherent cartooniness to Ub's work, in that inanimate objects were imbued with a natural rhythm and bounciness. Unlike his earlier work in the Alice comedies, in which backgrounds were merely a setting in which to place a character, the Flip settings became characters in themselves.

Adding a voice to Flip was one of the first major challenges that faced Carl Stalling, who left Van Beuren after a few short months to rejoin his old friend as the Iwerks Studio's musical director. Because all music, sound effects, and dialogue had to be recorded and mixed simultaneously—there were no multitrack recording systems at that time—Stalling treated the voice artist as merely another piece of the typically eight- to twelve-piece orchestra he used to score the Flip the

Frog series. Flip would never be a particularly verbal character, but at least now there would be more options available for the growing creative staff, which by the summer of 1930 numbered approximately twelve employees.

In addition to Stalling in the music department, Ub continued to recruit animators, storymen, and assistants. Storyman Bugs Hardaway and former Fleischer animator Rudy Zamora came to the studio around this time, as did a vibrant young woman named Dorothy Webster, who became Ub's secretary.

In New York, Pat Powers's adopted daughter, Eileen "Dot" George, also had great aspirations of being an animator. When she turned eighteen, Powers set her on a train and headed her west to the Iwerks Studio. To Dot's dismay, she was relegated to a position in the ink-and-paint department. It would be years before women would break out of the back room and into more visible roles as animators and directors. Dot spent four and a half years at the Iwerks Studio working as an inker with no chance for advancement.

Aside from providing his daughter to the studio, Powers was pressed by Ub into purchasing the best production equipment available, regardless of the expense. Powers fronted the capital for a high-tech recording console, the highest-quality microphones, new editing equipment, and an expensive animation camera. Ub's mind was increasingly focused upon technical matters. The new equipment would nurture and rationalize that interest. To accommodate the influx of new personnel and equipment, Powers rented new studio space at 9713 Santa Monica Boulevard in Beverly Hills. The second-floor studio had formerly been a dentist's office, and still contained some of the fixtures from that enterprise.

More important than the expanded, upgraded facilities was the studio's location adjacent to the Red Line train tracks. This provided not only a decent means of transportation but also made a fantastic horseshoe court for noontime horseshoe matches on the right of way. No matter how harried the schedule became or how strenuous the pace, the Iwerks Studio staff would always break for horseshoes.

Ub, the most adamant of the lot, reportedly attacked horseshoes with the same dogged persistence with which he attacked his animation.

The changes that were made in the new studio and in Flip were far from perfect to be sure—Flip would continue to evolve throughout his career—but they were sufficient enough, however, to entice Metro-Goldwyn-Mayer to begin distributing the series under Pat Powers's Celebrity Pictures banner. Flip the Frog would be MGM's first cartoon venture.

During these early 1930s, after the success of Mickey Mouse's sound debut, the major motion-picture studios began paying attention to the once novel idea of cartoon films. Suddenly the studios decided they needed their own cartoon factories to produce a steady output and to partake in the potential profits. Although the studios usually had to look beyond their own organizations for the necessary talent, once that talent was secured, the cartoons often exhibited the styles and preoccupations of the parent studio.

The Max Fleischer-produced cartoons of the 1930s (Betty Boop) fit in with the zany humor of the Marx Brothers and W. C. Fields as well with the eroticism of the films of Josef Von Sternberg and Mae West. At Warner Brothers, the early efforts relied heavily on music from the Busby Berkeley movies and plot ideas from the studio's features. At MGM, the watchword was glossiness. MGM spent more money per cartoon than any studio except Disney, and they made sure that it showed up tangibly on the screen. No one was happier about this than Ub, whose desire for top-quality product matched MGM's ability to produce it.

With distribution guaranteed, Ub Iwerks kicked his studio into high gear. The encouragement of the MGM contract gave him the push he needed. For inspiration, he looked to contemporary culture and current events as he had done with *Plane Crazy* and *Steamboat Willie*. In the late 1920s, a series of films starring William Powell as detective Philo Vance were released by Paramount. With titles like *The Benson Murder Case*, *The Greene Murder Case*, and *The*

Canary Murder Case, these dark films inspired Flip the Frog's 1931 offering, *The Cuckoo Murder Case*.

The Cuckoo Murder Case, utilizing all the glossy production values that MGM required, begins with an unseen perpetrator murdering a cuckoo-clock bird in an abandoned house. Before collapsing to his death, the cuckoo peers through the ghastly hole in his side, clutches a flower to his chest and falls dead. Not exactly Disney fare.

A horrified clock face picks up the telephone and dials "Sherlock Flip, Detective." Flip, replete with deerstalker hat, sleeps peacefully as the phone angrily rings behind him. "Damn!" The anthropomorphic phone swears, looking squarely into the camera. At the Disney Studio, a policy of self-censorship assured that the audience would not be offended on matters of taste. Disney would never have allowed questionable language of any ilk. At the Iwerks Studio, mild curses became commonplace.

Apart from blue language and unnerving subject matter, there are several scenes in *The Cuckoo Murder Case* in which Ub and his staff play with perspective with equal abandon. One such scene has Flip sneaking upstairs as the perspective of the staircase moves stealthily along with him. In typical cartoons of the day, the perspective drawings of the backgrounds remained fixed as the camera merely seemed to pan horizontally across them. The rules of three-dimensional perspective rendering were often ignored in the interest of expedience. To accomplish Flip's mobile perspective effect, the backgrounds had to be animated painstakingly frame by frame to keep up with a moving vanishing point.

The Cuckoo Murder Case ends with a single-vanishing-point effect. Flip the Frog finds that he is to be next on the Angel of Death's hit list and tries to escape by running through a cluttered hallway. As he runs directly away from us, Flip recalls practically every railroad-track, highway, or hallway chase that Ub had animated from Oswald's in *Trolley Troubles* to Mickey Mouse's in *Plane Crazy*. When Flip reaches the end of the hallway, he leaps into the void and disappears into inky blackness.

While Ub continued to work on improving the Flip the Frog cartoons in 1932, Pat Powers began to recruit the best and brightest from New York–based animation studios. From the Max Fleischer Studio, Powers enticed Grim Natwick, the source of much of Fleischer's style, to jump ship and join Iwerks in California. As the creator of Betty Boop, Natwick was recognized by his colleagues as one of the top animators in the business. As such, he had been heavily courted by Roy Disney as a replacement for Ub. Grim chose instead to work alongside Ub at the Iwerks Studio. Al Eugster, another Betty Boop stalwart, followed Natwick's lead and joined the Iwerks Studio shortly thereafter. The Fleischer animators recognized Ub as a kindred spirit, a technically brilliant artist whose craft manifested itself in fits of rebellious energy on the screen.

The addition of this veteran animation talent allowed Ub to rid himself of staff members who were simply not working out. One of the casualties was Chuck Jones, who had worked himself up from the lowly position of cel-washer to the somewhat more esteemed position of in-betweener. "By the time I got to be an in-betweener," Jones recalls, "I was bad enough to get fired."

Musical director Carl Stalling took a sabbatical from the Iwerks Studio to return to Disney, where he was put to immediate work playing the piano on "Who's Afraid of the Big, Bad Wolf?" in *Three Little Pigs*.

Reinforcements came again from out East. Stalling was replaced at the Iwerks Studio by Fleischer Studio's Art Turkisher. Turkisher drove to California from New York with fellow Fleischer refugee Jimmie Culhane, who was also joining his old friends on the Iwerks animation staff.

The most unwelcome personnel addition from the animators' perspective was Emile Offemann, who took the position of office manager. Offemann was seen by all as Pat Powers's henchman and was universally despised. Despite an utter lack of experience in the cartoon industry, Offemann acted as if he were a seasoned director. He was a harsh taskmaster who insisted that each animator produce thirty feet of film each week. "He began to drive the entire crew batty with unrealistic demands to increase our work output," Jim Pabian remembers. "He knew nothing about cartoon filmmaking, so his orders struck our studio people as worthless."

Newcomer Godfrey Bjork, who had been the frequent target of Offemann's scrutiny, referred to the Frenchman as the "result of the rape of a clapped-up whore by a syphilitic camel." Offemann hounded Bjork mercilessly for more footage.

According to Jimmie Culhane, "Godfrey had reason to hate Offemann heartily. The poor man was suffering from a slowly deteriorating heart condition, which often confined him to his bed. Emile would call him at home several times a day, ostensibly to find out how he was, but in reality to check to see if Godfrey had possibly gone off to the beach or the movies."

Even sick, Bjork was not free from his nemesis's grasp. According to Culhane's recollection, Offemann continued sending piles of work to Bjork's home with orders for Godfrey to finish them. Bjork tried gamely, but found that he was physically unable to do the work. A few weeks later, his exhausted heart gave out and he died at home in bed.

Presumably, Offemann was merely doing the job that he had been hired to do. It was his manner that was sorely lacking in tact. "He would come sneaking around, listening if we were working or not when we worked nights," Ed Friedman recalls. "You could see his shadow. We had these frosted-glass doors and you could see his shadow bent over trying to listen if we were working or not—a real character."

In private, Ub would occasionally socialize with Offemann. Their two families would meet to play bridge or go dancing, but within the studio, Ub did not appreciate the negative impact of Emile Offemann's interventions and the effect he had on staff morale.

The opposite was true of the talented Fleischer expatriots. From the moment of their arrival, they made a profoundly positive impact on the output of the Iwerks Studio. Grim Natwick in particular was instrumental in changing the tone and style of the animation. Flip the Frog changed yet again. His face became even more humanlike and he developed a more interesting and pleasant personality.

Other changes had some obvious roots. As Ub and Mildred's son Don approached toddler age, more and more juvenile characters began to make their way onto the screen at his father's studio. In 1932's *The Milkman,* while delivering milk—in a scene involving a complex curved, moving-perspective street background—Flip encounters a young orphan boy who quickly becomes attached to Flip and the hilariously cursing horse that pulls his milk cart.

The same orphan boy is used again in the next film in the series *What a Life!* He is a fun foil for Flip. Constantly, he gets the upper hand without making Flip seem weak or overly harsh in his reactions. In *What a Life!* Flip and the boy are street musicians hustling for spare change during the Great Depression. Ub's Flip cartoons did not skirt the issue of poverty nor attempt to hide the nation's troubles beneath idyllic parables or fables. They simply told it like it was. As had happened to so many people during the troubled 1930s, Flip and the orphan boy find themselves homeless and on the street. Hungry and cold, desperate for sustenance, they pawn their instruments. Just as they are ready to enter a diner, they hear a one-legged, blind street violinist and his howling dog performing for change. Magnanimously, they give up their last bit of change for the poor soul only to see him take the money and walk—on a previously hidden leg—into a waiting limousine. Flip and the orphan boy watch, resigned but not really surprised by this turn of events. The impression is that the two would do the same thing all over again given the circumstances. In this way, *What a Life!* was not simple cartoon escapism but instead offered a snapshot picture of the real world turned upside down, a world teetering on the brink of desperation, and therefore perfect for Ub's unique brand of anarchic animation.

The fresh style of these new Flip films bore the distinct mark of Grim Natwick's hand. Although he was only in his mid-thirties, Grim was already seen by his fellow animators as an old man in the industry. This perception, along with Grim's native skill as an animator, made him highly respected at the studio. He became Ub's right-hand man and trusted friend. The admiration was mutual. Grim raves, "If Christ hadn't been able to get into place, and you substituted Ub Iwerks, you'd have a pretty good substitute. He was a great guy and I don't think there was a dishonest bone in his body. He was a tremendous dreamer, and inventive."

Within a year of Natwick's arrival at the studio, Ub recognized Grim's own formidable gifts and offered him more of a supervisory role over the animation staff. This allowed Ub the freedom to explore his growing interest in the technical aspects of animation—the lenses, the cameras, the sound studio. Ub began to spend more and more time in the basement (or the technical workshop located just outside his office) and less time on the day-to-day activities of the studio.

Even as Iwerks began to pull away from animation, he remained a patient resource for his colleagues at the studio. "To learn the craft of animation from Ub Iwerks was the greatest thing that happened to me," recalls animator Jim Pabian. "His teachings to beginners like me, in all phases of animation, were so sound that in less than six months I was animating. . . . Ub was the unsung genius of the cartoon film industry."

Jimmie Culhane's learning experiences at Ub's hand were less beatific. He recalled that one of his first jobs at the Iwerks Studio was to animate a stagecoach for the cartoon *Phoney Express*, a Flip the Frog western written by Bugs Hardaway. "Iwerks came in to see what I was doing," Culhane remembers. "He was disgusted." Culhane had drawn the wagon wheels in a reckless manner that did not mesh with Ub's precision. "Ub sat down and drew perfect ovals on several wheels, fixed a few Flip drawings, and left with a very discontented look on his face." The Fleischer Studio may have been a hotbed of innovation and a fertile area from which to pluck potential animators, but Ub Iwerks could not tolerate sloppiness in the animation at his studio. His own innate perfectionism insisted on clean, precise draughtsmanship and technical accuracy.

The animators expressed their creative sides in other ways. As Flip the Frog matured as a character, they began to explore adult themes and situations more prominently in the films. In the pre–Hays Code films of the 1930s, subject matter frequently drifted into adult themes, but for an animated film to mine this territory was revelatory.

Risqué gags abound in 1932's *Room Runners*. In this delightfully naughty cartoon, Flip encounters a series of naked and near-naked women around every corner of the seedy Grand Slam Hotel as he tries to sneak out without paying his bill. In a dark hallway, one shapely lass scurries past Flip wearing only a sheer undergarment. A homely landlady runs her head through a painting and is shocked by the full-frontal nude depicted on the other side. Flip peers into an open window. "Hot dog!" He says, ogling the woman inside. He climbs through another window into a shower stall, which he finds is occupied by yet another naked woman. He peeks at one naked woman through a keyhole and he knocks over a dressing partition to reveal another angry, lingerie-clad lady.

The sheer volume of nudity in *Room Runners*—albeit much of it implied rather than shown—was in sharp contrast to the quiet, somber man who headed the studio. While Ub may not have instigated the ribald comedy, he certainly allowed it. Critics have recalled that in his early efforts with Walt, Ub frequently dabbled in barnyard humor, but rarely included the mature sexual content of *Room Runners*. Perhaps it was more the influence of the former Betty Boop animators than any real insistence on Ub's part. All of the women in *Room Runners* bear a familial relationship to Betty Boop, yet they attain little of her sensuality. Jimmie Culhane complained that although Iwerks now had the best Betty Boop animators on staff, "Ub was oddly indifferent to this possible advantage."

Once Ub even went so far as to redraw one of the sexier characters with more cartoony arms and legs. "She had all the sex appeal of a lawn mower," Culhane moaned. But it was not for lack of trying. *The Office Boy* featured only one female character, but she certainly made the most of her opportunity. Leonard Maltin, referring to *The Office Boy*, wrote, "Seldom has any cartoon concentrated so heavily on gags involving a young woman's derriere." The derriere in question was everywhere—in the face of the boss, stuck to a sign, wiggling and dancing lasciviously.

Chinaman's Chance (1934) was outrageous in other ways. It was a film that quite possibly very few cartoon studios could have—or *would* have—made. Racial stereotypes were prevalent in the cartoon industry at the time (Hugh Harman and Rudy Ising featured an African American juvenile, Bosko, as the first star of their Harman-Ising Studios), but *Chinaman's Chance* included the use of narcotics and dramatic imagery that made it startling, edgy, and unique.

Flip the Frog, once again in a detective role, tracks escaped prisoner Chow Mein to a Chinese laundry in Chinatown. In a surreal sequence worthy of 1960s psychedelia, Flip follows Chow Mein into an opium den, where he promptly partakes of the first pipe offered to him. Flip drifts into an opiate haze.

The screen image becomes distorted as Flip appears to be caught in a benevolent funhouse mirror. His head bulges, his legs stretch, his body wobbles and turns. According to animator Grim Natwick, the effect was achieved by projecting the footage of Flip onto a rolling plate of mercury and filming the resultant distortion. The scene is murky and dark, and particularly effective. It also served to focus Ub's attention on the technical side of animation yet again.

As the Flip the Frog series reached its third year of production, it was apparent that despite its unique style and lavish production values, Flip the Frog was not striking a chord with audiences. Ub asked Grim Natwick to make one last attempt to make the character more likable. Natwick drew up a new model sheet wherein Flip had made the evolution entirely into a boy, with no frog attributes at all. It was never used.

During its run, Flip the Frog turned a small but steady profit for Iwerks, but it was far from the landmark series for which Ub had hoped. Without the strong narrative and comic structures that Disney was developing, the Iwerks cartoons often meandered and too frequently relied on sight and sound gags for comedic impact. The competition in the animation world was strong and getting more sophisticated. The strongest competition of all continued to be the one character that Ub had designed himself: Mickey Mouse.

chapter 8

The Greatest Staff

Ub had experience a-plenty with the creation of new series and new characters. Dozens of characters in six series had been developed beneath his measured hand. As Flip faded from public view, Ub's focus began to shift to a new series that MGM would distribute. Ub relegated more and more of the story, gag, and character design to his growing staff.

Grim Natwick designed a cute little freckle-faced boy who exhibited every sign of being a young Baron von Munchausen. The character was named Willie Whopper. Natwick explains the choice of names: "A whopper is a lie and there were some untruths about Willie." Like Munchausen, the alliteratively named Willie Whopper was indeed the victim of his own overactive imagination. "So I called him Whopper, then just added Willie."

The opening titles for Willie Whopper featured Willie emerging from the center of a series of concentric circles. Ub's old friend from the Pacific Title Company, Leon Schlesinger, would use a similar title approach less than a decade later for his Looney Tunes cartoons series over at Warner Brothers.

The first version of Willie Whopper was pencil-thin. As drawn by Natwick, Willie could easily have been a nephew or younger brother to Natwick's Betty Boop. Willie shared Betty's more prominent features—well maybe not *all* of them—in a somewhat more masculine package. His first adventure was inspired by the growing popularity of aviation, thanks in part to the latest hero of the day—aviatrix Amelia Earhart. Like Mickey Mouse in *Plane Crazy,* Willie's first film exploits revolved around an airplane theme. In fact, *The Air Race* hearkened back even further into the Iwerks' archive, by borrowing liberally from Oswald the Lucky Rabbit's *The Ocean Hop.* That early effort featured a nearly identical opening sequence of various airplanes and their eccentric pilots getting ready for the race.

Unlike *The Ocean Hop, The Air Race* was filled with Iwerksian gags and puns. The name of the airstrip sponsoring the air race of the title was the Corn Field Air Field. The list of racers includes one entry named *The Spirit of Ammonia,* another called *The Perkle-8.* When we see the plane, it has coffee pots percolating around the propeller. Ub's enthusiasm for mechanical jokes required that each airplane have some pun or gag associated with it. One is a train locomotive with wings. One is a bicycle-powered contraption. One has a swirling Leonardo da Vinci–like whirligig propeller. Unlike Rube Goldberg's contrivances, which featured the elaborate interconnection of incongruous devices and gizmos, Ub's mechanical humor was based on the audience's recognition of his visual puns. Sometimes that humor required the audience to have at least some awareness of mechanics to get the joke. A funny joke to Ub was picturing an engine with nine pistons instead of eight. Another example of this style of humor is a scene in *The Air Race* in which the villain methodically "tunes" the engine with a tuning fork. When adjusted properly, the engine roars mightily—an Iwerks engine gag and a pun wrapped in one.

In a lapse of film continuity—but for the sake of a good gag—the villain is depicted in one sequence sporting a full beard, which he proceeds to shave off with the propeller of Willie's airplane. To Ub, anything was possible for the sake of a gag.

Willie's plane is so small that when the race is started, a piece of chewing gum the villain spits underneath a tire holds the plane fast. This, too, directly mimics Oswald's earlier plane adventure. Willie struggles to free his plane. Its outboard motor finally pulls free of the plane itself. It looks back at the plane. Determined to continue, the engine goes back and gives the plane a shove from the rear. Willie joins the race.

The air racers soar too close to a cloud on which St. Peter is standing with his thumb out hitchhiking. As they pass, the cloud and St. Peter's beard sail in the wind generated by the planes. Angered, St. Peter gives the finger to the reckless aviators. At this point in its career, the Iwerks Studio resolutely refused to censor itself or to be hemmed in by the strictures of society's mores. St. Peter's irreverently flipping the bird is another example of how anything in an Ub Iwerks cartoon could and usually would happen.

A few moments later in the same scene, a pilot is knocked from his plane by the dastardly villain. As he freefalls, he realizes that instead of a parachute, he has only a knapsack upon his back. As he plummets to his death, St. Peter haughtily invites him, à la screen vixen Mae West, "Come up and see me sometime."

Willie's plane spins out of control (as in *Plane Crazy* again), crashing into a live-action tower that collapses dramatically and humorously into a pile of dust. The live-action segment is almost gratuitous but cleverly done, and perhaps it gives a glimpse of the kind of scene Ub had envisioned for *Plane Crazy*. For *The Air Race*, Ub had the technical savvy, equipment, and time to be able to pull it off.

After knocking down the tower, Willie's plane continues to careen out of control. It flies into a fireworks stand with the word *FIRE-WORKS* written across the awning. The fireworks within explode in a great conflagration that sends Willie skyward and tears the fireworks stand apart. When the action settles, the letters of the word *FIRE-WORKS* have reassembled to spell *IWERKS*. The mustached proprietor of the fireworks stand peeks from out of the wreckage. This may be the one and only instance of Ub Iwerks being caricatured in cartoon form.

When Willie's bedraggled plane is propelled over the finish line, a ghastly-looking Amelia Earhart rewards him with a kiss. At this point, the daydreaming Willie awakens when a horseshoe falls on his head.

The Air Race was copyrighted on October 14, 1933, was heavily reworked, and not released until 1936, under the title *Spite Flight*.

In his next outing, *Play Ball*, Willie fared not much better in spite of a cameo appearance from the resilient Flip the Frog. Flip may have been gone as a series star, but Ub gave him one last bow in the spotlight in *Play Ball*. As part of a ticker-tape parade that feted Willie's stellar accomplishments on the ball diamond, Flip the Frog appeared alongside the considerably more legendary Babe Ruth in what amounted to Flip's final fleeting role.

Play Ball was also destined to be the swan song for Willie Whopper's first skinny incarnation as well. For the third cartoon, Grim Natwick transformed Willie from a male version of Betty Boop into a rotund little fibber. This newfound roundness offered a more sympathetic Willie to theatrical audiences. The resultant cartoon, *Stratos-Fear*, was copyrighted on November 11, 1933, and contains some of the most surrealistic imagery of any Iwerks film—which is saying quite a lot. In this space-age epic, a frightened Willie Whopper succumbs to laughing gas administered by his dentist, Dr. A. King. He floats through the roof of the dentist's office into the sky.

The unidentified Flying Willie soars higher and higher up through the clouds into space. He bumps into an angry moon, which warns him, "Go where you're looking. Go where you're looking." Willie lands upon a mysterious planet where he is beset by alien lunacy. In a secret alien laboratory, an evil, gibberish-speaking mastermind is testing a new laser device. He blasts first a cow and then a pig with the laser beam. The cow is rendered milk and steak, the pig is turned into footballs. One of the mastermind's henchmen has a telescope for an eye. He spies the hapless Willie entering the planet's atmosphere. The evil ones suck Willie into a giant vacuum cleaner, depositing him on the floor in front of them.

Taunted by surreal aliens at every turn, Willy surrenders to paranoia. Dropping through a hole in the floor, Willie slides across a dinosaur spine (a nice opportunity for Ub to use his xylophone effect), lands to find four robots singing in harmony and a band of musical instruments playing themselves—oboes, clarinets, pianos, violins, and even a caricature of Harpo Marx as (what else?) a harp.

"Hello, handsome," a vamp coos as she rises from a coffin. "Come up and see me sometime. Anytime. Right now." Willie is seduced. He follows her into an elevator. Upstairs, she turns into the villain. Willie leaps into a skeleton and is trapped within its rib cage. Struggling, he awakens in the dentist chair. The hallucination is over.

"Boy that's a whopper," the dentist says, examining the extracted tooth.

"Yeah," Willie replies. "But it's the wrong tooth!"

Leonard Maltin in *Of Mice and Magic* refers to the zaniness of *Stratos-Fear* as anticipating "Bob Clampett's *Porky in Wackyland* by five years."

In spite of the obvious improvement in quality that was evident in *Stratos-Fear,* the characterization of Willie was still primarily visual. His new body seemed much better suited to a more robust vocal characterization as well. The animators searched for a voice actor to play Willie. Instead, they found a precocious young *actress*.

Child star Jane Withers came to the studio to read for the part of Willie's girlfriend for a future cartoon. Jane, being the inquisitive charmer that she was, innocently asked Ub, "What's Willie Whopper like?" Upon being shown a model sheet of Willie, Jane exclaimed, "To me, he would sound like this." She proceeded to wow Ub and the assembled animators with her enthusiastic interpretation. "I was capable of doing all ages—men, women, children, animals, everything!" Jane recalled.

The animators adored the little girl with the Colleen Moore haircut. She won the part of Willie Whopper and the hearts of the staff in the process. Her slight native Georgian accent provided just the right touch of texture for Willie. Withers had once performed in a radio show back in Georgia entitled *Dixie's Dainty Dewdrop,* and was currently costarring in a weekly broadcast with a youngster named Mickey McGuire, who would later achieve international fame as Mickey Rooney.

At the age of five and a half, little Jane was already a seasoned professional. She may have needed to stand on a chair to speak into the microphone, but she certainly did not need a crutch to hit the right vocalization. Since she was unable to fully read the scripts, Jane's mother practiced long hours with her to help her learn the difficult lines. The result was a spontaneous energetic vocal characterization that defined Willie Whopper's character as much as Grim Natwick's new design.

To aid Natwick on the Willie series, Ub recruited Natwick's old colleague Berny Wolf from the Fleischer Brothers Studio. With an offer of better pay and the security of working again with his former mentor, Wolf leaped at the opportunity. When he arrived at the train station in California from New York, he was amazed to be met by a car from the Iwerks Studio. As he was driven though the streets of Beverly Hills, Berny marveled at the situation in which he found himself.

> I was twenty-two years of age and I was brought out there. You know, in those days it seemed like a movie star. Because they brought you out. Paid your wage. Picked you up at the station—we didn't fly out then—and took you out to the studio, which was in Beverly Hills. It was a small studio. That was the physical side to it. Another side was being all Alice in Wonderland to me. You know being a kid out of New York and going out there and sitting in a desk and looking out the windows and seeing palm trees. It was like heaven on earth going to California, a new land and all. I was making $150 a week to go out there. That was all kinds of money. I sent half the money home. I couldn't spend it.

Jimmie Culhane remarked that with Berny Wolf's arrival, the Ub Iwerks Studio now had on staff the top four Betty Boop animators: Natwick, Culhane, Eugster, and Wolf. Willie Whopper was the immediate beneficiary of this bonanza. Berny was paired with Grim on the Willies. Between the two veteran directors, they pummeled the unruly character into some classic comedy situations.

One of the first uses of Wolf's talents (his style and work ethic mirrored that of Natwick) was on the Willie Whopper cartoon *Viva Willie.* In this send-up of a western—with its not-so-faint echoes of *The Gallopin' Gaucho* to boot—Natwick and Wolf provided a roundup of gags revolving around Willie and his Betty Boopish girlfriend. Like Mickey Mouse with the drunken ostrich in *The Gallopin' Gaucho,* when Willie needs his horse, he finds his beast of burden too soused to function. Unlike Mickey's starch solution, Willie simply rides this one out, albeit not necessarily in a straight line.

In films such as *Viva Willie,* Berny Wolf's partnership with Grim Natwick provided a lively impetus for the success of the series. Together they were able to turn out mature cartoons more quickly and with a more consistent comedic styling than their predecessors had been able to do. This allowed Ub to back further away from the day-to-day operations of the studio. The situation quickly evolved to the point at which Ub was doing virtually no animation himself at all. He began to immerse himself in the technical aspects of film.

By the mid-1930s, Ub was bitten by the plane craze that he had used as inspiration many times before. He began making model airplanes for his young sons, Don and Dave. He frequented a hobby store on Melrose Avenue for supplies. A young clerk, Leroy Richardson, impressed Ub with his dedication to the hobby as well as with his machining abilities. Ub invited Richardson to the studio and showed him his new machine shop outfitted with a lathe, a drill press, and assorted tools that had been purchased but not yet put to use.

Ub explained to Richardson that until that time, any maintenance on the cameras, sound equipment, or other devices had been handled by the Acme Tool Company of central Los Angeles. Production was often held up while waiting for the Acme Tool Company to add the Iwerks Studio to its schedule. Needing a man to provide those services in-house, Ub offered Richardson the job for $18 an hour. Leroy was impressed with Ub's setup enough to join the staff as a jack-of-all-trades.

Ub assigned Leroy to work on a new camera stand. The old one had developed problems in its motor and Leroy soon worked out a solution. Leroy recalls:

> *Ub did a pretty good job of managing the different people there, the artists, the musicians, the sound recording. He had a genius for being able to do just about anything that anyone else could do. One day I was impressed when I walked back into the music room and he was playing the piano. He could compose music, write stories, he could do everything pertaining to the production of animated pictures. He was knowledgeable of photography, sound recording, processing, developing, you name it, he could do it all himself if he had to. For that reason, he knew how to relay what he wanted done to the other people, and he would do it in such a relaxed way that they felt they were working with him rather than for him. The atmosphere was very casual.*

In 1934, Chuck Jones was hired for a second time. In the short year away from Iwerks, Jones had managed to get fired from first Universal and then from Winkler's. "I tried to pass off some of Bill Nolan's animation as my own and they of course recognized the work," Jones explains. When asked how or why he got rehired at Iwerks, Jones surmises, "Ub must have had a short memory. I think he forgot, he was a little absentminded at times when he got to thinking about things that had nothing to do with animation."

Jones was not to last at Iwerks long. When he was given the ax for the second time, Ub's secretary, Dorothy Webster, did the deed. Apparently, Ms. Webster's charm softened the blow somewhat. Chuck and Dorothy began courting shortly thereafter. They were married two years later in 1935. Chuck Jones, of course, went on to great acclaim as one of Warner Brothers' finest directors. Dorothy was to be by his side through the Golden Age of Warner Brothers animation.

One has to wonder how the Acme Tool Company came to inhabit Chuck Jones's consciousness during his second stint at the Iwerks Studio. As low man on the Iwerks totem pole at the time, he would no doubt have had intimate dealings with Acme. It is all too easy to imagine the young Jones receiving the parcels of animation equipment with the fervor of his future alter ego, Wile E. Coyote.

Despite being fired from the Iwerks Studio, Jones recalls Ub's influence on his career. "For me the most important thing about Ub Iwerks was that he got me interested in animation and that became my lifetime. . . . I'm grateful to Ub because of that stimulation. Anybody that stimulates you to your life work should have, and does have, in my case, my unending gratitude. This is a good man and necessary to the entire field of animation."

Throughout these years, Ub's passion for games of skill remained as mercurial as ever. At times, his hobbies would spill onto the screen, providing the studio with comic material. An example of this was the wacky telescope the aliens used in *Stratos-Fear,* which reflected Ub's interest in astronomy. Instead of buying a ready-made telescope, Ub decided to build his own from scratch. He bought a special lens-grinding machine and ordered a piece of custom glass. He arranged for the glass to be aluminized to serve as a reflector. By the time the glass arrived at the studio, Ub's focus had shifted to a new, equally challenging hobby: archery.

At an Iwerks Studio picnic, Ub set up a bale of hay with a target on it. He told his willing accomplice Leroy Richardson to place a blank shotgun shell in the center of the hay bale. "Don't let anyone see you do this," Ub instructed. Richardson did as he was told. Ub urged the staff to try their hands at hitting the bull's-eye with the bow and arrow. One by one, the animators stepped up to give it a shot, but no one even came close. When it was Ub's turn, his first shot flew true, exploding the shotgun shell. The hay bale burst into flames.

What the staff did not realize was that Ub had been practicing archery with the world-famous Howard Hill, a legendary bowman. Ub had Richardson build special tools and fixtures for making arrows. For a time, it seemed to Richardson as if the studio was in the business of making archery equipment rather than animated films. "He became very skilled in target archery," recalls son Don. He became a friend of Howard Hill, and they practiced together. At one point, he even doubled for Howard in a filmed commercial that was shot in his backyard."

When Ub's interest in the bow eventually faded, it was replaced by the crossbow. Rather than buying a stock crossbow, Ub machined his own. He built the stock out of yew wood and had Richardson machine the track. When he took the new crossbow to a Beverly Hills archery range, the track malfunctioned. Instead of flying straight, the ten-inch bolt tumbled end over end. It knocked the hay-bale target over. Ub took the crossbow back to the studio for more work. He corrected the track problem. Knowing that Ub was not satisfied with the wood stock, staff member Wesley Farmer suggested that he use steel instead of yew wood for the stock. Ub took a leaf spring from a Model A Ford and adapted it to be used for the bow.

When he took it to the range, it took two people to pull the spring. Ub fired. The bolt went straight this time, clean through the target. Looking back, Richardson recalls, "We never did find the bolt."

Another hobby of Ub's was collecting, building, and restoring guns. Jimmy Cook, who worked as a cel washer at the Iwerks Studio, recalled that once when Ub received a pellet gun in a gift exchange at a company Christmas party, he sat down and proceeded to shoot every single ornament off the Christmas tree. "He had always liked guns," Don remembers. "When he felt the time was right and safe for us to be around them, he started to collect guns. His interest was in antique guns. He loved the old muzzle loaders, and joined a club where the members would go out to a range in Brea on Saturdays, and compete in target practice. He had a love for wild animals, fish, and birds, and had no interest in hunting or fishing. Taking an animal, fish, or bird just for the sport of it did not make sense to him. He was more inter-ested in perfecting his own skills as a target marksman."

On the animation front, Ub began playing at using color again. He filmed *Davy Jones Locker* and *Hell's Fire* in a two-color process called Cinecolor, a derivative of the Multicolor system. It was far from a perfect color system, but it worked. Because it was based on two colors, not all colors of the color spectrum could be replicated. Some colors looked remarkable, others looked like a lesser shade of mud. Ub experimented with his palette of colors until he had a working profile of how each color would look after being filmed using the Cinecolor process.

Hell's Fire features a colorful procession of evildoers cavorting in the belly of a volcano. Willie and his dog accidentally tumble into the volcano, but the other inhabitants of the inferno seem to have been placed there with purpose. Napoleon, Nero, Simon LeGree, Doctor Jekyll–Mr. Hyde, Ali Baba, a Roman Centurian with his courtesan, and a three-headed hellhound are some of the occupants tortured by the flames. Willie Whopper dutifully follows the devil's command by chasing a particularly loathsome fellow into a boiler room. Another good guy part for Willie Whopper was his role in *Good Scouts* as part of a multiethnic boy scout troop. In the upfront "reality" sequence, each scout steps up to the scoutmaster to tell of some good deed he has accomplished. The Asian boy, Chong, speaks only in Chinese gibberish; a German-Jewish boy named Izzy (an inside joke on assistant animator Izzy Ellis) stumbles over his words. "Oy!" he moans.

Willie Whopper steps up. He is an all-American boy. "Shucks," he says. "Them kids are pikers. Listen to this. . . ." Willie proceeds to tell his whopper of a story. Willie rescues a dog from the tin can tied to its tail, a young boy from a neighborhood bully, and an elderly woman from a busy street. All of Willie's attempts at good deeds turn sour. The dog brings all its friends with cans tied to their tails, the young boy defends the bully, and the woman steps into a puddle.

Good Scouts is also interesting for its soundtrack. Ub dusted off an old Jelly Roll Morton 78-rpm record that they had used for the Flip the Frog cartoon *Soda Squirt*. It plays throughout the entire film. Another highlight of *Good Scouts* is a scene in which Willie tries to thwart a kidnapping. He rides the spray of a spewing fire hydrant to the top of a skyscraper drawn in eye-popping perspective. The effect is dizzying. Willie totters on the edge of windowsills like a chubby, cartoony Harold Lloyd. Of course, in the end, Willie saves the girl.

Jane Withers continued to record Willie Whopper's voice throughout the series. One day, Shirley Temple, who had recently appeared with Withers in *Bright Eyes*, came for a tour of the Iwerks

Studio facilities. The biggest little star in Hollywood stopped by each animator's desk signing autographs and talking about their projects.

Withers, for her part, collected a little book of autographs of all the animators at the studio.

Among the more notable of these was Frank Tashlin. Tish-Tash, as he was called, was already a legend at the studio for being able to complete his quota of animation in the morning and to spend the afternoons drawing the comic strip *Van Boring*—a not-so-subtle jab at the Van Beuren Studio from whence Tashlin had come.

The list of animators and artists who worked at the Ub Iwerks Studio during this time and went on to later, greater acclaim is a veritable *Who's Who* of animation. Aside from Tashlin—who would later go to Warner Brothers and then to even greater acclaim as director of several Jerry Lewis movies (including *Artists and Models, Hollywood or Bust, The Geisha Boy,* and *Cinderfella*)—the Iwerks Studio staff included Steve Bosustow, who was later to found UPA, the home of Mr. Magoo and Gerald McBoingBoing. Fleischer's famed Betty Boop animators, Grim Natwick, Berny Wolf, Al Eugster, and Jimmie Culhane would all go to Disney after Iwerks and then on to legendary careers of their own. Cel-washer Chuck Jones would become one of Warner Brothers' most celebrated directors. Fred Kopietz would work on Donald Duck. Ted Sears and Otto Englander would join Disney's story department working on the animated features. Cal Howard and Earl Duvall would take similar story positions at Warner's. Sound technician Glen Glenn would form the legendary Glen Glenn Sound company. Little Jane Withers would continue a lifelong film career, including roles opposite James Dean and Elizabeth Taylor in *Giant* and appearing in a long-running series of commercials as Josephine the Plumber. Withers returned to voiceover work in 1996 when she filled in for Mary Wickes as the voice of the cantankerous gargoyle, Laverne. Wickes had died during the making of *The Hunchback of Notre Dame* for Disney.

Dick Bickenbach moved on to Hanna-Barbera. Berny Wolf

followed, achieving great success later as the director of Jonny Quest after a stint as a puppeteer for Buffalo Bob on the *Howdy Doody Show.*

Ub's close friend, Bugs Hardaway, also migrated to Warner's. A toothy gray wisecracking rabbit would achieve great fame when another animator labeled a drawing of the rabbit "'Bugs' Bunny." The name stuck. Over the years, Bugs Bunny would grow to iconic status second only to that of Mickey Mouse.

Carl Stalling likewise achieved greatness at Warner Brothers. Decades after his death, his music was still finding new audiences. Rock-and-roll groups such as Pearl Jam claimed Stalling as an influence. A tribute album of Stalling's music was released and was well received by a public that grew up with his music.

Ink-and-paint supervisor Mary Tebb returned to Disney with similar success. Mary Blair likewise took her stylish drawings to even greater heights at Disney. The "It's a Small World" attraction at Disneyland would feature Audio-Animatronics renderings of her colorful character drawings.

Despite the stellar quality of the staff, Emile Offemann continued to impose his controlling ways. Steve Bosustow once had the audacity to move his desk without first obtaining permission from management—that is, Offemann. The enraged Offemann ordered Ralph Somerville, who had taken on a few administrative duties, to go fire Bosustow. Somerville was unwilling to shirk his responsibility, so reluctantly he went into Bosustow's room. He told Bosustow, "I'm sorry, Steve, Offemann says you're no longer employed here." Well, Somerville recalls,

> Well, Steve got kind of teary and everything and you know it was such a shock to him and everything. Finally, I says, "Oh, hell," and I went back to Ub and I says, "Ub, you either reinstate Steve or I'm gonna quit." Ub sat there and laughed at me. He said, "You go back to your desk and start working and don't worry about Steve."

As he often was forced to do, Ub overruled Offemann's command.

When Ub left the Disney Studio, Walt Disney had commented, "I will sure feel sorry for Ub when he has any personnel problems. We know how gullible and easily led Ub is." Ub managed as best he could to control conflicts, intervening only when necessary. He farmed off more and more duties to Grim Natwick, even offering him a piece of the studio at one point. Natwick, however, turned down the offer. As an animation veteran, Grim was all too aware of the demands and pressures at that level of responsibility. He would help out Ub as best he could, but he knew that at heart he was an animator, not a businessman.

Not that being an animator was exactly devoid of pressure and responsibility, either—animation in those days was in many ways thankless work. Ed Friedman recalled that the animators amused themselves by playing practical jokes on each other. Some of the favorite pranks included the old standby of giving the hot foot to some unsuspecting animator. Another favorite trick of the Iwerks staff was putting Limburger cheese on the scorching-hot drawing table lights and waiting for the stench to stink up the place. A cup of water strategically balanced atop a slightly open door was another reliable prank, as was the old standby of taping a clear cell underneath a toilet seat.

Some pranks were much more elaborate. The floor that the Iwerks Studio now occupied had previously been a dentist's office. The fixtures remained in the wall. Ray Farranger connected a hose to a faucet, then threaded it into a hole in the drywall. Thinking that the hose had continued on through the wall unobstructed into the adjacent animators' room, he turned the water on. Farranger waited with anticipation for the uproar to hit. It did not come. He turned the water on full blast. Still no response. Suddenly the proprietor of the uniform shop on the first floor came barreling upstairs, screaming. The hose had taken a wrong turn and had flooded the shop below. Unfortunately, the uniform shop frequently took the brunt of the Iwerks Studio pranksters. Cigarette butts were routinely flicked out the window onto the awning of the shop, riddling it with small brown burn holes. Animator Merle Gilson told stories about stacking nitrate cels a foot high, setting them on fire and throwing them out the second-story window.

Once, a fire occurred within the studio itself. Film in the 1930s was made from a highly combustible nitrate stock. While working in the editing room, Ub accidentally dropped a lit cigarette into a bin filled with nitrate film scraps. It exploded in flames. No one was hurt, but the incident certainly demonstrated the dangers of the volatile film stock.

Typically, Ub himself stayed above the fray, rarely participating in practical jokes. Once, however, he asserted himself in a decidedly uncharacteristic way. He preferred a quiet atmosphere for his workers, so when they became especially loud one afternoon, Ub crept into the room and dropped a cymbal onto the floor behind them. The startled animators turned, amazed to see Ub standing there. He put his finger to his lips. "Shh," he said quietly. He had made his point.

One joke that backfired on the animators was a stunt in which they took Ub's tiny Astin Martin automobile from the parking lot and literally carried it into the upstairs hallway of the Iwerks Studio building. Ub was furious. He had built the Astin Martin from scratch, even going so far as to order special leather to reupholster the seats. It was clear to his employees that some things were better left untouched.

Ub was near obsessive about his automobiles. One of the fondest memories for many of the Iwerks animators was the image of Ub tooling around Beverly Hills in his brand-new silver Chrysler Airflow, reportedly the very first one to be sold in the United States.

Musical director Art Turkisher had a similarly high regard for his Terraplane automobile. This was the very same Terraplane that legendary bluesman Robert Johnson referred to in his immortal song of 1933, "Terraplane Blues." Turkisher's Terraplane has achieved almost legendary status itself among Ub's former animators, who often have greater memories attached to automobiles from the time than to the films they created. Like their creation, Willie Whopper, their memories of their cars have been exaggerated by time and hyperbole, but for those animators who were fortunate enough to work at the Iwerks Studio during this era, there could be no exaggeration of the quality of their peers on the animation staff. As Ed Friedman recalls, "Iwerks was the place to be!" Indeed. It was quite possibly the greatest animation staff ever assembled.

The bustling printing department at the Kansas City Film Ad
Company, 2449 Charlotte Street, provided the seeds of lifelong
inspiration. Ub is focused on a task, far left.

The gang at Buzzards Roost, the log cabin hangout in the east side of Swope Park, Kansas City. Ub and Walt are at far right with pipes. Photos and live-action footage have been found showing that this was a "set" for their skits and behind-the-scenes test shots.

The early Disney Brothers Studio staff (circa 1926). Ub, fourth from left, and Roy Disney, far right.

Mildred Henderson, Ub's wife-to-be, was born July 11, 1899.

Easter Sunday, 1926: Ub and Mildred pose in front of Mildred's house on Flower Street, Los Angeles.

Ub takes a seat on Mildred's front porch, Easter Sunday, 1926.

Walt and his wife, Lillian, on one of their weekend trips to Santa Barbara with Ub and Mildred. The photo was taken by Ub—the Iwerks Buick is in the background.

Young Hollywood mavericks: Walt Disney, Rudy Ising, Hugh Harman, and Ub Iwerks in front of a makeshift Hollywood set for the Alice comedies (circa 1925).

Producer Walt Disney and chief animator and partner Ub Iwerks in front of Hyperion Studio (circa 1928).

Ub's storyboard sketch of Mickey cartoon *Karnival Kid*, 1929. Even hot dogs had attitude. . . .

Carl Stalling leads the Disney staff in a rendition of the theme song, "Minnie's Yoo Hoo." Ub is in the top row, third from right.

The Walt Disney staff, in a publicity photo taken in front of Hyperion Studio: at center stage, Mickey's designer, Ub Iwerks, holds a Mickey cardboard cutout; Walt and Carl Stalling stand to his left.

The Iwerks family in the early 1930s. Left to right: son Don, Mildred, son Dave, and Ub.

The Iwerks Studio staff, early 1930s. Left to right: Meryl Gibson, unknown, Godfrey Bjork, Jim Pabian, Ben Clopton, Ub.

Ub engages in one of his many hobbies and games of skill—archery
(1930s).

Ub Iwerks, Kansas City Film Ad owner A. Vern Cauger, and Walt Disney pose with Disney cartoon figurines while reminiscing about their inspired Kansas City days twenty years earlier (circa 1943).

Ub and technical assistant Bob Broughton share a moment with the newly designed sodium traveling matte camera.

Eleven 16mm cameras compose Ub's 360-degree Circarama rig.

In the 1960s, Ub, Les Clark (Ub's apprentice during the late 1920s), and Walt Disney take time out to reminisce over the early inspired efforts of *Karnival Kid* storyboard sketches. Mickey had come a long way since Ub's initial renditions of the wiry, troublesome little mouse.

Ub enjoys a relaxing moment with his
youngest granddaughter, Leslie, in 1970.

Ub and Mildred pose in the backyard of their
home on Murietta Avenue in Sherman Oaks, in
1970.

chapter 9

Classics in Color

In 1934, the Iwerks Studio created a new cartoon series to run along with the Willie Whopper series. As he had done with the Silly Symphonies at Disney, Ub wanted to create a free-form series in which he could experiment with techniques, subject matter, and characters without being restricted by the personality of an identifiable leading star. The Comicolor Classic series would be the blank page on which Ub would be able to test and perfect many of his greatest innovations.

Each of the Comicolor Classics begins with an ornately decorated storybook opening to reveal a fable within. Two years later, the Disney Studio would use a similar device to begin its first full-length feature, *Snow White and the Seven Dwarfs*.

For his new series, Ub insisted on color. Disney, however, retained an exclusive contract with Technicolor for the three-color process, so Ub went back to the two-film (bi-pack) Cinecolor process, which had proved very effective in two of the Willie Whopper cartoons. The color palette was somewhat limited, but the results were quite vivid.

The Cinecolor process required two negatives to run through the camera simultaneously with the emulsions of each running back to back. Reds were recorded on one film negative and greens and blues on the other. They were then printed on dual-emulsion printstock. The result was an impressive array of rich colors.

When Ub presented Metro-Goldwyn-Mayer with the colorful new

series, the studio failed to show much interest. Based on the faltering success of Willie Whopper, they had just hired Ub's old Laugh-O-grams buddies, Hugh Harman and Rudy Ising, to head their newly formed animation division. Ub and his Comicolor Classics were pushed aside to make room for Harman-Ising's first series for MGM, the Happy Harmonies.

MGM understandably saw no need to compete with themselves for screen space, especially when both Ub's Comicolor Classics and MGM's Happy Harmonies were similarly conceived descendants of Disney's Silly Symphony series. Ultimately, Ub was forced to find distribution for his cartoons himself. He formed a new venture called the Animated Picture Corporation through which he would distribute the films. A company photograph of the Iwerks Studio staff from earlier that year was touched up to include the image of a hand-drawn building bearing the new Animated Picture Corporation name.

Unfortunately, the Animated Picture Corporation had none of the clout of MGM. With MGM coordinating the distribution, Flip the Frog had turned a modest but steady profit through the years. The Animated Picture Corporation had neither the resources nor the contacts to guarantee similar financial success for the new series. The quality of the films, however, remained first-rate from the start throughout each passing year.

The first Comicolor Classic to be put into production was *Jack and the Beanstalk*. Revisiting a tale that he had first filmed at the Laugh-O-grams Studio, Ub filled the Iwerks version with updated bits of business that showed how far the medium had come in the intervening years.

Ub, who had been responsible for a great deal of that progress, continued to press the boundaries of technical convention. In *Jack and the Beanstalk,* clever transitions signify the passage of time. In a scene in which a mysterious peddler sells Jack a handful of magic beans, the peddler holds the beans in his outstretched hand. The camera zooms in on the beans. The beans remain in focus but Jack's hand replaces that of the peddler. As the camera pulls back we see Jack holding the beans in the marketplace. The market background around Jack metamorphoses into the interior of his house. Jack remains in the very same pose, but now he is showing his mother the beans. The transition, simple as it may seem to a modern film-viewing audience, effectively set a new standard for a nonlinear, nonliteral approach to time transitions in animation and film in general.

The Willie Whopper directorial team of Grim Natwick and Berny Wolf codirected this first Comicolor effort, but for the second Classic, *The Little Red Hen,* Ub assigned Al Eugster and Jimmie Culhane to codirect. Along with storyman Otto Englander, the new directors sought a unique voice for the character of a selfish duck who would refuse to help the little red hen bake bread but was more than willing to help her eat it. Englander remembered a funny voice that he had recently heard on the radio. In the radio bit, a young milkman named Clarence Nash produced a hilariously sputtering impersonation of a singing goat. Englander called Nash in for an audition with animators Al Eugster, Jimmie Culhane, and himself. Nash impressed the Comicolor men with his hilarious nanny goat voice. They wanted to hire him immediately, but Ub was out of the office in the morning and would not be able to give the final stamp of approval until later in the afternoon. With his confidence buoyed by the excellent audition, Nash immediately called upon the Disney Studios and auditioned there as well. Walt hired Nash on the spot.

A few months later, Nash made his debut as the voice of a hot-blooded duck in Disney's *The Wise Little Hen.* Disney's *Little Hen* paled in comparison to the Iwerks Studio's version of the tale, but the duck character Nash introduced in the film was an immediate and overwhelming success. Donald Duck was to become one of Disney's most enduring and endearing cartoon characters, second only to Mickey Mouse. Clarence "Ducky" Nash would be the sole voice of Donald until the time of his death some fifty years later.

While animal characters such as Donald Duck were given glorified leading roles in most cartoons (even Betty Boop started as a dog!), the ethnic caricatures that found their way into the cartoons of the time were indications of the ugliness prevalent in 1930s America. Prejudice, maliciously intended or not, was rampant in the industry and in the nation. When Harman and Ising were at Warner Brothers, a blackface character named Bosko was their comic hero. Years later, Harman-Ising animators would recoil when pressed on the issue, only admitting that he was a mischievous little boy and downplaying his minstrel-like appearance.

The Fleischer Brothers recognized black culture by using the voices of Cab Calloway and Louis Armstrong for characters alongside Betty Boop. Similarly, Walter Lantz, in films such as *Scrub Me Mamma With a Boogie Beat,* used black jazz music for inspiration together with black stereotypes in his cartoons.

Ub—who had once received a letter containing a nasty use of the epithet *nigger* from Walt—had been raised in much the same environment as Disney and was no more generous in his treatment of nonwhite characters. His studio's racially insensitive work included Flip the Frog cartoons such as *Chinaman's Chance* and what was to be the nadir of the genre for Iwerks, the Comicolor Classic *Little Black Sambo.*

In *Little Black Sambo* the supposedly African characters speak in exaggerated black dialect from the Southern United States. The comedic situations emphasize the characters' ethnicity; for example, Sambo's mother warns him to watch out for the "mean ol' tiger. He sho' do like dark meat."

It is revealing to note that African characters in Iwerks cartoons are typically depicted in jungle attire or in subservient roles as butlers, footmen, guards, or indigents. Their archetypal features are grotesquely exaggerated, with large bulbous lips and bulging eyes. Regardless of setting, they speak in Southern black dialect. Positive black roles are typically assigned to incognito Africans. Often, one of Irv Spence's loose-limbed, scat-singing scarecrows provided the disguise. By obscuring the character's ethnicity in costume, the disguised characters were presumably more palatable to mass audiences.

Chinese men have slits for eyes and long braided topknots.

Hispanic characters are shown as slovenly, with large sombreros, crossed pistoleras, and large drooping mustaches. It is ironic that the same Iwerks Studio that featured these Pancho Villa–style Hispanic characters was also among the first to hire a Hispanic artist in a creative role. Rudy Zamora was a longtime animator at the studio and a deliciously colorful character in his own right.

Equally prejudiced (or even more so) is the studio's treatment of Middle Eastern characters and cultures. In the Willie Whopper cartoon *Insultin' the Sultan,* Mahatma Gandhi is unceremoniously and anachronistically thrown into the proceedings. The Gandhi character was only slightly less offensive than the bloodthirsty Arabs.

The Comicolor Classics were even more tilted in this regard. Despite delving into the rich folktales of *The Thousand and One Nights* for a trio of Classics—*Sinbad the Sailor, Aladdin and his Wonderful Lamp,* and *Ali Baba*—the Iwerks Studio treated the fables less as cultural icons and more as simple plot lines on which to hang a cartoon. The protagonists of each film were transformed into white-bread Americans thrust into lands populated by hideous dark-skinned villains. The heroes were indistinguishable from the European characters of Ub's earlier works.

The architecture of the Middle East lent itself well to the Iwerks Studio style of rounding the corners of every door and window. Minarets and colonnades flowed easily from Ub's fertile pen. As a guide to his layout artists, Ub built miniature sets of his concepts replete with keyhole doors and rounded windows.

In addition to the questionable treatment of minorities in the Iwerks cartoons of the 1930s was their treatment of homosexual characters. A running joke was to have a character appear briefly, swish wickedly, and mutter limpwristedly, "Oh, you nasty man," a catch-phrase coined in the 1930s by radio comedian Joe Penner. The rouge and pursed lips of these characters—not to mention the mincing, fey walk—would tip off the audience that this was a figure surely to be mocked. Such scenes occur in *Flip's Lunch Room, Mary's Little Lamb,* and *Sinbad the Sailor* among many others. During this time, making fun of gay and ethnic characters was a guaranteed comic hit.

While the studio drifted into the prejudices of its era, it balanced these lapses with moments of intense sensitivity. One example of that sensitivity is writer Otto Englander's sad tale called *The Brave Tin Soldier*. In *The Brave Tin Soldier*, a toymaker is seen painting tin soldiers and stacking them in a box like so many cigars. This was a common gag of Al Eugster, who was reportedly rarely seen without a cigar dangling from his mouth. Unfortunately for one soldier, he never makes it into the box. The toymaker accidentally drops him on the floor, breaking off one of his fragile tin legs. Being unfit to be sold as a toy, the tin soldier is deposited unceremoniously into the waste bin.

When the toymaker leaves for the night, the toys come to life. The one-legged tin soldier pulls himself out of the rubbish and hops on his one good leg across the toyshop floor. He is taunted by leering, jeering toys until a beautiful dancing ballerina doll takes pity upon him. The brave tin soldier falls in love with her immediately, and she with him.

A toy king rolls along and is awestruck by the ballerina's beauty. He wants her in a less-than-regal manner, but she is appalled by his advances and rebuffs him. The king takes her by force. The soldier hops to the ballerina's rescue. The king's soldiers defend their sovereign. In spite of the soldier's brave attempts at escape, he simply can't outhop all the king's men, and is captured. He is brought to a speedy trial. Despite a desperate plea by the ballerina doll, the brave tin soldier is ordered to be executed.

A firing squad gathers. Again the ballerina asks for leniency, but her cries fall upon deaf ears. The firing squad readies its weapons. The ballerina runs to the brave tin soldier and clutches him tightly. The firing squad shoots a barrage of corks at the lovers. The impact knocks them back into a roaring fireplace. Their bodies melt together into the shape of a heart. Steam rises from their melted bodies, and flies heavenward. At St. Peter's gate, their earthly bodies reconstitute themselves. The brave tin soldier's broken leg grows anew. The gates to heaven open, admitting its two newest toy inhabitants.

Arthur Turkisher's music beautifully underscores the somber underpinnings of the tale. The animation of Culhane and Eugster imbues Englander's story with just the right amount of pathos to allow the characters to tug a bit at audiences' heartstrings.

When Pat Powers was sent an obligatory viewing copy of *The Brave Tin Soldier,* he responded by firing off a tersely worded telegram to Ub that expressed his dismay at the film. In the telegram, Powers stated that he would tolerate "NO MORE UNFUNNY ENDINGS." After reading the telegram to Jimmie Culhane and Al Eugster, Ub did not say a word. He merely smiled his enigmatic smile. Perhaps Ub recalled Pat Powers's similar response to *The Skeleton Dance,* "THEY DON'T WANT THIS," Powers had written. "MORE MICE." Ub knew that *The Brave Tin Soldier* was a unique work that transcended the gag-fest that defined the cartoon industry of the mid-1930s.

Culhane and Eugster were incensed by Powers's response and sent off a reply to New York. In the reply, they excoriated Powers for his ignorance of the animation industry. To his credit, Powers did not respond to Culhane and Eugster's letter. If he responded to Ub directly, Ub never mentioned it to the animators. To this day, *The Brave Tin Soldier* remains one of the most critically acclaimed cartoons in the Iwerks Studio library.

The conditions under which an animator was required to work have often seemed idyllic to the outside world. Historians often write reverently of the Golden Age of animation in glowing, idealized terms. In truth, the joviality of the end product masked an often torturous path that the animation took to get there. Salaries were good for the Depression era, but benefits were practically nonexistent. The Golden Age may have yielded gold for the studios and distributors that profited from the success of the films, but for those who made them, it meant hard labor.

Work hours were long with few breaks allowed. It was not in the least bit unusual for animators to remain at their desks working well into the night. Men like Offemann ruled with iron fists. Weekend shifts were mandatory when production lagged behind schedule, which occurred more often than not. Offemann was reviled for his practice of walking into the animation room late on Friday afternoons to inform the staff that they would have to work the weekend to catch up.

Eventually the animators got fed up with the conditions and rebelled the way they always had—with their pencils and their wits. Lou Zukor and Ed Love earned Ub's wrath by allowing their frustrations to spill out on the drawing board. They posted a series of bitingly satiric drawings of an animator's life around the studio. Lou Zukor recalls that the artwork featured the multiple duties of an animator in the thirties: "It was some guy animating with one hand and doing something else with the other and he had a broom up his butt sweeping the floor. I guess Ub kind of took it hard. It was just a gag."

Lou Zukor's brother, Maury, who also worked for Iwerks, recalls that pranks and gags were the only outlet for a frustrated group of artists. "It got so bad at the studios, the conditions other than horsing around—it's the only way we could keep our spirits up. The money wasn't very good and you did work pretty hard."

This atmosphere pervaded the entire animation industry from the mid- to late 1930s. Several members of the Ub Iwerks Studio staff channeled their frustrations in impromptu discussions. These discussions, led by Grim Natwick and Jimmie Culhane, formalized themselves into a clandestine meeting at a beer joint on Western Avenue. Ten or twelve Iwerks employees attended this first meeting. Jimmie Culhane recalls that "the good Amontillado sherry sparked our indignation and we decided to form a union." They discussed who they should invite next.

Animators from other studios were no less interested in improving their conditions. A second and then a third union meeting were held. With each successive meeting, the number of animators seeking change grew. Select Warner Brothers artists began to join the Iwerks staff in the organization effort. Soon, the group was forced to move their meetings to the local Teamsters Union Hall to accommodate the large number of disheartened animators seeking representation.

When the studios learned of a fourth planned meeting, they attempted to thwart it by scheduling mandatory overtime for the night of the meeting. The only studio that did not use this union-busting tactic was the Iwerks Studio. Ub Iwerks chose to let his people attend. This is not to imply that he was supportive of the organizing efforts. Like all management of the day, Ub was "death to the unions," one animator recalls. Ub's anti-union stance was based purely on his business priorities as head of the studio. He had to produce high-quality product as quickly as he was able. Privately, however, Ub could certainly empathize with the plight of his staff, having been in their shoes himself.

Ub's top man, Grim Natwick, had also seen firsthand the demands of the animation industry from his time at Fleischer's. He had seen enough. Grim was not only one of the union stalwarts, he was the leader within the Iwerks Studio organizational staff and the man to whom Ub frequently looked to provide guidance and tutelage to the younger staff. It is more than likely that Ub gave the union efforts extra leeway because of his reliance on and respect for Grim Natwick.

As Grim's importance within the Studio grew and with Dorothy Webster and Emile Offemann handling the business matters in the mid-1930s, Ub retired to the refuge of the basement. The Iwerks animators saw him entering and exiting the building daily, but were kept entirely in the dark as to what exactly he was doing. According to Jimmie Culhane, "for several weeks he drove up to the studio with the backseat of his bedraggled coupe chock-full of gears and bits of steel shafting. The cameraman, looking very self-important, would help Ub unload, and they would both vanish into the cellar." For several weeks, Ub rarely made even token appearances at the noon horseshoe games. When he did, he refused to answer any questions about his activities in the basement. When Ub took on new projects they always took precedence over everything else in his life—his hobbies, his sports, his family. One day, the animators saw Ub pulling up with an automobile chassis in the backseat of his car instead of his usual heap of scrap metal. He dragged the chassis into his basement workshop.

Sometimes Ub would enlist the assistance of LeRoy Richardson on some aspect of the device. Richardson had no real interest in animation or even in the end product of the studio. He enjoyed working on his machines. He helped Ub put the finishing touches on the horizontal multiplane camera stand without fully realizing the significance of the awkward-looking device. When Ub finally emerged from the cellar, recalls Culhane, "We now had a brand-new multiplane camera, which Ub had built out of parts from an old Chevy that he had bought for $350! The damn thing worked, too."

The multiplane concept, as the name implies, involved using various planes of action to simulate depth of field. The first film to utilize Ub's new multiplane camera stand was *The Headless Horseman*. In the dramatic opening scene, a daydreaming Ichabod Crane imagines himself riding through a multilevel countryside background. The dark silhouette of Crane on his horse is in stark contrast to the layers of depth provided by Ub's multiplane. Mountains lie in the deep background, bushes are in the middle, the daydreaming teacher is in the foreground, and even closer are more bushes and trees. For an attempt at Ub's own version of the world's first multiplane camera, *The Headless Horseman* was a valiant effort, setting a new standard in animation.

Equally effective are multiplane scenes from *Don Quixote* in which the mad Don rides madly from left to right across the screen through a three-dimensional countryside in a manner not unlike that of Ichabod Crane in *The Headless Horseman*. *The Valiant Tailor* likewise contained effective use of the multiplane camera in a hectic chase scene through a mountainous landscape.

Because Ub's multiplane camera was horizontally oriented, it was well-suited for experiments in stop-motion animation as well as for the studio's typical cel animation. A stop-motion film entitled *The Toy Parade* was filmed but never released using the new multiplane technology. Ralph Somerville recalled working on a series of marching wooden soldiers that paraded tediously across the screen. Instead of changing drawings for each frame as in cel animation, in the stop-motion film, each wooden soldier had to be repositioned incrementally. After days of enacting this meticulous march, Somerville was more than ready to return to cel animation and the relative normalcy of the Comicolor Classics.

Chuck Jones recalls that Ub's penchant for embracing this type of technical experimentation often superseded his interest in creating cohesive story lines for his cartoons. "I think Ub was always seeking the magic of the mechanics of things—and he was brilliant, you know—but expecting him to be a storyman and expecting him to be what he was is like expecting Thomas Edison to write a comic strip. That's not what he did."

As the experiments continued, the humor of the Iwerks Studio became ever more eccentric. "The idea of the Comicolor series was to create kind of enchanting stories in the style of maybe the Silly Symphonies," animation historian Joe Adamson writes, "but they just couldn't help these bizarre flourishes. They kept veering from never-never land into the twilight zone. Things get really strange."

Balloonland was one of the strangest of the strange. As the name implies, the cartoon takes place in a land where everything (and every-body!) is made of balloons. Everybody that is, except the Pincushion Man. "I'm the old Pincushion Man, the terror of Balloony Land," howls the spiny, blue Pincushion Man. The cartoon was an isolation-ist tale, warning the fragile citizenry to stay where they are safe and secure, within the Balloonland boundaries. Taken in the context of the world situation of 1936, it was a cautionary tale of the times.

The sociological approach of the Iwerks Studio had changed sub-tly since Flip the Frog had realistically and comically faced the Great Depression. Like Disney's *Three Little Pigs* and *The Grasshopper and the Ants, Balloonland* is a parable. Symbolism triumphs over realism. Like its Disney counterparts, Ub's Comicolor Classics manage to be socially relevant without becoming overtly political or spoiling their innate entertainment value. Unlike Disney's films, however, Ub's films do not have the storybook innocence or sunny outlook. Ub's fables are bizarre tales that become surreal at times. With his drooping limbs and pinhead, the Pincushion Man would not have been out of place terrorizing the dripping clocks of a Salvador Dali painting.

Carl Stalling had taken a brief sabbatical away from the Iwerks Studio to help arrange *Three Little Pigs* at Disney's. When he returned to Ub a few months later, he suggested a series of films that revolved around the events of the seasons as he and Ub had done before with the Silly Symphonies. The best of these was the winter entry, *Jack Frost*.

Occasionally, the Willie Whopper directorial team, Grim Natwick and Berny Wolf, would slum in the Comicolor Classic neighborhood with frequently great results. The Natwick-and-Wolf-directed *Jack Frost* is an acknowledged masterpiece of the Iwerks Studio. Like many of its predecessors, its storyline revolves around little woodland creatures as they battle the harsh elements of the seasons. In this case, it tells the story of a naughty little bear who refuses to hibernate. He simply does not want to go to bed.

When viewed against the backdrop of the Great Depression in which it was created, *Jack Frost* like *Balloonland* seems to take an isolationist stance. Whereas Disney's fables seemed to extol the implied virtues of industriousness, the Comicolor Classics frequently warned against the dangers of leaving home. The little bear protagonist of *Jack Frost* will not comply. Voiced by Willie Whopper's Jane Withers, the little bear is a tad too big for his furry britches. Whenever he is faced with adversity, he cheerfully sings, "I don't have to worry; I don't have to care. My coat is very furry, I'm a frizzly, grizzly bear."

After being spanked by his mother for sneaking out of bed, the little bear risks his mother's wrath again by tiptoeing out of the house. Alone in the chilly forest, he is confronted by the gathering storm of winter as personified by Jack Frost and Old Man Winter himself. Old Man Winter chases the little bear through a stylized forest glade. Grim Natwick slyly drew the background trees as nude female figures. He recalled later that the inspiration had actually come from the ancient gnarled trees that lined the thoroughfares of Vienna, Austria, where he had spent some time studying art before undertaking his animation career.

Old Man Winter at his heels, the little bear seeks shelter wherever he can find it. He tries joining several of his forest friends in their homes, but they shun him. He is even rebuffed when he tries to stay with a skunk. Finally learning his lesson, the little bear returns to the comfort of his warm little crib. Safe at home. Safe at last.

Most of the colors in *Jack Frost* are sumptuous, but it took quite an effort to get them that way. The Cinecolor Process rendered most colors richly, but it was nearly impossible to create orange with the process. The vibrant orange coloring in the leaves and jack-o'lanterns of *Jack Frost* created myriad problems during the printing process. The lab tried several solutions, but was unable to come up with a solution satisfactory to Ub and Grim.

Quality was a constant concern. Al Eugster recalls, "We were much concerned with improving the product. With Disney leading the way, it was like a pack of racing greyhounds chasing a mechanical rabbit." Or mouse, as it were.

In the Comicolor Classic *Summertime*, Ub revisited familiar territory in a refreshingly new way. Similar to the Silly Symphony *Summer* and a companion piece to *Jack Frost*, *Summertime* nonetheless included enough innovation to be remarkable on its own merits. It begins with Old Man Winter still lurking about the forest glade. The sun is steaming mad at Winter's apparent impudence. It shoots rays of sunlight at the cowering Jack Frost. The sun rays then melt a snowman to reveal a sprightly, horn-blowing faun.

At the faun's urging, flowers emerge from the ground to dance as in Disney's *Flowers and Trees*. Black shadows of trees dramatically transform into shapely silhouettes of female forms dancing in astonishingly detailed profile. Rotoscoping has been frequently denied by former Iwerks Studio staff members, but the realism of the profiles of the tree dancers is sufficient to indicate that rotoscoping or a similar technique was used to create verisimilitude.

A group of centaurs playing polo is rendered much less realistically. The classical casting seems to be an inspired choice for displaying the annual rites of passage that mark the changing of the seasons. Old Mister Groundhog, fresh from his long Winter's hibernation, at first dances merrily through the forest welcoming Spring (most of the rituals of Summertime are actually Spring rites) when he is tricked by Old Man Winter into thinking he has seen his shadow. Frightened, he runs back into his home signaling the unwelcome return of Winter. The team of polo centaurs, however, do not accept Winter's return. They fight back with their mallets and snowballs. A group of fireflies joins in the effort. They attack Old Man Winter with tails aflame. He melts into a puddle of water.

It was during the production of the Comi-Colors in 1936 that Ub learned that his father, Eert Ubben Iwwerks, had died in Kansas City at the age of ninety-two. When the city asked Ub if he wanted to handle the funeral arrangements, his response was simple: "Throw him in a ditch!" The funeral arrangements were handled by the city and only three people attended the service. His apartment was sealed by Boss Pendergast; the final disposition of several of his oil paintings, his personal articles, and his two greyhound dogs is unknown.

Ub never fully explained his relationship with his father or the pain that he felt when Eert had left him at an early age. Even at the gentle urgings of his sons, Ub revealed little. Don recalls, "If I asked him questions about his father he'd say, 'We don't talk about that.' I think it was a tremendous hurt to him to have his father leave the family as he did and therefore during (Ub's) childhood he pretty much kept to himself. He didn't want to discuss it. He was influenced by the fact that his father had abandoned the family and he had to go to work. His mother was embittered about it."

Ub's early experiences stayed with him throughout his life. He knew the value of hard work and responsibility. "As I was growing up, his mother lived with us," Don remembers. "She contracted Parkinson's disease and as a result she was unable to care for herself, she needed the help of my mother and dad as well. It was tough, probably the toughest moment came when she needed enough care my mother couldn't provide, while raising my brother and myself and managing a household. My dad was faced with having to put her in a rest home where she could get daily care. I know it was really hard for him and it was really hard for his mother to accept that, but he had to do it."

As a father, his sons remember him as a disciplinarian who made it clear that children were to be seen and not heard. But Ub was loving and did enjoy involving his sons in his own work, providing early inspiration and insight into his own world. Don remembers learning of his father's skills as an animator in the 1930s. "I'd ask him if he'd draw me a cartoon sometime just as a treat, and he'd say 'sure.' We'd get a piece of paper and I'd sit on his lap and he'd start dashing off some kind of character. I wouldn't know what he was going to draw, but it was fun to see the cartoon start evolving in circles and lines and things. I wondered, What's going to come of this thing?"

In their home on Dixie Canyon in Sherman Oaks, Ub built a darkroom in the garage. Don was awed: "I remember the magic of seeing an image begin to form on a sheet of photo enlarging paper submerged in developer. With black-and-white printing, you could use a safelight, which provided a dim yellow light to observe your progress. In no time when he was showing me how to process film I had shot, and then how to print it. He was a perfectionist, so it took a number of attempts before I produced a print that he would approve."

Ub continued to come up with new techniques and photographic processes for his films, and spent less and less time defining story lines and characters. The Disney cartoons of the time were clear examples proving that strong plots and endearing characters, and not necessarily technical achievements on their own, were the key ingredient to a box office success. The Flip the Frog cartoons in 1931 turned a decent profit, but by the mid-thirties the margins were getting smaller. "These pictures that were made for $7,000 a piece were pulling in $300,000 on the first season," notes historian Joe Adamson.

"Pat Powers who was bankrolling them profited by more than $100,000 on the first season, so they were doing quite fine. That is why the other seasons existed because they were going great guns at first, but the profit figures actually went down as time went on, and of course the Depression got worse and theaters decided they did not need the Ub Iwerks cartoons. I know that Pat Powers in some years made much less than $100,000, so I'm sure he got less and less enchanted by Ub Iwerks idea of what made great animation." Ultimately it became harder and harder for Ub to maintain financial stability. By late 1936, he was forced to do the inevitable.

"We were finishing with a production," animator Ed Friedman recalls, "and we weren't even finished with it—this was on a Thursday. Ub came in and said just point blank with a serious face, no laugh, 'Sorry, you guys, this is it. We're finished. You're through as of tonight.'"

It seemed an oddly emotionless and sudden way to close the studio, but as Friedman recalled, "Those days, you see, there was no warning or anything. The boss—whatever he said, you did. And that was it." The Comicolor Classic they were working on, an adaptation of Charles Dickens' *Oliver Twist,* was left unfinished. The completed cels would never be filmed.

Though Ub had tried valiantly and though it had many successes to its credit, the Iwerks Studio ultimately failed. Historian Mark Kausler suggests that one reason for the studio's failure was that Ub was simply not cut out for the front office. "He wasn't a big salesman. He didn't feel comfortable being in the forefront of things. I think he'd much rather work behind the scenes and discover new things and discover new ways to do things." Throughout the Iwerks Studio's six-year history, Ub had learned this to be so. With independence, resources, and a constant spirit of experimentation, he had been given the freedom to explore both his strengths and his weaknesses. This restless enthusiasm continued through the studio's very last days.

The last film Ub released was *Happy Days,* the pilot for a new cartoon series based on the popular comic strip, *Reglar Fellars.* Created by Gene Byrnes, *Reglar Fellars* featured a group of young boys who resembled an animated version of the Our Gang Comedies featuring Spanky and the Gang. Using Byrnes's characters, Ub's artists had been extremely faithful to the comic strip, even incorporating its verbose style of dialogue. Never before had an Ub Iwerks cartoon been so relentlessly talky. Had they had the luxury of time, the Reglar Fellars series could have been a departure and a new direction for Ub and the Iwerks Studio. As it was, it marked a new direction in a different vein entirely. It marked the end of an era of independence. At this critical point, Ub Iwerks had no immediate plans for the future. He would have to do as he always had done, work with what he was given and improvise the rest.

chapter 10

Journeyman

The Iwerks Studio did not remain closed for long. Since he had state-of-the-art equipment with which to work, Ub opened his doors again as a commercial work-for-hire house. With a skeleton staff comprising Grim Natwick, Jerry Hathcock, and Paul Fennel, the new endeavor was called Cartoon Films, Limited.

Several commercial animation projects provided much-needed operating capital. Among these sustaining commercial projects were spots for an oil company and a series of films commissioned by a large British pharmaceutical company, Boots Chemists. *See How They Won* (1936) was a gothic tale directed by Grim Natwick that told the cautionary story of everyday citizen John Careless and his family as they battled the scourge of germs. The story opens at the Bad Health Headquarters, where the leader of the Microbe Army, a Napoleonic-looking commander, is strategizing how to attack John Careless. Flight Commander Fluenza and Captain Sorethroat watch with great interest as John Careless's dutiful wife offers him a jacket, which he refuses. John is attacked by germs at the office. Suddenly, his face becomes grotesquely distorted. The precision-ground distortion lens that Ub had developed for *Chinaman's Chance* was a simple but effective way of achieving the required disquieting effect. Obviously ill, John goes home to bed. Victorious, the Microbe Army looks for other victims. They attack John's daughter when she is scratched by her cat. Blood poisoning is the gruesome result—germ warfare at its worst.

Fortunately for John and his family, an army of Boots Chemists druggists, the Good Health Brigade, march in to eradicate the unpleasant beasts. Some of the white-coated good guys are armed with boxes of medicines, others carry atomizers presumably filled with pharmaceuticals. They chase the germs back home. A sequel, *Leave It to John,* continued the tale of John Careless, this time in the form of an animated warning on the importance of hand washing.

The Warner Brothers Studio's output was much less pedantic. The intent of the animators was to generate laughs, laughs, and more laughs, and they were becoming very successful in that endeavor. Leon Schlesinger had assembled a talented group of animators, which at the time included Ub's United Film Ad Service coworker Friz Freleng, Iwerks Studio alumnus Charles "Chuck" Jones, and Robert "Bob" Clampett. They joined Ub's old friend and colleague, musical director Carl Stalling, in the soon-to-be renowned Termite Terrace of Warner Brothers.

Separately, Schlesinger had promised both Chuck Jones and Bob Clampett that they would be next in line to fill an open director's spot at Warner Brothers. When the Iwerks Studio collapsed, Leon changed his mind and reneged on his promise. He signed a subcontract with Ub to direct the next two pictures using Cartoon Film Limited's state-of-the-art equipment. This did not sit well with Bob Clampett, who felt strongly that Schlesinger should have honored his word and made him the next director. "I went to see Leon and he told me what he had in mind was to put me with Ub, and then when Ub left, the job would be mine," Clampett recalls.

Despite his great respect for Ub, Clampett was miffed at the situation. Jones was no less disappointed. When Ub began running behind schedule on the two cartoons, Leon Schlesinger assigned Clampett and Jones to help get the films back on track. Once at the studio, Jones and Clampett were temporarily able to put aside their differences to work side-by-side with Ub on completing the slow-moving Porky Pig projects. In the official credits for the films, Ub Iwerks was listed as supervisor, while Clampett and Jones shared animation credit. In spite of the apparent parity of credit, Clampett had somehow convinced Schlesinger that he was worthy of higher pay, which aggravated Jones's competitive instincts. Bob Clampett and Chuck Jones would go on to become legendary directors in their own right, but the animosity that developed between the two created an unfortunate tension that persisted for years afterward.

An irony lost in the clamor surrounding the two animators is that the films were very funny, if not exactly critic-pleasing, films. *Porky and Gabby* featured a delightful new character from the mind of Cal Howard: Gabby Goat. One of the most misanthropic characters ever created by any animation studio, Gabby hates everything with equal zeal. He is part Daffy Duck, part Gabby the nightwatchman (from Max Fleischer's *Gulliver's Travels*, another Cal Howard creation), and 100-percent nasty. If Gabby had been a large, ponderous character like Peg Leg Pete, he would have been immediately off-putting. Instead, he was drawn tiny and cute and had a distinctive, squeaky voice that was as grating as it was endearing.

It has been rumored that one reason Ub ran behind schedule was that he simply abhorred the character of Porky Pig. That would perhaps explain why Porky is relegated to essentially a sidekick role in his own film. The irascible Gabby Goat steals every scene that he is in—nearly the entire film.

After directing a scant two cartoons for Warner Brothers (*Porky's Superservice* was the other), Ub quit. He had had his fill. Bob Clampett surmises that at this stage in Ub's legendary career, his "heart just wasn't in it." As Leon Schlesinger had promised, upon Ub's departure Clampett was made head of his own animation unit at Warner Brothers, a move that no doubt hurt Chuck Jones deeply. Chuck Jones would later come into his own as a director. His *What's Opera, Doc?* starring Bugs Bunny and Elmer Fudd has been cited frequently as one of the top animated short subjects of all time.

Like *Happy Days*, which Ub had animated using Gene Byrne's

Reglar Fellars characters, Ub's next venture borrowed an established comic character from England.

Ub had often found inspiration among British illustrators, and in the 1930s, one of the best was an Englishman by the name of Lawson Wood. Wood was renowned for a series of magazine covers featuring a grizzled old monkey and his youthful cohorts. Taking humorous stabs at golf, war, and the world at large, the character of Gran Pop Monkey was featured on a series of desk blotters, postcards, calendars, and covers of *Collier's Magazine* throughout the United States and Europe. Wood's fellow Englishman, Dave Biederman, contracted with Ub Iwerks to direct three Gran Pop Monkey cartoons. Lawson Wood himself drew models of the main characters, which were to be animated by Ub's minimal crew.

The character of Gran Pop veered far from Ub's usually distinctive character styling. Perhaps because of Wood's involvement, the films were wildly different from anything Iwerks had done before. Unlike Oswald, Mickey, Flip, or Willie, Gran Pop is far from Ub's prototypically self-confident, perky juvenile. Gran Pop is old, timid, and clumsy. Nonetheless, it is because of these very qualities that he proves an apt foil for some of Ub's classic gags. He is especially vulnerable to more complicated machinery such as typewriters, elevators, and Murphy beds.

Gran Pop starred in three cartoons, *A Busy Day, The Beauty Shoppe,* and *Baby Checkers.* Contributing to Gran Pop's demise was his appearance. Because Lawson Wood provided drawings for the character design, the elderly ape retained the drooping body, sagging face, and myriad wrinkles of his illustrated incarnation. None of these features were easy to draw once, much less repeatedly over time. Gran Pop faded away.

A similar fate befell a proposed series called The Way Outs, an animated travelogue that ended before it was ever completed. The demise of The Way Outs coincided with the moving of the old Iwerks Studio offices from 9713 Santa Monica Boulevard to a new location, 1704 Santa Monica Boulevard. There, Ub contracted to do animation for a former adversary, Charles Mintz. After taking Oswald the Lucky Rabbit from Disney's production team, Mintz had Oswald taken away from him in a similar manner by Carl Laemmle at Universal. The cartoon boomerang gag became a reality. Mintz settled at Columbia, where he revived Krazy Kat's career in sound cartoons and in 1934 helped to create the Color Rhapsody series of cartoons. The Color Rhapsodies, as the name implied, were yet another iteration of the Ub Iwerks/Carl Stalling Silly Symphonies formula.

One of the best of the Color Rhapsodies directed by Ub was *Merry Mannequins*. Drenched in swinging art-deco black-and-white, *Merry Mannequins* featured one of the liveliest musical scores of the post–Iwerks Studio era.

Another Color Rhapsody, *Skeleton Frolic,* revisits familiar territory for Ub. Like *The Skeleton Dance* and *Spooks* before it, *Skeleton Frolic* featured skeletons dancing in syncopated rhythm to the soundtrack music. Leonard Maltin in *Of Mice and Magic* comments, "The newer version was just a faint reminder of the first cartoon's originality and charm."

Set in a splashy carnival setting, *The Horse on the Merry Ground* is similarly charming and vastly more original than *Skeleton Frolic.*

While *The Horse on the Merry Go Round* is nominally a Color Rhapsody, it is largely the contrast between dark and light that gives the film its stunning look. Color is more implied than actual.

Although the Iwerks Studio cartoons had never brought audiences to the theaters in droves as he had once hoped, each contained its own moments of uniqueness in style, story, or technology. By the late 1930s, Ub's energy shifted toward the technological side of the business. More often than not, this fascination with the design of all things mechanical carried over into his home life. Since moving to California in the late 1920s, Ub had an avid interest in sailing. Wanting to pursue the hobby, he decided to build his own sailboat. He worked out of his garage, spending many nights and weekends drafting designs, manufacturing parts, and assembling the pieces. As the boat grew in form and size, friends and family, including his wife, Mildred, became skeptical when they suspected the craft would no longer fit through the doorway. Mildred warned Ub that he was not to cut a hole through the wall to extricate it. Ub was not concerned. When time came to remove the boat for launch, he merely tipped the sailboat on its side, removed the doorjambs, and slid the boat through the opening with a pre-calculated $^{1}/_{16}$ inch to spare.

"It was sixteen feet long, all wood with a beautiful varnished deck," Don Iwerks recalls. "The family drove with him to Balboa Island. He was very proud to be towing the new boat behind the car, and enjoyed the admiring glances from motorists as they would pass. He and Lee Richardson, his longtime friend and employee, rigged the mast and sails. Ub insisted on taking the maiden voyage by himself; in case something should happen, he did not want to have to be concerned about us. The sailboat worked like a charm, and soon we were all sailing with him around Balboa Bay. In those days, we could sail up onto the beach at any point we wanted. We really had fun."

After learning and mastering the technology of sailing, Ub abandoned the sport after only one season. The challenge was over.

This trait was a thread that ran throughout Ub's life and career. It was no wonder then that by the late 1930s his interest in animation would also come to an end. The Columbia cartoons, while providing much needed capital for Ub's studio during the late 1930s, were losing their luster. The challenge for Ub no longer resided in making the films, but in maintaining his own exuberance for producing them. He had completed thirteen Color Rhapsodies in all, many of which show the rubbery and loose-limbed style of his early efforts. *Midnight Frolics, Gorilla Hunt, The Frog Pond,* and *Blackboard Review* were a few of his last great efforts in animation before his steam ran out. *Wise Owl* was the last Ub Iwerks–directed release for Columbia on December 6, 1940. After a rigorous decade as an animation producer, Ub simply wanted to pursue what he loved most—film technology. "Animation becomes something you can get very good at, and then after a while the challenge is gone," notes historian

Joe Adamson. "Your interest is going to go into somewhere you can advance, where you can make progress, where you can have a new challenge. So that's really what happened, the challenge became technological for him."

In 1940, there was one major studio that was interested in improving the art form in that manner and had the resources to do so. The problem was Ub had left that studio ten years earlier. Now the question was, could he return?

11

The Return

Although Ub's desire to be a full-fledged animator had waned, the many enthusiastic artists coming into the field inspired him. When his friend (and Iwerks Studio animator) Ray Patin asked him to teach at his Ray Patin Animation training school, it didn't take long for Ub to say yes. He felt this was an opportunity to give back to the field and encourage new blood. Throughout his career, Ub had enjoyed show-ing younger artists the ins and outs of cartooning. Patin's studio offered him the chance to share his considerable knowledge of the field. For Ray Patin, having the renowned artist Ub Iwerks as an instructor was a great achievement.

With all of the new artists funneling into the Disney Studios to work on feature films and shorts, a well-trained staff was of prime importance. Since 1930, the Disney Studio had completed *Snow White and the Seven Dwarfs* and *Pinocchio*. The sheer mass of human resources required to make full-length feature cartoons precluded all but those with the deepest pockets from even attempting them. Only Disney and the Fleischer Brothers (with *Gulliver's Travels*) had released feature-length cartoons. RKO's Tat's Tales Studio had com-pleted principal work on an animated feature of *King Midas*, but had run out of resources before ever releasing it. With the lack of strong financial backing, Ub Iwerks had never given a feature film serious consideration at his own studio.

Many of Ub's previous employees and colleagues, however, had been hired to direct and animate the features at Disney, including Grim Natwick, Berny Wolf, Jimmie (now called "Shamus") Culhane, and Al Eugster. But there were also many young faces being called upon to animate who were in need of training.

Knowing that Ben Sharpsteen was involved in training at the Disney Studio, Ub called Ben and asked if the studio would be interested in sending over some students for instruction. Sharpsteen said that he would, but thought teaching to be demeaning for a man of Ub's talents. In an interview with historian Don Peri, Sharpsteen recalls, "I thought it was belittling, a step down. . . ."

> As I was very fond of him, I asked him to come over to the studio and have lunch with me. Now, I knew of no bitterness between Walt and Ub, so I made the casual remark to Walt that Ub had called me, what he had called me about, and that I had asked him to come over and have lunch. Walt just took it casually.

Ub may have had another reason for calling Sharpsteen. A few days earlier, Ub had spoken to Hugh Harman.

"Hugh," Ub said, "I have tossed in the towel. I can't go any longer at this business." Harman asked Ub how he could help. "I hate to mention this, but—do you think that if I made overtures or you made them for me to Disney that he would consider taking me back?"

Harman had occasional contact with Roy Disney and knew that Roy harbored no ill feelings toward his old associate. "Go down and talk to them," Hugh suggested. Ub telephoned Ben Sharpsteen later that day.

At their lunch meeting, Ub admitted to Ben Sharpsteen that in spite of his work at the animation school, he was seeking a stronger challenge. Sharpsteen recalls the meeting:

> I said to Ub, "You know, I've thought about you a lot, and I can't get it out of my head that you belong here." "Well," he said, "I suppose there is something to that," or something to that effect. I said, "You know there has been an awful lot happen here in the eleven years since you left, things are so absolutely different, and yet I have a suggestion to make.

There is a great weakness here in our technical set-up, especially in our checking department." Everything had to go from animation to ink-and-painting to camera, but the big place was between animation and ink-and painting—that was the big stopgap, checking. I said, "That's a big weakness and that's where I feel that I could hire you to take that job."

Mildred Iwerks encouraged Ub to return to Disney, knowing as Walt did that Ub would rather do things himself than supervise others. Ub also knew that with Ben being the intermediary, it would give Walt a chance to say no without embarrassment.

When Sharpsteen went to Walt Disney to explain his thoughts, Walt reportedly replied, "Don't come to me asking who you're going to hire or what you're going to pay him."

Walt's outward reticence toward Ub's return perhaps belied an entirely different emotion within. Disney had a well-documented lack of tolerance for anyone he felt had betrayed him or his studio. Ub's departure ten years prior had stung Walt deeply and certainly fit his criteria for betrayal. However, the shared history and obvious respect between the two men generated a different emotion that was far less negative.

When Walt Disney won his first Academy Award in 1932 for the creation of Mickey Mouse, Ub sent a telegram to Walt congratulating him on the honor. Even though Disney received hundreds of similarly congratulatory letters and telegrams, Ub's was reportedly one of the few he truly cherished.

Despite his curt response to Ben Sharpsteen, Walt Disney was far from emotionless on the subject of Ub Iwerks. For those who knew both men, it was obvious that Walt was glad to have his old friend back again. According to Don Iwerks, "Walt was astute enough to realize that bringing my dad back into the company was absolutely the right thing to do, that he could help this company and help Walt achieve those things he wanted to do. I think there was a great mutual respect between them. Past tense was past tense about what happened back in the 'thirties. It's here we are today, and here's where we're going, let's get on with it."

Ub Iwerks accepted Sharpsteen's offer of $75 a week (much less than he was accustomed to as a studio head) and returned to the Disney Studios on September 9, 1940. At the time, *Fantasia,* or *The Concert Feature,* as it was known around the studio, was in production, with most scenes already completed. The studio and the industry at large had been and still were developing at lightning speed. Ub was now returning to the fold in a whole new capacity, as technician, engineer, and inventor. He quietly began to prowl around in the production control department, which was responsible for scene planning and animation checking. This department, as Sharpsteen had said, filled in the crucial gap between the drawing and the ink-and-paint stages of animated film production.

Bcause Ub was a perfectionist of the most painstaking kind, he jumped into the role with vigor. Ruthie Tompson, who had known Ub and Walt in the early days when she appeared as an extra in the Alice cartoons, was now working at Disney in the ink-and-paint department. When she was transferred into Ub's department in 1940, the reunion was a pleasant one for both: "[Ub] was a great guy to work with. He had a twinkle in his eye and would tease anyone if they were gullible. If I had any dumb ideas, he'd listen and if he thought a suggestion was worthwhile, he'd try it and come back with an answer, good or bad."

During this time, Ub especially enjoyed the parts of his job that involved planning the movements of Disney's multiplane camera, which had previously been under the direction of Bill Garrity.

Having created his own multiplane camera from used-car parts in 1934 for $350, it was fascinating to Ub to see what he could do with the $70,000 vertical multiplane camera the Disney Studio had developed in 1937. Ub suggested to Walt that he could engineer a method of keeping the focus on all levels of the multiplane at a crystalline clarity. Walt argued that the technology was great, but by having backgrounds as clear as the foregrounds, the attention directed toward individual characters was lost. Walt felt that Ub's deep-focus technique would look artificial when compared to the soft focus prevalent at Disney at the time. In real life, it is impossible for the human eye to focus at various depths of field; Walt reasoned, therefore, that it should be no different in animation.

While Ub's multifocused, multiplane camera project never moved beyond the conceptual stages, it was precisely the sort of mental stimulus that he had been hoping for upon his return to the Disney Studio. Ub especially enjoyed the challenge of working with Walt again, being pushed by Walt, pushing him back, each man stimulated by the other to widen his own concept of what was possible. As they had in the 1920s, they continued to expand the boundaries of the possible.

Much had changed around the studio since Ub had left. In fact, the studio itself had changed. When Ub had left, the Disney Studio was located on Hyperion Avenue. Now the studio was installed in state-of-the-art facilities in Burbank. Aside from this obvious change, one of the greatest differences between the two studios was the number of new faces.

Aside from the Iwerks Studio veterans, the new generation featured many talented young men and women who were just beginning to make their mark on animation. Newspapers and magazines would laud Disney's Nine Old Men, the animators who were hand picked to represent the studio's best and brightest. Ub's old assistant Les Clark was the only one of the nine with whom he had personally worked at the old studio. The remaining eight were young upstarts with the talent to back up their distinguished nickname. Over the course of the next forty-plus years, the Nine Old Men would continue to turn out high-quality animation beneath the gaze of an ever more scrutinizing public eye. For Disney animators, competition came not so much from other studios as it did from the pressure they placed upon themselves.

As the original old man of the Disney Studio, Ub Iwerks's return meant different things to different people. To those who had thought the relationship between the two principals had been damaged beyond repair, Ub's return came as a complete surprise. But to others who knew both men well, however, it was a natural turn of events and made perfect sense. Ollie Johnston recalls, "When he came back, everybody had heard that Ub was back. We were all glad to hear it. We knew he'd be into everything. He was an important figure and genius at what he did with technical and mechanical stuff." Marc Davis recalls the reunion, "Ub came back, although not a partner with Walt Disney, he was back to his beginnings there, and I think this was very important to him, and I think it was awfully important to the studio."

A reading of Ub's article, "Movie Cartoons Come to Life," published in *Popular Mechanics* magazine, perhaps explains the allure that the Disney Studio held for Ub. In the span of a few pages, Ub breathlessly touches upon the Fantasound multispeaker sound system, the multiplane camera, animated rain effects, a curious device called the Sonovox, and the latest techniques for combining live action with animation. Most of these effects featured technical advances being developed by Ub and his department.

Apart from his tasks in the checking department, one of Ub's first jobs upon returning to the studio was to provide some combination-effects work for *Fantasia*. A scene was conceived that would feature Mickey Mouse shaking hands with the live-action conductor, Leopold Stokowski. "Well, this is how it was done," Ub recalls, concerning the merging of live action and animation for *Fantasia*:

> Stokowski was photographed first, shaking hands with thin air. Photographic prints of the scene were made and numbered. Then the animators placed drawing paper over the numbered photostats on a light board and matched Mickey's action to that of Stokowski. Mickey was inked and painted solid black to give the effect of a silhouette. When it came to photographing Mickey's action, a camera with a projection movement was used. In other words, the camera itself served as a projector. The camera was lined up on the camera crane and the film of Stokowski's action put in it and adjusted

until it synchronized with that of Mickey. Thus, with a
negative of both Mickey's and Stokowski's action, a double
printing of the two produced a "dupe" negative. To you in
the theater it appeared as if man and mouse were together
shaking hands.

For the most part, the challenge of combining live-action figures (such as Stokowski) with animated characters (such as Mickey Mouse) was in creating the illusion of believability. Ub's role in this process encompassed the visual aspects of filmmaking, but he was also involved with the auditory aspects of creating a theatrical experience that were the result of a technology that Disney referred to as Fantasound. In Fantasound, Disney was able to add the three-dimensional perspective in yet another realm: sound.

Leopold Stokowski had experimented with stereophonic sound for a 1937 Universal Studios production of *100 Men and a Girl*. In Fantasound, Ub wrote, the process went beyond stereophonic into multiphonic sound: "Realism is accomplished by placing loud-speakers at different points in a theater—behind the screen, along the aisles, or in the balcony." By recording an orchestra with multiple microphones, each directed toward a separate soundtrack, Ub wrote, auditory verisimilitude could be achieved. "In this multiplicity of soundtracks lies the secret of increased quality, volume range, and auditory perspective." In other words, fully three-dimensional sound.

The major problem with Fantasound was that in order for it to sound right, the proper equipment needed to be installed in each theater. Each unit cost $30,000 and few theaters could afford this expensive installation. When *Fantasia* opened at the Broadway Theater in New York City on November 13, 1940, ninety speakers had been installed to provide the full Fantasound effect. *Fantasia* played but a few venues using the full Fantasound process. It would be several decades before even stereophonic sound—much less *multiphonic* sound—would become commonplace in theaters nationwide.

In the spring of 1941, as *Fantasia* continued its first run in theaters, the Disney Studio was torn apart by a bitter labor action. The Disney strike turned the usually harmonious studio into a hotbed of tension, backbiting, and red-baiting. Strike leaders' pictures were banished from all Disney literature. Ub had received similar treatment when he left the studio in the 1930s. (Robert Feild's biography of Walt Disney and the Disney Studio featured not one mention of Ub Iwerks or his accomplishments in the creation of Mickey Mouse or the studio.)

Company literature was not the only arena where the strike took its ugly toll. The volatility of the strike atmosphere occasionally led normally docile people to violence and bitterness. Walt Disney and strikeleader Art Babbitt nearly came to blows when Babbitt catcalled Disney from the picket line. Disney reportedly hired thugs to pummel a group of strikers in an effort to intimidate them into ceasing their union activity.

Ub remained somehow immune to this animosity. According to one source, "[Ub] stayed quietly loyal and supportive during the strike, walking casually through the picket lines as if they were not there. . . . None of the strikers catcalled Ub when he crossed the picket lines." Such was the respect given him by his peers, that they restrained their anger when he passed. When he drove through the gates of the studio, the protesters would clear a path.

In the midst of the turmoil of the strike, the Disney Studio released *The Reluctant Dragon*. Essentially a backstage tour of the new studio facilities in Burbank through the eyes of humorist Robert Benchley, *The Reluctant Dragon* remains to this day a fascinating peek into the workings of the Disney Studio.

The obvious staging of some scenes does little to detract from the charm of seeing some of the greatest animation artists of their day at work on their craft. It is also a unique document in that, for once, Walt Disney does not dominate the film. Perhaps because of the animosity of the strike, Disney gave himself what amounts to a cameo-role in the film. His seemingly happy staff is given full credit, front and center.

In one scene of *The Reluctant Dragon,* Benchley visits the sound department, where lovely Frances Gifford demonstrates the use of a device called the Sonovox to create the vocal effects for Casey, Jr., an animated train engine in *Dumbo.* Created by writer-inventor Gilbert Wright, the premise of the device was that one sound (the train, for instance) could be fed through the Sonovox and then processed to filter the characteristics of a second sound (in this case, Frances Gifford's voice) to create a hybrid "train voice." It is a wonderful effect for Casey, Jr.'s voice, but Ub's idea of using the Sonovox to "transmute and remold motion picture voices into any language"—for example, translating Clark Gable's or Hedy Lamarr's voice into French or Russian—never came to pass. To modulate one set of voice characteristics into another simply proved too unwieldy.

In a way, the Sonovox amalgamation of voice and sound was not unlike the merger of live action and animation that Ub had long been a key figure in pioneering. While sound technology was of definite interest to Ub, he focussed primarily on the visual aspect of film.

Ub immersed himself in some special scenes for *Dumbo.* Animator Ken O'Connor had been working on a scene in which little Dumbo, feeling sad, inadvertently consumes a large quantity of alcohol and is now seeing pink elephants. To create the stark black background that was necessary to generate the eye-popping imagery of hallucinatory elephants, O'Connor used a swath of black velvet as backing. According to O'Connor:

> *There's nothing blacker than a piece of black velvet with no light on it. It is black! So that worked behind the characters and that was a satisfaction. There were all sorts of little things like that broke through in that sequence. I was pleased with it. Then Ub Iwerks did some juggling with color separation negatives where we had them skating back and forth, pink rim-light and green rim-light on the characters skating back and forth on black. He found a method of separating the records so he could print a pure magenta on the black and*

pure blue-green without it being muddied by the other two col-
ors. He separated out the records and got brilliance in the
effect that we hadn't got before. There were a lot of things
that I really liked, aside from it being really nutty and wild
and having plaid elephants and spotted elephants and all
sorts of crazy things we worked out pictorially, as well as Ollie
Wallace's music that I thought was keen.

The "Pink Elephants on Parade" sequence of *Dumbo* is justifiably one of the classic scenes in the entire Disney oeuvre. It has been imitated often but never equaled. Leonard Maltin in *The Disney Films* writes of this scene: "There is no way to overpraise the 'Pink Elephants' scene. It is one of the best things ever done at the Disney studio, and, to use a much overworked but appropriate phrase, years ahead of its time."

Dumbo was released in October of 1941. Whereas an Ub Iwerks cartoon might have satirized war and the growing world tensions, the simplicity of Disney's *Dumbo* provided just the right touch of innocent escapism in wartime. In director Steven Spielberg's much underrated World War II comedy, *1941,* the little elephant's impact (and that of escapist films in general) is demonstrated in a scene in which hard-boiled military man Robert Stack weeps openly in a movie theater while watching *Dumbo.*

A scant two months after *Dumbo's* release, in the early morning hours of December 7, 1941, the United States Naval Base in Pearl Harbor, Hawaii, was attacked by a squadron of Japanese war planes. The battleship USS *Arizona* along with three other ships was destroyed in the attack. For the first time since the Civil War, a war had come to American soil. The U.S. military responded swiftly and assuredly.

Late in the afternoon of that fateful day, U.S. armed services commandeered the Disney Studios in Burbank. When Walt Disney arrived at the studio, he was appalled to see that it had been overrun by five hundred military personnel. For a company that had been built upon fantasy, the harsh reality of the world had set in. Walt Disney's own office was taken over as command post for Naval Commander Raymond Farwell.

When they were informed that troops would be stationed at the studio indefinitely, Walt and Roy Disney traveled to Washington, D.C. Many companies had been forced to abandon their facilities to make way for military production. In exchange for producing a series of training films and inspirational cartoons for the government, Disney negotiated an agreement to maintain his studio and occupy his staff with war-related animated projects.

The war cartoons produced in this effort were as disparate as *Der Fuehrer's Face*—a wildly funny piece of anti-Nazi propaganda featuring Donald Duck (and Academy Award winner for Best Cartoon) —and *Four Methods of Flush Riveting*, a straightforward instructional film. Working with Henry Morganthau of the United States Treasury, Disney released *The New Spirit*, which starred a patriotic Donald Duck urging Americans to pay their taxes. *The Winged Scourge*, which featured the Seven Dwarfs, taught military personnel how to provide protection from mosquito infestations in countries that were at risk of malaria epidemics. *Education for Death* showed how little German children were indoctrinated into the Nazi way. Some of the other titles included *Food Will Win the War*, a particularly perverse film that used bizarre metaphors such as a sweater knitted out of pasta and wrapped around the world, to demonstrate how much food the United States produced annually.

It is noteworthy that after *Dumbo*, the next film distributed by Disney following the bombing of Pearl Harbor was *Bambi*. Made in the midst of the European and Pacific conflicts, these two features rank among the most simple, gentle, and good-hearted of the entire Disney catalog.

Bambi in particular is an incredibly simple film. It features a realistic rain effect by Ub's team of craftsmen. Ub explained his new technique for creating animated rain:

> *Falling water is photographed at night with a spotlight playing on it. The film is then put in a camera and enlarged prints made. Cartoon rain is added and the splatters are*

accentuated. The effect is much more lifelike than pen-and-ink rain, yet retains characteristics of animation.

It has been frequently assumed by film historians that once Ub returned to Disney, he never animated or directed again. He did in fact do both on occasion. Yet it is true that Ub desired to work mainly in the background and was always reluctant to take public credit for his past successes.

Although Ub did isolate himself at the studio to some extent, the notion that he was never involved directly in drawing or directing animation again is simply false. In truth, when Ub first returned, he was enlisted to help animate or direct several of the war shorts. The paucity of capable animators in the wake of the strike had left the studio temporarily shorthanded. Ub gladly lent his prodigious pencil to the effort.

In 1942, John Grierson of the National Film Board of Canada commissioned Disney to create *Stop That Tank: The BOYS Anti-Tank Rifle,* an instructional film for a new anti-tank weapon. The BOYS Anti-Tank MK1 Rifle was designed by a Canadian officer named Captain Boys in 1935. The rifle featured a .55 caliber, short bipod-mounted rifle with a bolt action and the ability to be fed from a five-round box magazine. It has been described as one of the most effective anti-tank weapons ever developed.

With this film, Ub's trademark scenes featuring engines and technical contraptions found a new audience. The war provided him with a whole new gamut of gags, machine parts, and contraptions. As a gun hobbyist with an avid interest in gunsmithing, Ub created all the intricately detailed technical drawings of the weaponry himself. He drew each mechanism of the MKI in minute detail, from the unusual recoil-reducing chamber at the end of the barrel to the adjustable sights along which the anti-tank gunner would aim.

As director of *Stop That Tank . . . ,* Ub recognized the value of allowing his animators to use their own creativity to enhance the film. Fortunately for Ub, he was assigned two of the most creative people at the studio, Fred Moore and Ward Kimball. Since Moore and

Kimball were between features at the time, they worked with Ub to punch up the comedy. Says Kimball:

> Ub had pinned up a basic storyboard that showed how the rifle was to be taken apart and how it was put back together again. It needed a little comedy, so Fred Moore changed things so that certain sections besides the serious instructional part would keep it light. How not to handle the rifle. We had fun with that. Ub just sat there and said, "Sure, that's good. That's good." He just said, "Hey, you guys know what you're doing." He sort of laughed about it. . . . We checked everything out with him, of course. We said it needs a little comedy, we can use the old trick we used on the Goofy—How to Play Baseball, how to do this, how to do that—by doing it wrong and showing the right way it should be done. We always had the idea that the narrator would go along telling how it worked. How to Ride a Horse—his narration was beautiful and always without any mishaps and here the Goof is going through all sorts of doing it the wrong way. That was the trick we had with the Goof and we used the same thing on The BOYS Anti-Tank because it needed a little comedy. Ub agreed. He just said, "You guys know what you're doing. I'll take care of the rest."

The October 1942 issue of *Popular Science* magazine contained an article about the film and the power of cartoons as a teaching medium: "Even civilians who witnessed the film were confident that they could pick up an MKI and blast a German tank out of existence."

A similar project involved a series of cartoons that educated army personnel in the crucial task of identifying military airplanes. The military concept referred to was called WEFT, for "Wings, Engines, Fuselage, Tail." If viewers could identify enemy aircraft quickly, they would have time to take appropriate fight-or-flight action before it was too late. Ironically, the technique of aircraft identification espoused in the WEFT film series was often less than welcome among the men in the field. They fashioned their own definition for the acronym *WEFT*: "Wrong Every F—ing Time." Despite this sarcastic response, the WEFT technique of aircraft identification is still taught to this day.

Ub's knowledge of aircraft was so comprehensive that he ended up writing most of the scripts for the WEFT cartoon series himself. Aviation had long been an interest of Ub's. In almost every era of his career, he had used aviation themes as the backdrop to his films. Oswald the Lucky Rabbit had *The Ocean Hop*, Mickey Mouse had his turn with *Plane Crazy*, and Willie Whopper had *The Air Race*.

Combined with his model airplane hobby, Ub's love of aviation may have yielded more tangible assistance to the U.S. war effort than education or propaganda alone. Chuck Jones recalls that when Ub was at his own studio, he developed a model airplane with an attached camera on board. Many have suggested that Ub's experimentation was a predecessor of modern aerial photography. Jones believed that this technique was used by U.S. airmen in the Pacific theater during the war, although this claim has not been confirmed.

In his provocative book, *Victory Through Air Power*, World War I commander and aviation theorist Alexander P. De Seversky championed the use of aircraft in all aspects of the war effort. Seversky claimed that "The MOST significant single fact about the war now in progress is the emergence of aviation as the paramount and decisive factor in warmaking." Walt Disney thought that this was an important idea, and set out to create a full-length feature film based upon De Seversky's theories.

Unlike the cheery entertainment offered by most animated films, *Victory Through Air Power* had the singular, gravely serious intent of attempting to influence public opinion and, subsequently, governmental policy. Ub subcontracted his former Iwerks Studio colleague Leroy Richardson to provide several model airplanes for the film. Each airplane was constructed in excruciating detail to match the distinctive features of the full-size aircraft.

Shown throughout the nation in 1943, the sixty-five minutes of *Victory Through Air Power* proved to be too much propaganda for audiences to bear in one sitting. In Roy Disney's words, the ambitious film was "a big flop" with the general public, but it was, however, highly successful as "a patriotic gesture." Franklin Roosevelt was reportedly introduced to the film by Winston Churchill in a private showing that influenced Roosevelt's handling of air support for the strategic D-Day invasion.

With international tensions mounting and with pressures at the studio reaching a fever pitch, it seemed an odd time for Walt Disney to embark on a foreign trip with a cadre of artists at his side. In retrospect, the trip could not have been timed better. Walt Disney and his entourage toured Latin and South America at the request of Nelson Rockefeller, who was then the United States coordinator for inter-American affairs. Rockefeller proposed the goodwill tour as part of the department's "good neighbor" policy.

The good neighbor policy was intended to maintain a positive image of the United States among South Americans and to inoculate them against communist and Nazi ideologies. Whether Walt's trip accomplished these grandiose goals is unclear, but it soon had the residual effect of easing internal tensions within the studio.

With brother Walt safely out of the country, Roy Disney settled the animators' strike through arbitration. Walt's absence allowed him to end the labor stalemate while not losing face or appearing to acquiesce personally.

The trip was also beneficial in that it rejuvenated the spirits of the weary Walt and his fellow artists. The 16mm film that was shot during the trip was edited for use in the creation of the film, *Saludos Amigos,* a small but fulfilling pastiche filled with vivid color and visual energy. Divided into four sections that corresponded to the countries that the Disney entourage visited, *Saludos Amigos* allowed Ub the chance to experiment again with combining animated characters with live-action backgrounds.

Ub had not engineered the combination of live action with animation on this scale since the Alice comedies some fifteen years earlier. The technology, he found, had changed relatively little since those seat-of-the-pants days. In 1933, Linwood Dunn's horrifying special effects in *King Kong* had been produced using essentially the same simplified traveling matte processes that Ub had used in the Alice films. The equipment had improved slightly, but not the theory. Walt Disney recognized the gap between the equipment and the processes in film technology. He summoned Ben Sharpsteen to his office.

Disney's outward lack of interest when Ub had been rehired was now replaced with a protective concern. Despite his forays into other projects, Ub remained as part of the checking department. "You've got Ub there checking," Disney chided Sharpsteen. "I think you're wasting him there."

Sharpsteen replied, "Yeah, but I didn't know, bringing him in after all the years, where to indoctrinate him."

"Yeah," Walt responded, "but you know you can't go out and ever hope to hire a man who was as well schooled in optics as Ub. He's a genius." On September 11, 1943, Walt made Ub the head of the newly developed Disney Optical Printing Department. Ub had previously been working on the development of the double-headed optical printer, which the studio dubbed Optical Printer #2. Its purpose was to create various types of special effects, superimposition of titles over backgrounds, reversing action, as well as slowing down and speeding up action. It was the first double picture head optical printer that employed a lens system to optically superimpose two separate film images upon each other. The camera would then photograph the combined images. Printer #2 was the "workhorse" optical printer from 1943 through its retirement in the early 1980s. The effects shots in virtually every Disney film up to the mid-1960s were accomplished on Printer #2.

The Three Caballeros, the sequel to *Saludos Amigos*, was one of the first films in which Ub's process was put to use. Throughout *The Three Caballeros*, Donald Duck, along with his amigos, Jose Carioca and Panchito, interacted seamlessly with colorful live-action characters. The blend is particularly seamless in two scenes in which Donald Duck attempts to win the heart of the wonderful Latin songstresses Aurora Miranda and Dora Luz.

In a scene set in Brazil, Donald and Jose stroll alongside Aurora Miranda as she sings "Os Quindins De Yaya." The two animated characters weave in and around the live-action actress, vying for her attentions. Live-action musicians join the scene, eventually breaking into a riveting dance number. As the dancers mimic fighting, they metamorphose into animated roosters engaging in a mock cockfight. The combination of the animation with the active camerawork of the scene transforms what could have been a standard musical number into a stunningly evocative film moment.

A scene in which Donald woos Dora Luz is similarly well handled. As she sings the beautiful ballad "You Belong to My Heart," Donald flutters about her like a bee around a flower. As Leonard Maltin relates in *The Disney Films*:

> *The girl appears in his eyes . . . he dances among the stars . . . everything he sees becomes a neon sign, then flowers and wildly colored geometric figures . . . then silhouettes, gradually turning into shadows of his dream girl, who evolves back into a flower.*

The sequence is every bit as crazy as Maltin describes. Much of the overall fun of *The Three Caballeros* stems from scenes such as these, which Disney promotional materials hailed as "the most startling advancement in motion picture technique since the advent of sound."

The sequence in which an animated duck dances and romances a human actress was so realistically rendered that some critics took the scenes too seriously. *The New Yorker* in particular was appalled at the scene:

> *In the first place, a somewhat physical romance between a two-foot duck and a full-sized woman, though one happens to be a cartoon and the other pleasantly rounded and certainly mortal, is one of those things that might disconcert less squeamish authorities than the Hays office. . . . It might even be said that a sequence involving the duck, the young lady, and a long alley of animated cactus plants would probably be considered suggestive in a less innocent medium.*

The Three Caballeros, proved that technology had caught up with imagination. In many respects, the pressure was now on the writers, since Ub's inventions had made previously difficult ideas feasible.

Donald Duck missed an opportunity to share the screen with a more masculine companion when Roy Disney turned down a request by Metro-Goldwyn-Mayer for Donald to perform a tap dance number alongside Gene Kelly in *Anchors Aweigh*. The part went instead to Jerry the Mouse from MGM's Tom and Jerry cartoon series. Jerry's whimsical dance with Kelly is justifiably viewed as one of the classic dance sequences from Kelly's storied career.

The *Anchors Aweigh* proposal was not an unheard-of request for Disney. Occasionally, Walt Disney had indeed loaned out his characters to other studios. Mickey Mouse, Disney's most valued character, was featured in a cameo role in the 1934 Jimmy Durante musical comedy *Hollywood Party*. Alfred Hitchcock borrowed scenes from the Silly Symphony *Who Killed Cock Robin?* for the climax to his suspense thriller *Sabotage*.

In 1944, Walt subcontracted with the Goldwyn studio and film director Elliott Nugent to provide an animated segment for the Danny Kaye/Dinah Shore comedy *Up in Arms*. Walt suggested using Ub to animate an eighty-second newsreel sequence for the ending of the movie. In his film debut, Kaye plays a hypochondriac who, after getting drafted into the war, accidentally smuggles his girlfriend aboard his Pacific-bound troopship. When the Japanese attack and take Kaye prisoner, a series of funny escapades ensues in which the neurotic hero finally escapes and even manages to nab some enemy soldiers. In the final scene, a newsreel plays in the background. An animated segment of the newsreel depicts a small worm eating its way through the emulsion of the film, ultimately breaking through the fourth wall of the newsreel and of the movie itself. Just before the film is entirely chomped through, the worm says (to the audience), "I'm the only one who knows how this picture ends and I'll never tell!" He takes the last bite and the screen turns to white. For reasons unknown, however, the scene was ultimately edited out of the final film. It languished for years in the Disney Film Library before it was discovered by Disney senior manager of restoration, Scott MacQueen, and identified with the help of Leonard Maltin.

Ub continued to immerse himself in any aspect of the Disney enterprise that needed his assistance. His efforts in the 1940s included effects work, animation, direction, sound enhancements, mechanical engineering, optics, color processing, and even writing on occasion. As was true in all aspects of his life, he took the biggest challenges, and wrestled them into submission. He refused to play the ambitious parlor games of the corporate world.

Behind the scenes at the studio, however, were other men and women who operated on the more subtle political level. One of these men was Ub's immediate supervisor, William "Bill" Anderson, who had arrived at the studio in 1943 as head of production control. As Ub and Anderson crossed paths over production issues, conflicts in personality and methodology arose. The chemistry between the two was bad from the start. Having once served in the position now held by Anderson, Ub found it demeaning to report to a man who showed him no respect. According to associates close to Ub, he considered Bill Anderson to be one step up from a used-car salesman. Tension between the two grew so severe that Ub once reportedly offered to take their discussion outside to the parking lot and settle the matter there. Becoming aware of the animosity between the two, Walt Disney personally intervened on Ub's behalf several times. In 1945, he moved Ub away from Anderson into a position in the process lab, a move that pleased both men immensely.

With all the Disney cartoons and live-action features in production in the 1940s, there became an increasing need to provide high-quality color still prints for marketing and publicity purposes. The print reproduction methods the studio was using often had problems with color fidelity. Kodak introduced a patented process in the 1930s that became the premier method of making color photographic reproductions, a system termed the Kodak dye-transfer process. Realizing that the studio could use such a process, Ub brought it into the studio in the 1940s to test. Through the use of masking techniques, he redesigned the three-color system to improve upon its saturation and contrast range. According to sources who worked with Ub during that time, after he got it up and running, it became the superior system for paper-print reproduction. When engineers from Kodak inquired as to how his system produced such good results, Ub would not allow anyone from the company to view it. Ub was always protective of his work when it came to keeping Disney at the forefront of film technology.

While at Disney, Ub continued to be in demand elsewhere. In 1946, director King Vidor requested Ub's assistance for process work on *Duel in the Sun*. The western drama starred a veritable *Who's Who* of actors, led by the always steady Gregory Peck and the luminescent Jennifer Jones as his half-breed love interest. Peck and Jones were joined onscreen by Walter Huston, Harry Carey, Joseph Cotten, Lionel Barrymore, Lillian Gish, and Butterfly McQueen. Location shooting for the film had been completed, but the final dramatic scene required that the camera appear to track from a tight shot of the couple to a high extreme wide shot of the landscape. Nowadays the effect would be executed with a helicopter and a zoom lens, but for *Duel in the Sun,* Ub achieved the effect optically.

Bob Broughton recalled watching the footage in the Disney Studio process lab. The projectionist would run the film forward and then reverse it when it was finished. As the figures on the screen moved backward, the fatally wounded Jennifer Jones gathered herself and rose again. Jones's undulations looked vastly different in slow-motion reverse than they did when viewed at full speed forward. "It [the reversed sequence] was the sexiest thing you ever saw in your life." Broughton recalls. The engineers played the scene over and over again, transfixed by the vision of the lovely Jones.

While the engineers were quite enthralled, Ub never noticed Jones's gyrations at all. As Bob Broughton would later recall, "There was no playing around with him in the middle of one of these things. He had tunnel vision. But that's the kind of challenge he accepted.

Here's something that's not quite right, it's not working right, there must be something that can be done."

This was Ub's daily challenge—seeking all those things which were not yet "quite right" and making them so.

chapter **12**

Animating Life

The Disney war effort had proven to Walt Disney that he could keep many different groups of artists occupied on several different projects at once. When the war ended, Disney moved the artists from mass production of propaganda films to mass production of a series of educational and commercial films. Feature films were extremely costly and time-consuming to produce, while the commerical films often used limited animation and shortcuts that cut costs and hastened production time. Also, like the war films, these were works for hire. Corporate or academic sponsorship dictated the content and theme of the films. Walt supplied the manpower and technical wherewithal, corporations supplied the cash. Having produced commercial cartoons at his own studio, Ub could relate to Walt's need for generating cash flow.

A Walt Disney Productions manual from this time period highlights this need:

> COST-PER-FOOT *is a horrid phrase but it's got to be put up with, like hot spells and taxes. The suggestions in this manual should help to keep old man CPF where he belongs— and still maintain the Disney quality which is our most vital asset.*

The manual further stated that anytime they questioned how best to do this, Disney employees should consult Ub. "Ub's ingenuity can usually contrive to get an effect or shoot material that stumps the more staid, conventional camera crane." Many times simple solutions to film problems were referred to as "Ub gags."

Among the industrial films created at Disney were *The Dawn of Better Living* for Westinghouse Electric Company and *Bathing Time for Baby* for Johnson and Johnson. Other films were created for Firestone and General Motors.

The Iwerks passion for perfection and his focus on getting the job done could be exhibited in many different ways, depending on the circumstances. According to Bob Broughton, "[Ub] was the fastest eater I ever knew. He would start getting nervous during the last two-thirds of the meal, wanting to get back to work." Don Iwerks remembers his father acting the same way during their evening dinners.

> My mother used to get on his case at times about that too, he'd sit down at dinner and he'd be through with it in about five minutes and he was ready to get up and get going again. My mother and I and my brother would always eat in a normal manner, we'd always be there fifteen, twenty minutes after he'd gotten up to go on and do whatever he was going to do. She used to say, 'You're eating too fast, you're going to get indigestion!' but he wouldn't pay any attention to it. He was so focused on what he was doing, solving problems and moving forward.

His impatience with his staff was no different. When Virginia Summersfield, one of his trio of secretaries, would calculate long strings of numbers on her adding machine at her desk, Ub would stand behind her and finish the sum in his head—correctly.

The problem inherent in the production of educational and industrial films was that the Disney Studio did not retain full control over the output. Because they were works for hire, the films were owned by and controlled by the companies that commissioned them. This lack of control coupled with a low profit margin erased any enthusiasm for this kind of film.

After nearly two years of creating these films, Walt Disney had had enough. According to Roy Disney, "Walt, in a huff one day, said, 'Oh, to hell with it! From now on let's make the word *educational* a dirty word around here. Let's stick to *entertainment*. He abruptly closed the Educational and Industrial Film Division and following that he proposed to give audiences "'sugar-coated educational stuff.'"

The "sugar-coated educational stuff" Walt had in mind was a series of nature films. For a first project, he turned his live-action cameras loose on the frontiers of Alaska. A talented married couple, Alfred and Elma Milotte, veterans of industrial and educational films, were commissioned by Disney to spend a year filming the Eskimos and wildlife of the frozen North with 16mm cameras. The 16mm film would then be blown up to 35mm for theatrical presentation.

Having experimented with blow-up work on *Saludos Amigos*, Ub was certain that this effort was technically flawed and would fail dismally. Ben Sharpsteen recalls Ub voicing his concerns to Walt. "'You cannot run sixteen-millimeter pictures on these big screens. Once you blow them up to thirty-five-millimeter and then the grain will start and people will not hold still,'" he said. "'If you're going to do it, you've got to send out thirty-five-millimeter cameras.'" Ub feared that any small imperfection on the film would look huge when blown up for the large screen and would be distracting.

Walt believed otherwise. "No," he replied. "They cannot have those great big cameras and carry them around and get them into those places and run them. They have to be run with electricity and they're going to have batteries and everything." Walt continued, "We can't afford to supply them with film. These people have to be patient and sit there hours and hours and days and days, hoping to get a shot. It's going to be costly enough with sixteen-millimeter, but they've got to shoot thousands of feet of film for every foot that they use. So it's got to be the cheapest film." Ub understood the financial reasoning, but was not satisfied with the quality of the process. He was determined to figure out a solution on his own.

The 16mm footage began to come in from the Milottes at regular intervals. At first, Disney was not certain in which direction the final film would head, but when footage came in of several sequences of seals filmed on the Pribiloff Islands, Walt had found his direction.

"Why don't we take what we have and build a story around the life cycle of the seals," he suggested to Ben Sharpsteen. "Focus on them—don't show any humans at all." The result was twenty-seven minutes of captivating footage of seals living in large herds on the islands. Walt called his landmark film *Seal Island*.

Aware of Ub's fears concerning the film and struggling to convince RKO to release the film to a national audience, Walt suggested a test screening at a large theater. In December of 1948, the Crown Theater in Pasadena booked *Seal Island* along with a regular feature. Harper Goff was present for the screening:

> I thought, God, look at those scratches in it, you know, but we do our regular publicity thing and we go down [to the theater]. They run this special True-Life Adventure and it knocks the people right in their bloody hat. Nobody ever noticed the lousy film! Walt said, "Nobody's going to—if they look and see the quality of the film, we're dead! But they're going to be entrenched with these animals." And he was right. So he knew. He knew.

The audience had been enchanted. Walt knew that he had another hit on his hands. *Seal Island* would go on to win the 1948 Academy Award for Best Live Action Short Subject and to initiate the successful True-Life Adventure series.

Despite its commercial and critical success, Ub was not satisfied with the technical aspects of *Seal Island*. The scratches deeply offended his sense of order. His solution would become one of the greatest achievements in the history of filmmaking.

Roy E. Disney remembers witnessing the results of Ub's experiments:

> I was working on a film called Mysteries of the Deep, which was one of the twenty-five-minute True-Life Adventure films. We had it all finished, had it all blown up to 35mm, the music was written, and at the last possible moment, somebody brought in some film of a live birth of a baby porpoise that was shot down in Marine Land in

Florida. The birth was the first to be captured on film and it was a rotten old black-and-white negative. We said, "Well we can tint it," so we tinted it blue, and it looked pretty good. We cut it into the film, wrote some music for it, and when we got back the blow-ups, there were the worst scratches running down the middle of this footage that you ever saw in your life—big black lines through all of it. We were all sitting there in the sweatbox and Ub was sitting in the back of the room where he always sat, and the lights came on, and we said, "We've got to throw it out, it's no good, it's just horrible film." So then Ub said quietly, "Give me about a week." We all said, "Okay, you know something we don't know." So he took the film and about a week later he called us and said, "Come back and look at this stuff again." We all gathered in the sweatbox again and we ran it and it was like new film, there were no scratches. We said, "What did you DO?!" He had invented something that became common practice in the business ever since, now known as the Wet Gate.

Ub reasoned that much of the distraction of the scratches could be eliminated by passing the film through a liquid called perchlorethylene, which has the same refractive index as film stock. The liquid would flow into and fill the scratches without harming or softening the resolution of the image. Bob Otto, one of Disney's mechanical engineers, did the work for Ub. "It was done on an existing printer. We designed this slip-in head that would allow the film to be run through a liquid clear through the optical path." The process remains a standard in the industry today.

While the creation of the liquid optical printer was an advancement in the quality of the True-Life Adventures, there was yet another aspect of the nature films that required Ub's attention: color. Because film footage for the True-Life Adventures series was shot in different locales during different seasons, scenes that could be edited together to form a coherent story line often had jarring incongruities when viewed in sequence. For example, a scene of a rabbit running desperately from a bobcat in the succulent green of sunny spring might be spliced together with a scene of a similar-looking rabbit diving into a hole against a dusky brown autumnal background. The action of the scene makes for an exciting story, but the juxtaposition of lighting and background between scenes can be startling. One of the roles of Ub's process lab was to help blend these incongruities. A master of color, Ub's crew would selectively enhance the balance of colors to give the viewer the illusion that this was indeed true life that was being observed and not manufactured events.

In some cases, scenes were created in the controlled environment of the studio to match missing segments or to provide close-ups for the lead animal actors. These re-creations—while anathema to naturalists and documentarians—provided necessary thematic and dramatic continuity. For the sequences, Ub matched the tonal qualities of existing footage to create a smooth transition between the artificial contrivances and the natural scenes.

Bob Broughton has estimated that two-thirds of all the color effects work that was done was so subtle that the audience could not even tell it existed. Sometimes, however, it was not subtle enough. Walt Disney had an innate sense for when technical imperfections would impede an audience's enjoyment of a film. In dailies one time, he insisted on shooting a time-consuming scene again. The director disagreed. "Ahh, come on, Walt," he said. "We can show that scene to a thousand people and not one of them will spot that."

Walt responded, "You're damn right they won't. But all of a sudden they'll be aware they're sitting in a theater and they're out of the picture. That's why we're gonna do it over."

That sense of detail enhanced the 1948 feature *Melody Time*. Another in a line of films that were comprised solely of seemingly unrelated short subjects, *Melody Time* was nonetheless a quiet tour de force for Ub and his crew. Melody Time is filled with vivid color and effects work.

The standout segment of *Melody Time* is "Bumble Boogie." The mere concept of the musical arrangement is ingenious in itself. The animation equals the music's ingenuity.

In the next segment, "Little Toot," Ub concocts his best rain effect since *Bambi*. When the tiny tugboat, Little Toot, is banished to an area beyond the twelve-mile limit, he mopes sadly alone. As he paces morosely through the water, his reflection glistens elegantly atop the surface. Unfortunately, the quiet melancholy of the scene is shattered by a horrendous rainstorm.

The rain is not simply a torrential downpour; it also thrashes dramatically from side to side. The realistic rain and water effects enhance a sense of fear and drama.

Following "Little Toot" is Fred Waring and his Pennsylvanians' musical adaptation of Joyce Kilmer's classic ode to Mother Nature, "Trees." Ub's influence on this segment is so complete that he is often referred to as the segment's director in film biographies. From beginning to end, the segment is nonstop effects animation at its finest. In subject matter and in tone, it resembles the Silly Symphonies with forest settings that Ub had directed some twenty years earlier.

"Trees" begins with fireflies shimmering amid a stylized landscape. Aside from the fireflies, a few deer, and several squirrels moving slowly through the woodland scene, Ub's effects provide the visual energy of "Trees." A single leaf falls from a tree, sending austere ripples through the pond. Rain follows, less realistic, more poetic than in "Little Toot," but equally effective. Wind blows the rain, birds, and leaves in many directions. The "camera" pulls back to reveal that the landscape we have been observing is contained entirely within a single drop of dew upon a leaf.

A nearby spiderweb is veritably glistening with dewdrops. To compare the "Trees" spiderweb with the spiderweb from the Silly Symphony, *Summer* is to observe how far the artform had come in two decades—and how far Ub had come along with it. When the segment concludes, with sunset changing the color of the sky, the trees silhouetted against the sky are revealed to symbolize the cross at Calvary. As an audience, we are fully aware that we are seeing a mature artform being used by mature artists in a beautifully serious manner.

Another sequence in *Melody Time,* "Blame it on the Samba," utilizes the same characters and colorful imagery that were used in *Saludos Amigos* and in *The Three Caballeros.* In this case, as the Dinning Sisters croon sadly on the soundtrack, Donald Duck and Jose Carioca are seen literally beset by the blues. They saunter into the Cafe de Samba run by the Aracuan Bird who appears to be owner, bartender, and waiter wrapped into one.

As Donald and Jose mope, the Aracuan Bird concocts a mixed cocktail that grows into a large glass filled with a churning rainbow of colors swirling around the organist extraordinaire, Ethel Smith, who is cheerfully playing a perky samba. Animated bubbles swirl in and around the characters, both live-action and animated.

First one, then three, and then a screenful of swirling Ethels fill the screen. As the tempo of the music accelerates, so does the frenzy of activity. Finally, in a swish of color, the birds gleefully blow her up with a stick of dynamite. When gravity is restored, the characters swirl back down in eddies of color before melting back together again in the glass of bubbling wine.

Throughout *Melody Time,* with enough rain and wind, sleet and snow to daunt a legion of postal workers, Ub's talented effects men treated water as a paintbrush with which to paint the canvas of the film.

In the latter part of 1949, a small film was released by Disney that featured very little animation. *So Dear to My Heart* was Walt Disney's heartfelt paean to his and Ub's Midwestern roots. When they were in their teens, a race horse named Dan Patch had been a regional and national legend. Walt explained his nostalgia for the horse, by saying, "The great racehorse Dan Patch was a hero to us. We had Dan Patch's grandson on my father's farm." Long before Secretariat or Seattle Slew, Dan Patch had caught the imagination of young boys throughout America.

Despite the beautiful seeming simplicity of the scenes, the amazing thing about the animated sequences of *So Dear to My Heart,* however, is that, as Leonard Maltin aptly says, "one wonders how necessary they were." For a Disney film to raise this particular question was a landmark event in the studio's history and a definitive turning point for Ub Iwerks.

So Dear to My Heart was a small success for the studio, enough so that the modest little live-action venture virtually sealed the direction of the studio's future. Walt Disney decided to make the leap to live-action films. For Ub, this meant an entirely new set of challenges to pursue. He welcomed the opportunity while maintaining his heavy workload supervising the process work on the animated features.

Following the October 1949 release of the delightful *The Adventures of Ichabod and Mr. Toad,* which met with modest box-office success, on February 15, 1950, Disney released the animated feature *Cinderella,* which was a certified box-office sensation with audiences of all ages and seemed to signal a return to the high-quality animation of *Snow White* and *Pinocchio.* Film critic Leonard Maltin referred to the film as "one of Walt Disney's best animated fairy tales." Supervised by Ben Sharpsteen with strong animation from Marc Davis and Ward Kimball and with tasteful musical direction by Oliver Wallace, the color, animation, story, music, and backgrounds combine to create fantasy at its finest. It also contains a classic bit of Ub Iwerks optical effects and animation.

For the sequence in which Cinderella is seen scrubbing the floor before the ball, Ub designed an elaborate soap-bubble effect sequence.

As the beleaguered Cinderella plaintively sings, bubbles rise from her soapy brush. As each bubble forms and floats gently about her, her image is reflected within them. As one of the early pioneers of so-called "personality animation," Ub made sure his effects animation always served to propel the personality and emotion of the characters and scenes in which they appear. To his credit, they are never merely effects for effects' sake.

With *Cinderella*'s financial success, Walt Disney distanced himself further and further from the animated features. "We realized that as soon as Walt rode on a camera crane, we were going to lose him," one animator muses. He was right. More and more, Walt Disney involved himself in the live-action films.

The first of the new films were produced in England. Even though World War II had ended years earlier, profits from the European distribution of Disney films remained frozen. The moneys could be spent in England but not transferred to the United States. Disney hired a crew of talented Englishmen to head his live-action technical staff. The most important of this group was a man who would achieve legendary status as a matte artist, Peter Ellenshaw.

Treasure Island featured child actor Bobby Driscoll as young Jim Hawkins in a faithful retelling of Robert Louis Stevenson's classic adventure tale of swashbuckling pirates and hidden treasures. Largely because of actor Robert Newton's performance and his incredible interaction with young Bobby Driscoll, *Treasure Island* was a critical and popular success. The live-action films that followed—*The Story of Robin Hood, The Sword and the Rose,* and *Rob Roy, The Highland Rogue*—were also produced in England using the frozen European assets. The response to these films was less enthusiastic than for *Treasure Island,* but respectable nonetheless.

Ub visited the sets frequently to advise the effects teams and study how he might enhance the process. During his visits, Ub watched Peter Ellenshaw at work. For *The Sword and the Rose,* Ellenshaw created more than sixty separate handpainted mattes which, according to director Ken Annakin, gave the film "a much broader sweep visually than it ever could have had" otherwise. From Annakin's experienced vantage point, Peter Ellenshaw "knew how to modify reality and make it look even realer than real."

The import of this was not lost on Ub, who realized that the success of the process was due in a great part to Ellenshaw's paintings. The photographic process itself, however, was quite cumbersome, and Ub felt he could improve it. When he returned home, he made tests to composite the matte and live-action elements optically. Red, blue, and green positive separations of the action film were combined with the matte painting. In the matte room, a stationary stop-motion camera was mounted on a rigid platform focused on a framed glass upon which the painting was made. In the area of the painting where the action film was to be located, the glass remained clear. A frosted cel was placed on the back of the glass in the clear area, where the three positive separations (red, blue, and green) were projected and photographed. After the red separation was photographed, the film in the camera was rewound to the start and the blue separation was photographed, followed by the green. After the live-action photography was completed, the film in the camera was again rewound to photograph the illuminated painting. The four passes of the film through the camera completed the process of combining the matte painting and the action film. The advantage of Ub's color separation system was to allow precise control over color balance, density, and contrast in each color record. The results were greatly improved matte shots and realistic effects for the many Disney films to come.

When the European frozen assets had been fully liquidated following the production of the fourth British production in 1953, *Rob Roy, the Highland Rogue,* the production of live-action features returned to the United States. Many members of the production company followed a short time later, including Peter Ellenshaw, who was given a lifetime contract with Disney, and novelist Lawrence E. Watkin, who had scripted the British Disney films.

Watkin was a former English professor whose novel *On Borrowed Time* Walt Disney enjoyed greatly. Watkin's script for *Treasure Island* was faithful to Robert Louis Stevenson's original while adding the requisite Disney touch (a happy ending) and was a major reason, along with Newton's wonderfully overblown performance, for the film's success.

Not all critics were overjoyed at Disney's foray into live-action fare. Some critics (as well as some members of the studio staff) complained that the films were aimed more toward adult audiences, not children. Walt Disney recoiled at the presumption. He felt that both his animation and live-action films were aimed at a mass audience of all ages. "All my films are for grown-ups. Some people don't ever grow up and some are old the day they are born. But most of us retain a love for fantasy and heroic adventure to the last day we live. These are the people we make movies for—and I don't care how old they are!"

chapter **13**

Ubbeland

In the early 1940s, Walt Disney undertook fatherhood with the same enthusiasm and vigor that he showed for his work at the studio. Walt particularly enjoyed what he referred to as Daddy's day, Saturday, when he would take his two daughters on outings around Los Angeles. Often, they would visit local amusement parks. Disney, while enjoying the time with his daughters, found that he and the other parents were often bored sitting on benches, eating popcorn, and watching the kids on the rides. Added to this growing discomfort was the general squalor of many of the establishments.

Walt developed a new vision during these outings. At first, his plans involved building a small amusement park across the street from the studio. Mickey Mouse Park was conceived as featuring only a handful of rides and attractions but it would be designed to appeal to both children and adults. Disney explained that it would be "something of a fair, an exhibition, a playground, a community center, a museum of living facts, and a showplace of beauty and magic." As Walt began to investigate the project, it snowballed into a fully themed amusement park that began to be reverentially referred to as Disneyland. As he was later to explain at the eventual park's grand opening, Walt had envisioned Disneyland as being a happy place where children and adults could both enjoy themselves thoroughly. "Here," Disney said, "age relives fond memories of the past, and here youth may savor the challenge and promise of the future." By spending time away from the office with his daughters, Walt had come upon the germ of an idea that would take root and shape his company for years to come.

The Disneyland theme park had started out to be an expensive side venture, but it seemed to be growing more and more expensive with each new innovation that Walt Disney envisioned. Not content to copy the slapdash parks that had so offended him, Walt enlisted the studio's creative personnel to push their talents to the limits in terms of technology and ingenuity. To finance such a mammoth undertaking, Roy Disney negotiated a deal with ABC television to broadcast an hourly television show entitled simply *Disneyland*. At the time, critics who saw television as direct competition to motion pictures, decried the move as being counterproductive and bad business. The Disneys disagreed; they needed the capital.

For ABC's Leonard Goldenson, it made perfect sense as well. For a scant $500,000 investment in Disneyland, a 34.48-percent share, he was able to purchase the rights to a new television show bearing the highly marketable Disney name. In one fell swoop, Ub Iwerks found that he had not one, but two new avenues in which to use his talents, and the talents of his colleagues, including his sons.

Throughout the years, Ub involved his sons in his own activities, hobbies, and work. Don Iwerks, after graduating from high school in 1947, parlayed Ub's informal teachings into a job with LeRoy Richardson in his camera shop. Several years later, Don followed in his father's footsteps by going to work for him in the Process Lab running optical printers and developing machines. David Iwerks joined his brother at the studio in 1953, where he soon became part of the Special Effects Division.

"One of the enjoyable parts of my childhood was the fact that he had a shop and that he would teach me, as soon as he felt I could handle it, how to run his machine tools, whether it be a lathe or a saw or a drill press. So I became interested in doing the same thing, in inventing and so forth." Don remembers that when he was in fourth grade, the students were asked to build a Chinese checkers board with holes that were countersunk to hold marbles. "Everyone at school was drilling the holes with some little hand drill. My dad let me take his power drill to school to do the countersinking work. It was such an exciting thing for such a little kid to be able to handle that tool."

Each son was a member of a handpicked team that followed Ub wherever his myriad projects took him.

If someone had told Walt Disney in 1935 that he would someday produce a live-action adventure film directed by the son of Max Fleischer and featuring the special effects wizardry of Ub Iwerks, he might have laughed at the notion. The Fleischer Studio and the Iwerks Studio were in direct competition with Disney at the time. Thirty years later, the combined efforts of Richard Fleischer, Ub Iwerks, and Walt Disney created motion-picture magic.

Director Richard Fleischer was known at the time for having directed the 1952 suspense thriller *Narrow Margin,* which Leonard Maltin in his *Video and Movie Guide* referred to as "one of the best B's ever made—fast-paced, well-acted, impressively shot in a claustrophobic setting." Since *20,000 Leagues Under the Sea* needed exactly those elements to be successful, Fleischer was an inspired choice to direct the film. Fleischer merely substituted for the confining atmosphere in the train of *Narrow Margin* the wonderfully rendered submarine *Nautilus* in *20,000 Leagues.* B-actors were replaced with the estimable A-list actors Kirk Douglas, Peter Lorre, James Mason, and Paul Lukas.

Along with his optical effects work, which included mattes, miniatures, and glass shots, Ub also lent his hand in the animation. In a scene where fish were supposed to be seen swimming past a large underwater window, off-screen fish wranglers struggled to throw captive fish into camera range. The results were often less than stellar. Ub jazzed up the final version of the film by adding realistically rendered animated fish to the still waters. This short bit of animation continued Ub's string of cameo appearances as an animator while effectively filling in for the lackluster performances of the live fish in the scene. Ub would continue to moonlight with cameo appearances for years to come.

In the early 1940s, Ub took up bowling. He joined a league with Disney colleagues, including his secretary, Virginia Sommerfield, and Roy Disney. In fact, Sommerfield recalled that when she was interviewed to be Ub's secretary, he seemed more interested in her bowling handicap than he was in her secretarial skills. It was during a Saturday afternoon of bowling with friends that Ub threw the first 300 game that the Lankershim Lanes in North Hollywood had ever witnessed.

The *Valley Advertiser* newspaper on July 18, 1941, displayed a front-page photo of Ub, "the bowling sensation," receiving his awards. The story, headlined "Gifts Shower Ace Bowler" went on to say, "a high-scoring bowler, U. B. Iwerks of 4047 Dixie Canyon Avenue, Sherman Oaks, today had so many honorary gifts in recognition of his prowess that he didn't know what to do with them. He rolled a 'perfect' game, or 300 score, at the North Hollywood Bowling Center, and the first prize, a $50 check from A. A. Sherman, owner, was immediately turned over to the Children's Hospital by Iwerks. From various North Hollywood merchants who had pledged prizes for the winner of the month's highest score, Iwerks today had a $40 suit, a gold wristwatch, four tires, two café dinners, 10 gallons of gas, a grease job, a pair of shoes, a camera, a horseback ride, two cleaning jobs for the suit, a bouquet of flowers, and a barbering job."

Don, who was twelve at the time, remembers his father's reaction. "He came back on a Saturday afternoon and said, 'I bowled a 300 game.' He rolled a strike on his last ball of his first game, and then had to roll twelve more, and ended up with thirteen strikes in a row. But what was interesting was when he came home, he put his ball in the closet, and didn't take it out again, that was it. Once he achieved 300, there was nothing more to do."

According to Bob Broughton, "He was like that. When he had

his eyes set on accomplishing something and accomplished it, that was it, he didn't want to go back and dwell on it." When Ub had mastered animation, he left it behind, making only brief cameo excursions into the craft. Iwerks Studio animator, Al Eugster, felt that Ub had simply become *too* good. Animation was no longer challenging. Likewise, when he had conquered bowling, he sought other challenges.

Ub bought a bicycle to ride to and from work during the gasoline rationing of the war years. Leaving early in the morning from his new home at 4500 Mary Ellen Avenue in Van Nuys, he rode across the San Fernando Valley through orange groves and vacant lots, to the studio in Burbank. He also rode the bike to get to and from appointments on the lot. Bob Broughton remembers Ub's constant frustrations, when, after leaving production meetings he would walk back to his office with fellow employees, forgetting he had left his bike behind. Hours later, he would need his bike again, only to forget where he had left it.

As he had done during his twenties in Kansas City, Ub purchased a motorcycle to speed up his journey to and from work. When the war was over Ub lost interest in the motorcycle, eventually selling it to refurbish more of his beloved antique cars.

Ub often sated his restless mind with relentless research. A voracious reader, he was known to saturate himself in technical manuals and self-improvement books, only on occasion dipping in to the random novel. If a book or project did not interest him within a short period of time, he would discard it and move on. Don Iwerks remembers his father valuing time as being "very precious—he didn't want to waste it."

Many of his greatest innovations were the adaptations and perfection of concepts that he had first read about in journals. After fully conceptualizing a theory, Ub would often put away the books and solve the problems using his own native intelligence. Ken O'Connor once commented, "Ub was a dilettante. A dilettante floats from one thing to the next, often abandoning it. In about five minutes he'd become a professional. In about ten minutes he'd design the whole damn system."

Ub was aware of the shortcomings of process photography. The results of composite imaging were rarely convincing. He had read about a process called the Sodium Traveling Matte Process that had been invented and patented by J. Arthur Rank, an English company.

Through the Motion Picture Research Council, a group supported by the major motion picture companies in Hollywood, he contacted the Rank Organization to learn more about the process. He found that it had been perfected to a degree, but was still in need of improvement. The Motion Picture Research Council was permitted to work on improvements with the goal of perfecting it for use by the member studios. An improved camera prism was the key element in the process. Various tests were done and the results looked promising. A short time later, studios that supported the council decided to disband the council and the various assets were divided among the studios. Ub saw to it that Disney received the sodium prism and all of the test data that had been created to date.

The problem with existing blue-screen technology was its inability to accurately render fine lines such as blowing hair. By incorporating the prism into a three-strip Technicolor camera, Ub was able to do his first test on one of the sound stages at Disney. He shot two people waving a fishnet in front of a sodium screen. When he combined the final fishnet footage with a background element, the sodium process eliminated the matte lines that were problematic in the blue-screen process.

Ub was successful with his tests, and Walt enthusiastically agreed that the sodium matte process could become the standard for combining live action with animation. The system began to be implemented in their upcoming features.

Other projects for Ub came from Disney's television show. For *20,000 Leagues Under the Sea*, Walt Disney had found that television was a near-perfect publicity-generating mechanism. Two separate episodes of Disney's TV show featured backstage, making-of footage of *20,000 Leagues*, which served to generate general interest in the film. One of the episodes, "Operation Undersea," even went on to win an Emmy Award as the best television show of the year.

The *Disneyland* TV show offered much more than hour-long commercials for Disney's feature films, it also offered top-shelf original entertainment filmed directly for television. The most phenomenal of these was the remarkable, "Davy Crockett, King of the Wild Frontier" series. As with all of his products, Walt Disney insisted on a high level of quality in every aspect of his television shows. Disney insisted that Peter Ellenshaw paint the mattes, and that Ub Iwerks be placed in charge of special processes.

Because of a compressed production schedule, there are some obvious shortcuts in the final telefilm. For example, all interactions between human actors and wild nature occur either offstage (such as Davy fighting a bear) or via jump-cuts (alligators from the True-Life Adventure *Prowlers of the Everglades* are edited next to footage of Davy and George wading through the muck of backwater Tennessee). Other scenes are constructed with Ub's and Peter Ellenshaw's matte compositing.

Because they had filmed the *Davy Crockett* segments in full color, the Disney Studio was able to release the combined sequences, with additional transitional material, as a feature film. The success of the film had an enormous impact not only on Disney, but on a number of other industries as well—including the coonskin cap manufacturing industry.

In his book, *The Crockett Craze,* Disney historian Paul Anderson writes, "As the popularity of the Davy Crockett TV series grew, it created a merchandising bonanza that has never been surpassed, with the only comparable merchandising being that for the *Star Wars* movie sagas." At its height, over 4,000 officially licensed items were produced that bore the Davy Crockett name and image. Everything from Davy Crockett ice cream to Davy Crockett tool kits bore the coonskin-clad phenomenon's image.

Because of this unprecedented popularity, it was perhaps inevitable that a sequel to *Davy Crockett: King of the Wild Frontier* would be made in spite of Walt Disney's personal aversion to doing sequels of any sort. Unfortunately for those who were pushing for more Crockett, the last scene of the first movie ended with Davy and George fighting valiantly to their deaths at the Alamo. To overcome this slight problem, the producers created a prequel, *Davy Crockett and the River Pirates*. Like its predecessor, the new Davy would be released first on television and then moved to motion picture theaters in a full-color version.

Expectations for the new film raised the budget and hence the quality of the production values considerably. Peter Ellenshaw and Ub worked together to create beautiful effects work, including a scene that combined location footage from the raging Ohio River with painted mattes and process effects. The integration of actual footage with the manufactured scenes was seamless.

Because of the success of the two Crockett films, Fess Parker was instantly catapulted to stardom as Disney's most marketable nonanimated actor. Immediately he was cast to appear in a string of western films that capitalized on his rugged charm and his sincere good looks. In *The Great Locomotive Chase*, *Westward Ho, the Wagons*, and *The Light in the Forest*, Ub Iwerks and Peter Ellenshaw created believable settings that at times seemed to shine even brighter than the films themselves.

One afternoon in 1955, while working on *Westward Ho, the Wagons*, Ub paused in a hallway to share a bit of conversation with Walt Disney. They discussed the challenges that faced Ub in working with the Cinemascope process, which had been introduced to the studio with *Lady and the Tramp* and *20,000 Leagues Under the Sea*. Walt suggested that while the large format and curved screen of Cinemascope were indeed great innovations, especially for the current westerns, he thought that the process could be taken even further. Walt encouraged Ub to give some thought to designing a screen that did not just curve around the front of the audience, but one that wrapped around through a full 360 degrees. In 1901, at the World's

Fair in Paris, one of the earliest versions of the 360-degree film had debuted. Walt thought that such a film would be an innovative addition for the theme park.

Some thought was never enough for Ub. He gave it *much* thought. The concepts that Ub came up with were integrated into a process that was dubbed Circarama. Basically the concept of Circarama involved eleven 16mm Cine Kodak Special cameras (much smaller and lighter than 35mm cameras) mounted on a pedestal pointing outward. By synchronizing the projector motors, the films could be projected completely around an audience, giving the illusion that the audience was immersed in a 360-degree environment. The only problem with the eleven-camera process was that, because of the focus angle, blind spots were possible. A person or landmark could suddenly disappear into one of these blind spots only to magically reappear on the adjacent screen.

One theoretical solution to this problem was to plan each shot carefully to eliminate as much foreground material as possible. This was a viable solution for grandiose exterior scenes of canyons and mountains, but was far from acceptable for any close-up action that could fall into the blind spots. To solve the problem, six-inch-wide black strips were placed along the edges between each of the eleven screens to mask the slight overlapping of seams.

Disneyland would prove to be the greatest venue for the Circarama technology, which would later be showcased to great acclaim through-out the world. Over the course of thirty-odd years, Disneyland saw several different 360-degree films, including several spectacular travelogues of the United States.

On opening day, July 17, 1955, an American Motors–sponsored Circarama attraction opened at Disneyland. The eleven-camera 16mm film was entitled *A Tour of the West*. As the name implies, the film featured a travelogue tour of the rugged west as directed by Peter Ellenshaw. The landscapes of the American west proved an apt subject matter for the first Circarama effort. Whether the setting was huge expanses of desert, the craggy mountains' majesty or the bathing beauties in Las Vegas, the 360-degree process proved an audience delight.

Ub's singleminded focus on matters of work was not without its liabilities. One night in 1957, Ub came home after a long day, feeling exhausted. The number of projects and the incessant workload compounded his fatigue. Ub's old Iwerks Studio friend Bugs Hardaway and his family had remained close to Ub and Mildred. Bugs's wife, Hazel, was at the Iwerks house visiting. As a practicing nurse, she took one look at Ub's gaunt face and realized that something was seriously wrong with him. She recognized that Ub was in the throes of a severe heart attack, and they rushed him to the hospital. More than likely, her quick action saved his life.

While Ub was recovering, William Anderson had all of Ub's furnishings and personal items removed from his office and deposited into a new office upstairs. With the approval of Walt Disney, who was concerned for Ub's health, Anderson replaced Ub with his loyal assistant, Eustace Lycett. Lycett recalls that when Ub returned to discover what had transpired while he was away, "All hell broke loose."

Eustace Lycett would remain with Disney for the remainder of his career. He would win many honors and award, but Ub Iwerks never forgave him for his role in the forced departmental coup d'état. He reportedly never spoke to Eustace again. When he was reminded that it was Anderson and not Lycett who was responsible, Ub replied tersely, "He could have said no."

Despite the ignominy of the method in which he had obtained his new position, the new role allowed Ub to report directly to Walt Disney, not to some disrespectful subordinate. Since Ub's heart attack, Walt restructured the job so that Ub was able to more fully explore his role as jack-of-all-trades—and master of most—without maintaining the day-to-day rigors of production work.

It was after the close call of his heart attack that Mildred, family, and friends convinced Ub he needed to take some time off. For a man whose work was his pleasure, it wasn't easy. Ub and Mildred took numerous trips and cruises around the world. Snapshots from Switzerland, Germany, Canada, Asia, and many areas of the United States, showed Ub carrying his prized Leica camera. He always returned with boxes of slides, which he would organize into shows for family and friends. These photographs, rich in color, detail, and stark compositions became subjects for Ub's lifelong interest in painting.

Preferring to work in oil on canvas, with brush or palette knife, Ub deployed his eye for detail to capture landscapes, buildings, skies, and people. An oil painting he created for son Don on his birthday shows sheep grazing amidst the rolling green hillsides of Ireland. Another painting of a desolate street in the ghost town of Bodie shows an elderly couple peering through windows of an abandoned building. There weren't many artists Ub was influenced by or of whom he spoke admiringly, except one—Peter Ellenshaw, Disney matte painter and colleague.

Mildred was also creative. Having always had an interest in flowers, plants, and gardening, and a good sense for design, she joined the local Laurel Gardening (Flower Arranging) Club in the 1950s. Mildred could be found outside in the garden or in the workroom with flowers and plants strewn around in creative flurry. Vases, dried branches, and a plethora of plant life filled the storage units alongside her husband's camera equipment. Their travels around the world allowed Mildred to gain knowledge of different plant life and incorporate them into her designs, with which she won numerous competitions.

Upon returning to the studio after his heart attack in 1957, the projects that needed Ub's attention had stacked up. The live-action films, animated features, television shows, and Disneyland Park all had technical issues that he needed to address. Ub bounced from one project to another.

William Beaudine, Jr., who directed the second photography unit on the film *Johnny Tremain* for his father, William Beaudine, Sr., remembered Ub being heavily involved in a sequence of the film in which a British ship is being tossed about an angry ocean. Shooting the scene on location would have required a tremendous cost and organizational effort. Richard Fleischer had expended a great deal of each when he shot and then reshot a similar rainstorm sequence for *20,000 Leagues Under the Sea.*

It was far easier and just as effective for the Beaudines to shoot the scene on a soundstage with the raging storm added through Ub's photographic effects. Ub appeared on the set periodically to ensure that the effects he was creating back in the lab would match the actions of the actors in front of the sodium-screen backdrop.

Whenever Ub would drop in on a soundstage, though he rarely spoke, his reputation and stature preceded him, and he commanded a level of sincere respect usually reserved for Disney.

Ub's innovations soon began to garner attention around the world. The success of his 360-degree Circarama theater at Disneyland proffered a request from the U.S. government to use the system and accompanying film at the Brussels World's Fair, scheduled to open in April 1958.

The new film was a nineteen-minute extravaganza entitled *America the Beautiful,* which, like *Tour of the West,* showcased the 360-degree process by glorifying the landscape and vistas of the United States.

A portion of the footage for *America the Beautiful* was shot from a specially equipped airplane. Ub's son Don was assigned to be the camera technician, and traveled with the plane. The eleven 16mm Circarama cameras were suspended beneath the plane on a retractable hydraulically operated mount.

By April, the new, improved Circarama exhibit opened at the Brussels World's Fair amid much anticipation. Because of its limited capacity, only 3 million people were able to see the attraction during its six-month run.

The late 1950s was an era of fads. Disney's Davy Crockett had set off a craze of coonskin cap dementia that dwarfed any other popular trend of the day. Hula hoops and bobby sox each had their moments of glory. In motion pictures, the fad of the 1950s was

3D. Audiences wanted to be thrilled by the sight of the *Creature from the Black Lagoon* coming right toward them in the theater. By wearing either polarized or bicolored glasses, effective illusions (not to mention innumerable headaches) were generated for the thrill-seeking audiences.

Even the legendary Alfred Hitchcock created a three-dimensional film, *Dial M for Murder,* which stands as one of the more aesthetic renderings of the technology fad. Walt Disney would not be left behind. The studio, still producing an occasional educational film, was in the process of working on a series of cartoons about music for schools. The first of these was called *Melody.* Walt approached Ward Kimball about turning it into a three-dimensional film, and said, "You know they've got this new 3D thing. Do you think we can take that *Melody* picture and convert it into 3D and put it in theaters?" The answer was Ub.

Ub calculated the precise positions needed for the camera crane and then photographed the artwork twice—once from the left-eye position and once from the right-eye position. The combined effect created a three-dimensional image.

Melody was to be the first 3D cartoon. A few months later, the Donald Duck–Chip and Dale cartoon *Working for Peanuts* became the second and last of the genre at the studio.

Unlike *Melody,* which was a two-dimensional cartoon adapted to utilize the 3D process, *Working for Peanuts* was conceived as a 3D film, and hence featured several gags that took full advantage of the process. Veteran director of the Donald Duck films Jack Hannah, along with brilliant animator Bill Justice, filled *Working for Peanuts* with scenes of peanuts flying through three-dimensional space. The premise of the story was that Chip and Dale were trying to steal peanuts away from a zoo elephant named Dolores and her zookeeper, Donald Duck. As peanuts are being tossed into the air, they seem to float above the bespectacled audience.

The film was well received, but for several reasons, Walt opted not to launch any more into production. First, the rush of studios latching on to the 3D craze during the 1950s created a surge of 3D films that were not very good. People began to lose interest. The other reason was that technicians in 3D theaters frequently did poor jobs in maintaining proper alignment on the projectors, and audiences were left leaving the theater with headaches. Within a span of several years, 3D had come and gone.

Although Ub was no longer immersed in the challenges of 3D, the next project he undertook was one that made him see spots—literally. Millions of them.

chapter **14**

Elephants, Dogs, and the Birds

Throughout the years, Walt Disney had often joked with his animators, "I'd like to have a machine to replace you SOBs," he would say. Although he was kidding, there was an ever-mounting concern at the studio about the increasing costs of animation production. Given the cost of maintaining a large staff of trained inkers on the animated features, the thought of streamlining the workforce was a welcome idea.

Unbeknownst to Walt, Ub had been dabbling with that very idea. When the first Xerox copiers came to the workplace in the 1950s, Ub realized immediately their application to the art of making animated films and the possible cost savings therein.

Ub traveled to New York to visit Xerox and discuss how the xerographic process could be applied to cartoon production. Inking seemed to be an ideal place to utilize the new technology. Artists would animate each drawing in pencil on a sheet of paper, and in the inking stage, the inker would trace these lines onto a clear cel. Warner Brothers' director, Chuck Jones recalls:

> Sometimes the animator was only as good as the inker and
> the inkers in those days only drew the line, but no matter
> how careful they were, they varied a little bit and a

thousandth of an inch was what made the difference
 between a good-rate line and the line you intend, and
 the line that is then transferred by a slight variation. It's
 like what Mark Twain said about the difference between
 the right word in writing and almost the right word is the
 difference between lightning and the lightning bug. . . .
 'Cause you're dealing with a thousandth of an inch in
 that case and it could make a whole difference.

Phyllis Craig of the Disney color department recalls that when Ub returned from New York, he came to her and explained his concept. While she was encouraged by the idea, she told him she did not think it would work. Within a week, Ub presented Craig's department with a prototype machine for testing. After trying it several times, she was able to explain to Ub the problems that she was experiencing. He took the device away for another two weeks of fine tuning. When he returned it, all of the issues had been resolved. "You never told Ub that it couldn't be done," she remembers.

In Ub's concept, all black lines on the original animation draw-ings were copied to a metal plate through an electrostatic process. Ultimately the Xerox equipment would become a large project that occupied several rooms of a building. The first dark room housed a lens and shutter inset in the wall. The lens focused the image onto a selenium-coated aluminum plate. The operator would photograph an image, create an electrical charge, and then run the result through a cas-cader machine, which applied black toner powder that adhered to the electrical charge, forming rich black lines of powder. The plate was then put on a conveyor belt and moved to another room where the black pow-dered lines were transferred onto cels. A chemical vapor fixative then permanently affixed the image onto the cel. After the plate finished its process, it was then run through a revolving drum coated with rabbit fur to brush the toner residue off its surface. The cleaned plate was then conveyed back to the initial room to repeat the process.

On July 29, 1957, Ub filed a request for patent with the United States Patent Office for his revolutionary Xerographic Fusing

Apparatus. Because the device used technology proprietary to the Xerox Corporation, it was the Xerox company and not the Walt Disney Company that was assigned the patent to Ub's invention.

When Ub's testing of the new Xerox apparatus had been completed satisfactorily, he showed his results to Walt. Disney, while enthusiastic about the potential savings, was skeptical that the process could provide the quality of line he was accustomed to. Nonetheless, he approved the process to be used on a limited basis. As they had often done with new technology, Disney artists tested new animation ideas in their short films before giving them full exposure in the feature films. The Walt Disney Studio's multiplane camera had been tested in this manner in *The Old Mill* before being used—even in a limited manner—for the wishing-well scene in *Snow White and the Seven Dwarfs*.

The first film to benefit from Ub's new Xerox process for its entirety was a short movie entitled *Goliath II*. Based on a Bill Peet story, *Goliath II* told the delightful tale of a tiny elephant trying to survive in a large and unfriendly world.

Xerography simplified the process of reusing scenes from other movies. A scene of the crocodile from 1953's *Peter Pan* made a cameo appearance in *Goliath II* intact. As was hoped, the line drawings retained their inherent hand-inked look throughout the film. Taken in the context of the animation of the time, the effect was seamless.

Despite the film's artistic and critical success, animator Ollie Johnston recalls that at first Walt Disney was not entirely satisfied with the results. He felt that the breadth and consistency of the animators' lines were proving too difficult to replicate. In the first Xerographic efforts, thin lines often disappeared entirely. Ub continually modified the machine to get better results. In 1959, Ub patented an additional invention, the Xerographic Developing Apparatus, which improved on the consistency of the development process. From that point on, the detail of drawn lines of all widths remained consistent. "In addition," Ub wrote in the patent summary for the new device, "it was found that certain of the artist's shading effects, that were normally lost in the manual tracing, could be retained by the careful application of xerographic techniques to improve the quality of the finished cartoon."

Not only did the animators use the xerography process to create character animation for *101 Dalmatians,* but they also used the process extensively to enhance the backgrounds for the film. Ken Anderson, *101 Dalmatians* production designer, felt that by creating both foreground and background images using the same xerographic process, he could forge a happier marriage between the flat foreground and the beautifully drawn backgrounds. He felt that they would be stylistically akin to one another.

The xerographic process had limitations in the use of color. Prior to Ub's xerographic inventions, in features such as *Sleeping Beauty,* colored lines are used to enhance and soften specific attributes of character designs. The delicate yellow ink lines used on Briar Rose's blond hair soften the edges, as do the red ink lines that define her cape. Even when the lines appear to be mostly black, as in those of the jet-black Scottie dog in *Lady and the Tramp,* they are in fact subtly contrasting dark gray outlines that allow leg and head movements to be discerned clearly against the black fur of the dog. Animation had come a long way since Ub had drawn Julius the Cat entirely with black ink, using stark poses and silhouettes to delineate the image of the figure.

Now, with the xerographic process, all lines were by default solid black. Ub's Xerox process was in many ways a stylistic shift backward to advance forward technologically. Despite the seeming strictures of the process, the top-level animators welcomed Ub's innovation. For the first time ever, it was *their* actual work that was being exhibited on the screen, not that of the inkers. Disney animator Marc Davis recalls the impact of the xerography process on his creative output: "I did Cruella De Vil, and I had every scene of her. To see my own drawings up there was a very exciting experience. And this was Ub Iwerks, you know, he was the one who figured out how to do that."

Walt's continued skepticism over the new process was dampened somewhat by the daunting prospect of producing 113,760 frames and 6,469,952 spots for *101 Dalmatians*. Disney may not have liked the style, but he certainly took full advantage of the cost savings. As Chuck Jones explains: "If I had suggested doing *101 Dalmatians* [at Warner Brothers], everyone would have thought I was crazy. Even a dog named Spot, with one spot, would have been out of the question."

This obvious difference in *101 Dalmatians* from any previous animated film that had not used the Xerox process was stark and profound. In *Sleeping Beauty*, artist Eyvind Earle had striven for (and achieved) beautifully rendered painterly backgrounds. With the new process, the painterly was replaced with linearity.

Because Walt Disney did not care for the aesthetics of this look, for the next animated feature, *The Sword in the Stone*, the background artists retained a bit of the xerographic process but mostly reverted to the more painterly techniques they had used prior to Ub's invention. Once again Ub's technology had, in Walt's eyes, exceeded the scope of the story needs.

By the time *The Jungle Book* was in production some eight years later, the xerographic lines had all but dropped out of the background drawings. While the possibility of using Xerox lines for character outlines remained as an option, artists had learned to use the process selectively to best suit the needs of the film. Ollie Johnston, who was responsible for animating the little girl who entices Mowgli to come back to the man-village at the end of *The Jungle Book*, chose not to use the Xerox process for lines around her mouth. Instead, he opted to have them hand-inked in color.

Indeed, 1959 was a banner year for Ub in many regards. Along with his successes with the Xerox process, he devised an anamorphic wide-angle lens that allowed for the photography of *Sleeping Beauty* in the wide-screen format. Ub also worked his magic on *Darby O' Gill and the Little People*.

Ub, with engineer Bob Otto, created a nodal-point perspective camera that was used to shoot the forced perspective effects of leprechauns interacting with lifesize human beings. With this camera, an actor in the foreground was shot actual size, and, performing with the correct sightline, could interact with characters (actually in the distance on an oversize set) who would appear in miniature. Visual effects supervisor Richard Edlund recalled the breakthrough concept. "They'd shoot *Darby O' Gill* in the foreground on a set piece that was built to blend with a set piece of a different scale in the background, so that the little guys were in the background dancing." The nodal-point camera combined the two set pieces in the frame and created a combination that appeared seamless. The process was no easy task. Since Ub's camera was shooting twenty-four frames per second and required enormous depth of field to carry focus across the stage, the amount of light needed was enormous. "I think on *Darby O' Gill* they must have had every light in Hollywood rented for the thing," Edlund recalled, "they were shooting with a slow-speed film, and had to close the lens down to correct the large amount of depth of field." The city of Burbank assigned a substation to deliver enough power to operate the many lights, and numerous air-conditioning units were brought in to cool down the set. City fire marshalls were on ready alert in case of any electrical problems. Ultimately, the shoot was a success and the mark the visual effects made upon the motion picture industry was groundbreaking.

"One thing about the Disney effects department was that they were very secretive," Edlund remembers. "All the studios during that time usually had special photographic effects departments—MGM, Paramount, Universal, Fox—and they were competitive, and everybody was very secretive about the processes they came up with. Whenever somebody created something, and it was the first time it was done, soon people would be able to look at it and be able to deduce how it was made. You can always take something apart once it's made, but building it is a whole different thing. Today people are copying things that Ub either stumbled upon or thought through, and it's interesting how much of what he did has become part of the grammar of film."

In 1959, Ub was honored in the industry for his design of the

Triple-Head Optical Printer (#10), an improvement over the existing Double-Head Printer (#2) the studio had previously been using to combine sodium traveling matte shots. He received a technical Academy Award from the Academy of Motion Picture Arts and Sciences for an "improved optical printer for special effects and matte shots in color."

The Disney film *Pollyanna* utilized the newly adapted Triple-Head Optical Printer. Based on the book by Eleanor Porter, *Pollyanna* featured a winning performance by Hayley Mills in the title role and solid supporting work by Karl Malden, Adolphe Menjou, Jane Wyman, and Kevin "Moochie" Corcoran. *Pollyanna* included a scene of the young Corcoran putting his face into a river to look for fish. The camera angle switches from above the water to beneath the water. The point of view becomes that of the fish looking up at Kevin. It is a simple scene, but it required a great deal of technical scene planning. *Pollyanna* also included classic bits of matte work. For one example, the building selected as "Aunt Polly's" house was in reality only a single-story structure. Ub integrated a Peter Ellenshaw matte painting of an additional second story into the existing footage to give the building a larger, emptier feeling. It is difficult to discern the difference between the real first story and the painted second story.

In 1960, Ub was honored with the Herbert T. Kalmus Gold Medal from the Society of Motion Picture and Television Engineers (SMPTE) for his outstanding contributions to the technology in equipment and processes for the making of color motion pictures. The president of SMPTE, Norwood L. Simmons, personally presented Ub with the award while W. E. Gephardt, chairman of the award committee, read the citation, which outlined Ub's achievements in creating the double-headed optical printer, the color-correction masking process, the xerographic process for animation and the 360-degree Circarama system.

It has often been said that when working on a project, Ub had tunnel vision and required nothing but 100-percent effort from his staff. Don Iwerks, working with his father in the same department for many years, saw that Ub did not have patience with people who made the same mistake twice. When a mistake was made, Ub would spend time with the person explaining the correct way to do the task in question. However, if the mistake was made again, everyone knew the unfortunate soul might be read the riot act. According to Don, one person in the department used to take a pill to calm his nerves when he realized that Ub was upset about something. It jokingly became dubbed the "Ub Pill."

Ub had always shared Walt Disney's belief that quality, thoroughness, and attention to detail were important. When he was focused on an idea, he had little patience, and wanted to see it implemented immediately. One afternoon when Don was on the telephone in his office, Ub walked in and stood in the doorway thumping his foot impatiently, waiting for him to finish the call. "It was as if he was saying to me, 'Get over this, I have something important to talk about,'" Don recalls.

It was that afternoon that Ub had finally conceived a solution to the problems with the Circarama system. He told Don: "There's probably once in a lifetime when you can solve a problem when it is the one and only perfect solution, and I have found it."

After years of consternation and concern, Ub had indeed come up with a better method of filming 360-degree motion pictures. In Don's office, he sketched out a circle of mirrors mounted around the top of a camera pedestal. He drew nine 35mm cameras turned upward toward the mirrors, shooting the reflections. The reflected images by nature had no seams, no apparent blindspots. Don Iwerks refers to Ub's moment of Eureka as "a thrill of a lifetime to come up with an idea that solves a problem." Ub's invention became the standard for all future 360-degree films at Disney and was renamed "Circlevision."

The Parent Trap (1961) featured a clever gimmick in which Hayley Mills portrayed twin sisters. Based upon a German story, "Das Doppelte Lottchen," by Erich Kastner, *The Parent Trap* tells the contemporary story of twin sisters who have been separated through divorce but are reunited at a summer camp.

Ub used the double exposing split-screen technique and the sodium-vapor process to create the illusion of the twin Hayleys. *The Parent Trap* was the first major studio use of the sodium process in the United States. First Hayley would perform each scene in front of the yellow sodium screen. When the resultant film was developed, it would then be bipacked back into the camera, whereupon Hayley would shoot the entire scene again as the other twin. Working from timing sheets (an old animation device) Ub created an effect that is entirely believable. The audience never becomes aware of the contrivance.

For Lucien Ballard, director of photography for *Parent Trap*, however, it required too much preplanning. He recalls that he was in favor of abandoning the special-effects shots entirely in favor of the more expeditious technique of using a double for Hayley:

> They'd worked out this whole film using an English process, [the sodium-vapor process] much like the old blue backing process, to get the twins into various scenes. It involved double-exposure with the backgrounds and it was very complicated. Plus, when you were shooting, you could never tell the girl which light to look into or anything. I told them it was too complex, and asked instead for a double.

Ballard shot several scenes with Hayley Mills' look-alike. The real Hayley would face the camera while the double was seen only from the rear. When Walt Disney discovered what was going on, he insisted that Ballard use Ub's sodium screen process. Ballard mused later that he thought the reason Walt demanded using the sodium screen was that Walt liked technical things. The truth was that the double exposures simply made for more effective storytelling, with both twins' faces reacting at the same time, than awkward and obvious shots with a camera looking over a double's shoulder. According to Ub's assistant at the time, Bob Broughton, Walt held high regard for Ub's judgment on technical matters and would defer to his recommendations. "I got to sit in the background, behind each of them, and they just had nothing but total respect for each other. Ub took care of the technical end of things, and every time he had an idea or when to do some research, Ub had a complete go-ahead. In those days, we [the Process Lab] didn't have a budget—the project was the whole thing, and both Walt and Ub were of the same mind."

In an interview with Ub Iwerks in 1971, Lawrence Watkin recalled Ub's comments. "Walt will gamble, and it takes him only five minutes to make up his mind. On a million-dollar project Walt will tell you yes or no like that! Anyplace else they have committee meetings after committee meetings; they'll talk a project to death." It was clear to Watkin that "Ub was devoted to Walt Disney. He considered him a brilliant administrator, who treated his men with respect. He spoiled them for working anywhere else. Ub credited him with a spacious intelligence; Walt not only knew good art when he saw it, but could grasp an intricate engineering idea the minute he heard it. If I questioned Ub about anything that put Walt in a bad light, his eyes would flash and his mustache bristle and he would exclaim with disgust: 'What does he know about it? He wasn't there!' Then he would give me the story straight, for Ub wore no man's collar but his own."

In a conversation with Walt Disney, Lawrence Watkin recalled the admiration Walt felt for his longtime friend, "Without any prompting he characterized Ub as a natural engineering genius and one of the nicest guys that ever lived. He shook his head as if it were hard to believe and said, 'Gosh, he can do anything.'"

Ub Iwerks liked to work in quiet—he did not tolerate extraneous noise in the shop areas. Dave Smith, Disney archivist, recalls, "when I first met him, his office was not near anybody else's office, it was back in the corner of the ink-and-paint building, all by itself; nobody was around him, he had no secretary, nothing around him. Here he went every day and here he worked all by himself in that office. I think that was very much the style of Ub Iwerks, I think he was very independent, very devoted to his work."

Ub, however, didn't always have a choice when it came to being interrupted. Bob Broughton recalls that Walt would often bring dignitaries or heads of corporations through the process lab and would have Ub walk them around the lot to show off the latest projects. "When Ub would come into the lab, he took me aside the first time and he said, 'Bob, now when I bring tours or visitors through here, I'm going to turn to the man that I'm bringing in and say, "I'd like to introduce Bob Broughton." Then I'm going to turn to you, with my back to him, and if I say "I'd like to introduce you to Mr. Wereewerewerr," don't ask me what I said because I've forgotten the guy's name.' He did that time and time again, and he *got away* with it!"

Not every name that came into the process lab, however, was forgotten. Virginia Sommerfield, Ub's secretary in the early 1960s, was startled one day when a loud commotion broke the usual silence of the office. She recognized a large man in the midst of the crowd. Alfred Hitchcock, himself, walked up to her desk and asked for Ub.

Hitchcock had long been a fan of Disney films. In several of his films he had included sly references to Disney animated scenes. Hitchcock used sequences from the Silly Symphony *Who Killed Cock Robin?* in the climactic finish of *Sabotage* (1936) and he appropriated the music from *Hell's Bells* as the theme song for his television anthology series.

While Walt Disney and Alfred Hitchcock may have appeared to have been in some ways polar opposites, they both shared an obsession with quality, story, and control. Their personal attention to the smallest detail extended to the technical aspects of film. Like Disney, Hitchcock had turned his filmmaking ventures into a veritable cottage industry that encompassed not only motion pictures but extended into television and even included *Alfred Hitchcock's Mystery Magazine*. One day in the late 1950s, while reading the latest issue, Hitchcock read a short story by Daphne DuMaurier.

From this story Hitchcock created a film in which a small New England town is besieged by attacking birds. The story describes a community beset with an environmental disaster of nearly biblical proportions. The normally docile birds of the community turn vicious and wreak terror upon the unsuspecting citizens. Hitchcock felt that the story could be crafted into a disturbing and memorable motion picture. To pull off the more horrific aspects of the film, the audience would have to believe that the birds represented a true danger to the townspeople of Bodega Bay, the San Francisco–area town where the film was shot. Bird wranglers could be used throughout the film, but the sheer mass of birds that Hitchcock envisioned would require the best special-effects work the industry had to offer. He called on Ub.

Master visual artist Albert Whitlock had observed Ub's mastery of optical effects during his tenure painting mattes and creating titles at Disney in the 1950s. As head of the special photographic effects department at Universal, Whitlock recommended Ub for the complex special-effects work on *The Birds*. Hitchcock agreed, asking Walt Disney to subcontract Ub's services and the necessary equipment.

As he had done for *Up in Arms* and for *Duel in the Sun,* Ub began work on his third non-Disney live-action project. Once again he was called upon to create stunning matte and effect shots, this time to shock and startle the audience. What lay ahead of him were 83 matte shots and 163 hours of technical work for which Hitchcock was billed $1,125 per week. Of that money, Ub received $150 on top of his regular weekly salary.

To help Ub create similarly complicated exterior scenes and finish the work on a tight schedule, he recruited a who's who of the industry's most talented experts. L. B. Abbott came from 20th-Century Fox, where he was head of special effects. Veteran Linwood Dunn had been involved with the optical effects of *Citizen Kane* and *King Kong,* to name but a few of his many notable effects projects. Bob Hoag joined *The Birds* from MGM, where he was in charge of photographic effects.

The Birds was indeed one of the more horrific movies that Hitchcock would make in his career. To pull off the foreboding effects, Hitchcock met with Ub for daily planning sessions. Actress Tippi Hedren recalls their creative collaboration: "I loved watching Ub and

Hitch working together because so many directors would just say 'okay, you do it,' but the two of them would talk and really get into the whole process of how it would be done. I know that when Ub came to the set, he was much revered. I mean, everybody felt that this was a very fine artist and technician, and he had invented this wonderful process that made the special effects areas of films unique and very believable." Ub's sodium system was the only technology that could achieve the desired results. Art director Robert Boyle recalls, "In *The Birds,* we were faced with superimposing living, moving things around our characters. Using the usual blue-screen process, sometimes fringing occurs—shadowy lines created when the two matrices are not exactly aligned."

One of the more confounding challenges facing Ub was a climactic scene wherein Tippi Hedren, Rod Taylor, Jessica Tandy, and the young Veronica Cartwright find themselves prisoners in the living room of the Brenners' house. For this scene, Hitchcock had envisioned thousands of birds pouring through the fireplace and terrorizing the Brenner household.

In the finished scene, the room appears to be almost completely overcome by swallows, finches, and buntings. They pour in through the fireplace and fly with abandon around the room. To contain the birds, Hitchcock had the set sealed with a translucent plastic so that the birds could not escape, but light could still penetrate. He then instructed his wranglers to keep the birds moving by having them shoot air at the frightened birds every time they attempted to roost. Mingling with the live birds were a handful of mechanical birds whose realism heightened the menace of the scene.

Despite the earnest attempt at creating a flock of angry birds, the effect was not quite pulled off in production. It was clear from the outset that Ub's handiwork was needed to make the scene more believable. To this day, stories persist of Hitchcock practically torturing the young Tippi Hedren by inundating her with hordes of bloodthirsty live birds. Truth be told, on the set the birds were far from the vicious beasts that they were reported to be. In fact, Hedren recalls a different story. "The finches were supposed to come down the fireplace you know. They all came down and we were ready to fend them off and that sort of thing, and they—well, they sat on the hearth, and a few of them jumped up on the coffee table and they were sitting on the edge of the sofas and they'd sit there and we'd go, 'Okay, now what?'"

To compensate for the birds' lack of activity on the set, Ub filled a soundstage on the Disney lot with birds flying against a sodium-screen background and filmed them with his sodium camera. By multiplying, reversing, and optically compositing the various film elements together onto one strip of film, he combined this footage with the footage of the handful of live and mechanical birds shot on the living-room set. Consequently, many hundreds of birds appear to burst from the fireplace and fill the room in the final scene.

Tippi Hedren recalls seeing the finished composition: "To see the scenes in which we were reacting to absolutely nothing, to see them filled in with Ub Iwerks' magic was a thrill, because then the whole scene worked. You know, real fright [at] what was happening was right there."

Not every effects shot undertaken, however, went as perfectly as the Brenners' living-room scene had gone. One scene was planned in which a group of disturbed crows attacks a group of children on their way home from school. Again, Ub shot hundreds of feet of birds flying against the sodium screen. This time, however, the birds were filmed flying through a wind tunnel. This footage was added to existing photography of the schoolchildren running. Visual-effects supervisor L. B. Abbott recalls the unique problems of the crow attack scene, which took over five weeks to construct:

> Our two biggest problems were perspective and size ratio; we had to optically make the birds appear to be swooping down at the kids by moving them into the frame, at the same time adding a slight zoom to bring them in closer. We had to play around a lot with increasing and decreasing the size of the birds to make them look right in relation to the children.

They also had to be optically multiplied, to make the mass appear larger than it was.

It has long been assumed by film critics that the crows that chase the children from the schoolyard in *The Birds* were slightly underexposed during the printing process. This theory supposedly explained why some crows appear as somewhat shadowy silhouettes flying at the frightened schoolchildren.

Bob Broughton, however, recalls that the actual reason for the indistinct appearance of the birds was that in some cases they are the reversed images of *white* birds that were shot at the Disney Studio for expediency's sake. Black crows were difficult to obtain; white pigeons were plentiful.

> *We shot a bunch of white pigeons out on Stage 3 [of the Disney Studio] with no lights except on the birds. . . . We had a bunch of black drapes hanging, so these white birds were flying in front of these black drapes. Well, we took the negative of that. Now we got black birds over clear film. And we bipacked those in front of the backgrounds in the picture.*

Despite the challenges that faced him, Ub's special effects broke new ground in the horror genre. The results of the months of labor that he, Dunn, Hoag, Abbott, and the others endured were justly nominated for an Academy Award in 1963 for Special Effects.

Hitchcock and Ub maintained a casual acquaintance over the years. Ub always remembered *The Birds* as one of his most enjoyable experiences. Mildred Iwerks recalled the afternoon shortly after completion of the movie when a long black limousine made its way down the steep driveway of the Iwerks house on 4024 Murietta Avenue in Sherman Oaks. Out of the limousine stepped a chauffeur dressed in black carrying an elegantly wrapped package to the door. When Mildred opened the door, the chauffeur handed her the package and simply said, "A gift from Mr. Hitchcock," and departed as quickly as he had arrived. The gift, a thank-you present to Ub, was a crystal martini set purchased from the Bullocks-Wilshire department store in

Beverly Hills. Mildred displayed it for years in their china cabinet alongside the gold-rimmed crystal stemware given to them as a wedding present in 1926 by Walt and Lillian Disney.

Usually Ub's department was involved in creating new special-effects shots for films and television, but occasionally they were called upon to troubleshoot and fix problems with existing projects. Disney's charmingly nostalgic *Toby Tyler, or Ten Weeks in the Circus* was a classic case of this type of project. When the soundstage shooting was completed on *Toby Tyler*, the director, Charles Barton, noticed that in one scene a cameraman had failed to position his camera at the right angle. At the top of the image was a strip where the backdrop ended and the rigging of the soundstage began. The cost of reconstructing the set to reshoot the scene would have been exorbitant and would have pushed the film well over budget and hopelessly behind schedule.

To hide the mistake, Peter Ellenshaw painted a matte to mask the top two inches of the scene. When Ub optically integrated the painting into the existing footage, the effect was unnoticeable. The skillful blend of matte and optical work had saved the studio a considerable amount of time and money.

Another area that required Ub's keen troubleshooting abilities was Walt Disney's Mickey Mouse Club television show, which was filmed on a very short schedule with little or no time for reshoots. With 260 one-hour episodes and 130 half-hour episodes scheduled, Ub was asked to come up with a solution for the problem of quickly editing the Mickey Mouse Club television show. Since the show was filmed with three cameras, Ub devised a means of interlocking three film editing machines together, allowing an operator to view the same scene in synchronization from all three separate camera angles at the same time. Each editing machine had its own monitor; an electronic switching system allowed the operator to edit and switch back and forth between the three versions, recording a running record of the final edit.

Like his three-editing-machine innovation for the Mickey Mouse

Club, Ub's myriad projects for Disney during the early 1960s more often than not set new standards in technical achievement. With Disneyland, television, feature animation, and live-action films, the new challenges seemed endless. But Walt Disney was about to drop an assignment in Ub's lap that, if Ub could pull it off, would invariably propel the Disney Studio to the forefront of technical excellence.

chapter **15**

Grand Finale

Only Ub Iwerks would (or could) follow the macabre experience of creating special effects for Alfred Hitchcock's *The Birds* with the fancy of doing the same for *Mary Poppins*. Since being introduced to the series of books by his daughter, Diane, in the late 1940s, Walt Disney had wanted to do a screen adaptation featuring P. L. Travers's children's book series heroine Mary Poppins. A nanny of redoubtable abilities, Mary Poppins would have been a suitable lead female role for a full-length animated feature of the 1940s. In the early 1960s, however, live action was the medium of choice for Walt Disney.

After considering a slew of talented actresses for the role, including Bette Davis, Mary Martin, and Glynis Johns, Disney was swept off of his feet when he saw Julie Andrews in her sensational Broadway performance as Queen Guinevere in Lerner and Loewe's *Camelot*. Andrews had recently won great acclaim for her performance as Eliza Doolittle in Broadway's *My Fair Lady* and was obviously a star in the making.

Disney personally courted the budding young actress for his version of *Mary Poppins*. As was often the case, his powers of persuasion were formidable. When the producers of the motion-picture version of *My Fair Lady* chose Audrey Hepburn for the lead role of Eliza Doolittle, Julie Andrews agreed to do *Mary Poppins* for Disney.

With the luminescent Andrews aboard, *Mary Poppins* would excel on many levels. The unprecedented effects work demanded by the script pushed many of the Disney craftsmen to the peak of their art form. Some of the live-action scenes featured subtle photographic effects (Mary Poppins floating up a banister, for example, filmed in reverse) to prop effects (the "Spoonful of Sugar" scene created with delightful stop-motion animation by veteran animators Xavier Atencio and Bill Justice) to animatronic effects by Wathel Rogers (a robot robin that duets with Mary). But the film's success would rely on the seamless integration of live action and animation.

During a walk in the park with Mary Poppins, the Banks children encounter Bert, the Chimney Sweep, portrayed with comic brilliance by Dick Van Dyke. Bert is busy practicing the lost European art of sidewalk chalk painting. In a series of pastel tableaus, Bert illustrates forgotten landscapes of childhood. Bert hints to the children that it is possible to visit these lands even though they are constructions of pure fancy. The children beg Mary Poppins to take them there.

In one of P. L. Travers's books, the author writes a succinct little scene describing what happens next:

> "Mary," Bert said, "why don't we go there right now?
> Together, into the picture . . ." Pff! There they were, right
> inside it!

As Leonard Shannon in an article in *Disney* magazine, "Poppins Revisited," so appropriately stated, "It took only twenty-one words from the original book to trigger the whimsical 'Jolly Holiday' sequence in *Mary Poppins*." At first Disney envisioned the scene with human actors against an animated backdrop. This would have been a routine matte job for Ub and his crew, but the scene quickly took on a life of its own.

Walt was discussing the scene with the Sherman Brothers when he was struck with the idea of replacing the live-action waiters with penguins. "Why don't we have penguins as waiters?" he suggested. "We'll animate the penguins—in fact, we'll animate everything except the principal characters!" It was a moment of inspiration that infused the scene with a spirit and eloquence that elevated the entire motion picture to a new level. The ideas Travers had hinted at in the book would now be realized.

When the child's nanny sends the group into a drawing of a pastoral English countryside, they land—somewhat chalky from their journey—in the midst of an entirely chalk-drawn world. The animation was created by a contingent of Disney's renowned Nine Old Men: Ward Kimball, Frank Thomas, Ollie Johnston, Eric Larson, Milt Kahl, and John Lounsbery. Bill Justice and Jack Boyd joined in to make the "Jolly Holiday" sequence a completely collaborative work of art.

The animated character moved in and around, through and by the live-action actors with a remarkable grace that belied the difficulty of the process used to create it. Previously, Ub had performed his live-action-animation magic primarily in planes that existed either in front of or behind the actors. Rarely had he been required to do both at once. Along with Pietro "Peter" Vlahos and Wadsworth E. Pohl, Ub developed the traveling-matte process to such a degree that animated figures could appear to move from the background to the foreground and back again with no apparent conflict.

Academy Award–winning special effects supervisor Richard Edlund recalls Ub's achievement: "I think if you look at *Mary Poppins*—which is the best example of its use—the matte shots in that are quite good, and photochemical mattes (as opposed to the modern digital mattes that we're doing now) were much more cantankerous. Photography is a cantankerous process, it's not something that yields up the results real easily, you have to use all kinds of tricks and manipulations and get out of it what you want." Ub got what he wanted.

Throughout the scene, chickens and rabbits dart in and around Bert's legs. As Mary and Bert dance their way across an animated bridge, Bert bends to pick a bouquet of animated flowers. Turning into colorful butterflies, they flutter from Mary's hand, hovering in front of the live actors. Near the end of the sequence, Ub reverses the process by having an animated character give Mary Poppins a bouquet of real flowers.

For the "Spoonful of Sugar" sequence, the actors were first filmed snapping their fingers before an empty sodium screen. The resulting image was then combined with Xavier Atencio and Bill Justice's stop-motion footage of toys, furniture, and clothing all moving about the room.

When Mary Poppins snaps her fingers; a bed makes itself. Jane Banks snaps her fingers, causing a dollhouse to come to some semblance of order. By combining traditional stop-motion animation with the sodium process, as well as reverse printing, the studio pushed the envelope one step further.

Even more effective in a cinematic sense is the classic "Feed the Birds" sequence. For this scene, Ub was assigned to add footage of birds flying around a cathedral spire. With the improved traveling-matte process, Ub created the impression of hundreds of pigeons soaring in and around St. Paul's Cathedral spires, utilizing the same optical techniques he used for decidedly more malevolent purposes in *The Birds*. The image of Jane Darwell singing the Sherman Brothers' plaintive song "Feed the Birds" while Ub Iwerks's special effects swirl about her proved to be one of the greatest combinations of effects, music, and acting achieved to that date. The scene was destined to become one of Walt Disney's personal favorites.

Mary Poppins was nominated for thirteen Academy Awards, including Best Picture. It won five of those awards, including Best Musical Score, Best Song ("Chim Chim Cheree") and Best Actress for Julie Andrews. In addition, Ub Iwerks, Pietro Vlahos, and Wadsworth E. Pohl were honored with the Scientific and Technical Oscar for the conception and perfection of techniques for color traveling matte composite cinematography. It was the second Academy Award for Ub, and his third nomination by the Academy.

The 1964–1965 New York World's Fair featured several new Disney attractions with which Ub was actively involved. One of the more intriguing of these was titled *Great Moments with Mr. Lincoln*. Sponsored by the State of Illinois, the attraction was planned to feature an Audio-Animatronics figure of Abraham Lincoln himself. Walt Disney's idea for the attraction dated back over a decade, when he had wanted to create a small dancing figurine for a traveling exhibit intended to show miniature scenes from the motion picture *So Dear to My Heart*. For this exhibit, Disney asked Davy Crockett actor and former dancer Buddy Ebsen to be filmed performing a loose-limbed dance in front of a gridwork backdrop. From this, Disney technicians created a small mechanical figure that was programmed to precisely mimic Ebsen's motions. The success of this little figure, nicknamed "The Dancing Man," prompted Walt to expand this initial concept into a life-size robotic Lincoln. This fully synchronized combination of mechanical automatons with sound was dubbed "Audio-Animatronics."

Along with Roger Broggie and Wathel Rogers, Ub's created a photoelectric control system that allowed the Audio-Animatronic Lincoln to move and speak realistically. The figure's movements were synchronized using a large light-activated cam unit that ran on a spindle. Each feature that required mobility, such as fingers, knees, etc., required a separate hand-cut cam to activate the machinery.

Walt's original thought had been to create a room full of presidents, each interacting and talking aloud with the others. Because of the extreme costs of such a venture, the Hall of Presidents project was quickly scaled back to be a Hall of President, incorporating only the single figure of Abraham Lincoln.

Disney imagineers molded several of their own hands out of Duraflex as models for the animatronic Abe Lincoln. The hands eventually chosen to be used for the Great Emancipator at the New York Fair were those of Willie Gillis. After installation it was determined that Gillis's hands were too large for Abe. (When the attraction moved to Florida years later, Don Iwerks's hands were chosen as more realistic replacements.)

Due to the extreme pressure of time and the difficulties encountered when programming the mechanical Lincoln, it was decided to limit his actions on stage. To make up the back story that would enhance the believability of the presentation, the beginning of the show was culled from a series of large murals that were projected onto a separate screen and cross-dissolved into one another.

When the preshow ended, the curtain rose majestically to reveal a singular seated figure. Elegantly silhouetted, the unmistakable visage of Abe Lincoln appeared. As the stagelights began to warm and illuminate the figure, the illusion became real. The figure moved slowly at first, seemingly took breath, and then spoke. Into a structure constructed of Duraflex, wires, and imagination; life had begun again for Abraham Lincoln.

Ub worked on a special lighting effect for the finale of *Great Moments with Mr. Lincoln*. Using an image of the United States Capitol building silhouetted against a beautiful cloud-filled sky, Ub used a bank of ten-by-ten-inch projectors fitted with turntables that slowly moved special colored gels into the light path. A spiral was cut into the gel. When rotated into the light path, the color and pattern were projected onto the screen. The clouds on the cyclorama behind the Capitol building dissolved into Old Glory. (When Ub would later adapt the attraction for Disneyland, he would paint the flag himself.)

Walt Disney saw only the promise of the exhibit. He quickly requested that plans be made to move the attraction to Disneyland in an expanded exhibition. He also laid plans for an even more extensive version of the animatronic Lincoln to be used for a new project that he was envisioning on the East Coast. The 1964 World's Fair had proven to Disney that Eastern audiences would flock to high-quality entertainment with the same fervor as the hordes of visitors that regularly made the journey out west to Disneyland.

After the success of the 1964 World's Fair, Ub spent much of the next few years concentrating on various aspects of new attractions for Disneyland. At one point, he got the idea that by combining Audio-Animatronics with film projections, he might be able to produce some special effects for a proposed attraction called the Haunted Mansion. One day, he brought in a white Styrofoam wig stand to test his ideas. The wig stand was shaped like a human head only with no facial details. Ub projected a film of a talking human face onto the wig stand. Bob Broughton, who was present for the experiment, recalls the response. "We both about fell off our seats. My God, it looked real. It was just simply round—a general shape of a head. There was no nose, no mouth, no anything, but the image when we made it fit right on to this thing, it looked just like it!"

By modifying the head to give slight definition to the features, the effect was complete. Don Iwerks and Yale Gracey worked with Ub on a test. They showed it to WED Enterprises (the Disney design group) management, who were very excited with the effect. They agreed to use Ub's concept for the disembodied head of Madame Leota in the Haunted Mansion attraction. With the face of Disney costume person Leota Toombs and the voice of Eleanor Audley eerily emanating from a speaker built into the table beneath the head, the simple seance scene became one of the highlights of the ride.

"We found out that if you just project onto something that is 3D, it looks like it is the regular shape," Broughton recalls. The effect was so frightening that Ub joked that he was going to "get the diaper concession at the end of that ride." Broughton recalls that they were even told "to tone it down. They figured all the kids would wet their britches."

WED was so enthusiastic about the new technology that they used it in a second section of the Haunted Mansion attraction. A quintet of humorous singing busts was created using essentially the same effect.

By the mid-1960s, Ub and the Disney Studio were headed full speed toward the future. Walt Disney wanted to continue to build upon the successes of the 1964 World's Fair by forming further alliances with corporate and governmental sponsors to present exhibitions around the world. In September 1962 Ub had provided the technical assistance on the CircleVision 360 film *Magic of the Rails*, which was commissioned for a 1965 exhibition in Lucerne, Switzerland. Sponsored by the Swiss Federal Railways, and directed by the renowned photographer and filmmaker Ernst Heineger, *Magic of the*

Rails featured a dazzling train tour through Switzerland that served as an international postcard for Disneyland and Ub's technology.

The trips to Switzerland allowed Ub and Mildred to explore the country and become close friends with Ernst and his wife, Jeanne Heineger. Jeanne recalls fond memories of the operas and cultural events she and Mildred would attend while their husbands were working. In-depth technical discussions, she recalled (with a sigh), always spilled over into the dinner outings they would have as a foursome.

Not content to rest upon the myriad successes of Disneyland, in the early 1960s Walt Disney began surreptitiously scoping out sites for a new theme park to be built in Florida. With the assistance of Card Walker, Admiral Joe Fowler, and Roy Disney, Walt selected a prime location near Orlando on which to build the new park. Unlike Disneyland, Walt was delighted that this new park would have the "blessing of size." Also unlike Disneyland, Disney would retain complete control over all aspects of the park and the surrounding area.

The new park, dubbed simply PROJECT FLORIDA at this juncture, was planned to house several new lands and conceivably a fully operational city. The Experimental Prototype Community Of Tomorrow (or EPCOT) was to be the featured attraction of this construction. While the great plans were being laid for the Florida Project, Disneyland in California continued to grow and to evolve. One of the most popular new rides installed at Disneyland during this time was the Pirates of the Caribbean. Unlike standard amusement park roller coasters, which relied on the thrill of speed and breathtaking turns to generate excitement, the Disney "dark" rides were designed to immerse the passengers completely within the structure of a story. The sights, sounds, and even the feel and smell of the environment were carefully controlled for maximum effect.

Ub designed electronic candles for use in the Pirates of the Caribbean ride. Dabbling in electronics in his spare time, he devised a circuit that made lightbulbs flicker realistically, as if they were indeed blowing in the wind.

Many of the attractions at Disneyland utilized film projectors for various photographic effects and each one had to be attended by separate operators. Early in 1966 Walt decided to update the Tomorrowland attractions, including the *Trip to the Moon* ride. An idea he envisioned for Mission Control was to have a wall of monitors wherein each screen showed different moving images of the launch activities. The obvious problem with the idea was that each monitor would require a separate projector and projectionist to run the film. The operational costs were prohibitive. Walt called Ub to a meeting to discuss the need to use films in the park. When Ub returned to the shop, he simply said to his crew, "Well, we've got a task."

Ub began with an analysis of why the projectors were breaking down, required high maintenance, and had excessive wear and tear. Tests showed the commercially available projectors the studio was using were not designed for the continuous operation needed in the park. The second important finding was that the method employed to run the film in a continuous loop without rewinding resulted in excessive scratches on the print. The longer the show ran, the more scratches there would be.

Ub's first task was to find new projectors. The 16mm film projectors being used by the U.S. military had been designed to be rugged and take abuse, and he reasoned that spare parts would always be available. A military projector was purchased and tests began. He discovered that if the optical sound head was removed, the film would no longer have to ride over the sound drum. The soundtracks were recorded on separate magnetic film, which ran on a 35mm sound reproducer in synchronization with the film. Ub had his team build a new 16mm projector that would be easier to operate, require minimum maintenance, and withstand the long operational hours in the park. The projector dilemma was solved, but the scratching of the film remained.

Efforts were made to improve the currently used flat platter storage system, but the results were not encouraging. Ub suggested adapting the film storage cabinets that were being utilized in the motion-picture film laboratories. After film was processed and washed, it entered a long cabinet containing banks of rollers over which the film was threaded. The cabinet was a dry box with warm air that dried the film before it was wound in a roll. Ub reasoned that the same technique could be used to store film in an endless loop. The film did not touch any surface or itself and was transported through the projector, then back into the cabinet where it ran over rollers until the head of the film reached the projector again. A prototype was built in the machine shop, and the test results proved successful.

Ub was finally able to show Walt the results of his team's efforts. Don recalls that one late afternoon Walt came walking through the shop. "My dad asked him if he had a minute, that he wanted to show him something. Walt looked at his watch and said, 'I'm running a little late, and I've got people up in my office, but okay, yeah, I've got five minutes.' So we went next door where we had the projector and film loop cabinet set up and my dad asked me to turn it on and run it for him. Walt stood there and watched in total awe and disbelief. He put his arm around my dad's shoulder and said, 'Ub, this is real progress.' He was really excited about it and immediately asked Ub, 'Could we do CircleVision this way?'" With nine 35mm projectors operating reel-to-reel and three operators running three projectors each, the task was no small feat. But Ub didn't hesitate. "Sure, we can do it." Don recalled, "Walt looked at me and asked, 'Could your shop finish them in time?' and you didn't say no to Walt. You said yes, and you made it happen."

Within eight months, the projectors and film loop cabinets were designed and built for both the Tomorrowland attraction, the new CircleVision theater showing *Trip to the Moon*. The systems continue to operate in all of the Disney parks today.

Although their schedules were always busy with myriad projects, both Walt and Ub enjoyed taking moments to reminisce. In the early 1940s, A. Vern Cauger, their first boss in the animation world at the Kansas City Film Ad Service, visited Walt at the studio. Walt immediately called Ub to come to his office for a visit. Photos from that afternoon show Ub, Walt, and Cauger, with Three

Caballeros figurines in hand, laughing and conversing—remembering those early days when that first collaborative spark was lit.

From their early years as naïve young boys struggling for a foot in the door, to the experienced and confident grown men now leading their craft, Walt, Ub, and Roy could look back on their lives with pride. Not only did they take the industry by the horns and define it anew, but they changed the way the world saw itself through entertainment. Walt and Ub traveled the same road in the 1920s, diverged on their own creative paths in the 1930s, and reunited again in 1940. "Ub Iwerks and Walt Disney were a wonderful team throughout almost their entire working lives," historian Mark Kausler recounts. "When they were in Kansas City, they learned together how to animate. They created Laugh-O-gram Films. It didn't work, and they split up. They then combined again in Hollywood, made the Alice comedies, Oswalds, the early Mickey's and Silly Symphonies. Then when Ub and Walt were apart from each other, they developed strengths and skills of their own. Ub's tenure as a cartoon producer gave him the chance to stretch his wings creatively, do things his way, and develop his interest in the technical sides of things that he gradually evolved into. And Walt, being on his own, was forced to push himself, push his studio, sell his product more effectively, make it more appealing to more people. When they reunited again in 1940, Ub and Walt had both developed a set of strengths that made them even stronger together than they were apart."

Author Lawrence Watkin, in his unpublished manuscript on Walt Disney, explained the dynamics that fueled both men. "Ub was like Walt in many respects, but in nothing more than in his answer to a challenge. Both loved their work and both were stubbornly persistent when facing the impossible. If anyone told Walt it couldn't be done, he'd say, 'We'll see . . .' and when Ub was approached with long-faced negativism, he'd recite: 'According to aerodynamics the bumblebee cannot possibly fly.'"

❖   ❖   ❖

In 1966, the work continued steadily toward the undisclosed park site in Florida. Along with the live-action and animated feature films, television programming, World's Fairs and Disneyland, EPCOT was consuming a greater and greater amount of Walt's energies.

Unfortunately, he would not live to see this particular dream come to fruition. In the fall of 1966, Walt Disney entered St. Joseph's Hospital with a nagging cough. He was soon diagnosed with lung cancer. His left lung was removed in an effort to stall the spread of the cancer—but it was sadly too late.

On November 30, 1966, Walt entered St. Joseph's Hospital again. On the morning of December 15, 1966, Walt Disney died. Suddenly, the world had lost a legend. Ub's lifelong friend was gone.

Don Iwerks remembers his father's reaction:

> He happened to be down on the shop floor when it was
> announced. It had come in over the radio, and our secretary
> went over the P.A. system and announced it through the shop
> over the loudspeaker system that Walt had just passed away.
> So that was kind of a tough way to learn of it—being so
> close as he was to Walt all those years—to hear of it that
> way. He and I sat in my office a little later—they dismissed
> everybody, the whole place went home right away—and we
> were there for a little while. He came up in my office and sat
> down, and he was obviously upset that that had happened,
> and his words were, "That's the end of an era." My dad's
> view, I think, is that he didn't have anybody to please any-
> more. Not only did he lose a friend, but he lost that person to
> whom he was dedicated to please.

The death of his boss and one-time partner saddened Ub Iwerks greatly. For all the complex shared history between the two, it was obvious to all that Ub loved Walt.

While the differences between Ub and Walt were indeed real, there was an unspoken admiration between them. During their later years, they had demonstrated a mutual respect for each other that transcended differences. When asked one time if there were any animosity between Walt and Ub over the years, Roy Disney replied forcefully, "Poppycock. Pure Poppycock." To Roy, Ub was family— Disney family. In the latter years, Ub and Walt had on occasion appeared together in publicity photographs. A photograph of Les Clark, Walt, and Ub captures the old friends examining their old drawings from *Karnival Kid,* an early Mickey Mouse cartoon they all worked on. The unabashed joy that radiates from their faces indicates their shared joy. After all the years, they seemed to genuinely enjoy themselves and each other.

Roy O. Disney's son, Roy E. Disney, comments on the relationship between the Disney family and Ub: "There was enormous respect that was very, very clear and evident between both Walt and my dad and Ub." Ub by then was working in the process lab in quite a different capacity than he was as an artist earlier. But there was clear fondness for him from them and I remember that very, very well." With Walt gone, Ub could only continue to strive for the satisfaction of knowing that his accomplishments provided value to the company, but according to Bod Broughton, he felt "it was going to be a challenge to keep going."

Through the 1960s, Ub's technologies were used in virtually every Disney film. One of the films was a movie based upon the exploits of a Volkswagen Beetle named Herbie. *The Love Bug* starred Dean Jones, Michelle Lee, and Buddy Hackett in a madcap chase-and-race caper that featured numerous special-effects and matte shots.

Partway through the filming of the numerous sodium effects shots on *The Love Bug,* Ub was finally able to resolve a longstanding worry he had had for years with the sodium prism—there never existed a backup prism. Ub struggled for years to find the original designer of the optics. He tried to commission other optical houses to build a new one, but manufacturers declined because of the difficulty in creating the specialized coating. On every film since 1957, the "sacred prism," as it became known, had to be carefully handled— if it were ever dropped, scratched, or damaged, the multimillion-dollar production would be shut down. Ub's only solution was to finally design one himself. In 1969, Ub designed and had constructed a new version of the sodium prism, to the great relief of many producers. Ironically, the backup prism was never needed, and the original was used until the sodium camera was replaced by newer technology in the 1980s.

Another film to utilize the sodium camera in the late 1960s was the feature film *Bedknobs and Broomsticks*. Walt Disney had begun working on *Bedknobs* before he died. Rights to the story were initially purchased well before the rights to *Mary Poppins* had been secured. On the overall, *Poppins* may have surpassed *Bedknobs and Broomsticks* in both ambition and achievement, but there are moments in the latter that were just as memorable as its predecessor. Nowhere is this more apparent than in a combination animation–live-action sequence set on the mysterious Isle of Naboombu.

Directed by Academy Award–winning director-animator Ward Kimball, the Isle of Naboombu sequence is a cousin to the "Jolly Holiday" sequence from *Mary Poppins*. In the sequence, the live-action characters—the apprentice witch, portrayed by the Tony Award–winning actress Angela Lansbury, the con man portrayed by David Tomlinson, and a trio of children who resembled dusty cousins of the *Mary Poppins* kids—seek the mysterious Star of Astoroth to complete a magical incantation that would enable Eglantine to enact the "Substitutiary Locomotion" spell, i.e., to make the inanimate come to life.

Ward Kimball stuffed over 130 gags into the 22-minute scene. The laughs come so fast that the audience is unaware of the technology driving the scene. The combination of the live actors with the animation is seamless. Ward Kimball explains:

> The technique is really quite simple once you get the hang of it. You photograph the live action with a masked-off camera, then you fill in the masked-off area with animation. Then you put them together. Presto! There you have it—live action and animation combined! Of course, I might have left out a couple of details. To assist actors with conceptualizing their scenes, large cardboard cutouts of the animated characters

were used. Angela Lansbury remembers the adventures of acting with cardboard. "Half the time you're acting to the big cardboard cutout of a lion or a large bird and the various cartoon characters, so that at least we have an idea of the size and the dimensions of the cartoon drawing that will eventually be on the film beside us."

The animators used Ub's xerographic process to maintain the look and feel of a storybook artist's drawings. Each animated character was detailed and retained a penciled-in look that was fully in keeping with the storybook illustration effect.

Combining live action with animation was merely a detail. The Disney Studio had long since accustomed itself to Ub's innovations and used them to their fullest technical capability. This meant that the process was no longer an obtrusive device but an accepted technique that allowed the story to be told more effectively than ever before.

Another innovation was the improvement of the projection equipment used in many of the attractions at the parks. The use of commercially available classroom overhead projectors had become the staple for projected effects work, but one of the difficulties in using them was that they were not designed to readily attach accessories. Furthermore, they were difficult to service and repair. Ub and the studio machine shop decided to design a new projector that would be as maintenance-free as possible and completely modular in design. The various attachments could be easily mounted and an automatic lamp changer insured that the projector could always remain on. The lamp change mechanism would signal the show's monitoring computer that the projector was on its spare lamp. A new lamp would be installed after the park closed at night. This projector became the standard for special-effects projectors in the parks. For Epcot and Tokyo Disneyland, 400 projectors were produced by the studio machine shop.

In the early part of 1971, the U.S. Travel Service, a division of the U.S. Department of Commerce, approached the studio with an interest in leasing the CircleVision film *"America the Beautiful."* One of the missions of the Travel Service in foreign countries is to encourage travel to the United States. They owned an inflatable dome structure that was left over from the 1970 World's Fair in Japan. Ub was asked to conceive how a portable, traveling theater system could be constructed, easily assembled, operated, disassembled, and shipped to new locations. The studio machine shop was again involved in producing the projectors, sound system, film loop cabinets, portable platforms, and screen system. The U.S. Travel Service toured the world for five years, showing the *"America the Beautiful"* CircleVision film to millions of people. Once again, Ub's prolific work allowed people from all over the world to enjoy Disney entertainment.

Although Ub did not retire, age did force him to wind down a bit. He spent more time with Mildred, his son's families, and his grandchildren. As the new generation grew to understand and appreciate his many roles in the industry, Ub was reticent to share much of his past. His son, Don, recalls, "In all of his work, my dad was one to put yesterday behind him. He was never focused on yesterday or his accomplishments or any of that. It made no difference to him. He once said of Mickey, and he said it to me on numerous occasions, because people asked him, 'Well, how do you feel that you created Mickey and you didn't get any credit?' He said, 'It isn't creating it; it's what you do with it.' And he gave Walt full credit for making something of Mickey that he did in the 1930s. He said, 'We could sit around, draw characters all day long, but unless you do something with it, it doesn't amount to anything. And Walt did something with it.' The fact that he [Ub] was able to create it, I'm sure he was proud of that fact, but it isn't anything he's going to go around patting himself on the back—he'd never pat himself on the back for what he did. If he enjoyed his accomplishments, he did it privately, he could smile and feel really good about it, but it wasn't like, 'Look what I did,' he wasn't that kind of person."

Mark Kausler once shared an elevator with Ub Iwerks and Roy Disney at the Disney Studios. Kausler had written an article on Ub when he was fourteen years old and maintained a strong interest in the history and works of all the great animators, including Ub. When he complimented Ub on his character, Flip the Frog, and asked him a question about those earlier years, Ub simply smiled and put his finger to his lips. "Shh," he said. "We don't talk about that around here."

For the opening of the 1967 Montreal Expo, Ub flew to the event on Disney's private plane with animator Ward Kimball. Although Kimball had worked on projects alongside Ub throughout the years, there had never been the opportunity to enjoy a private conversation or relax with his fellow Disney veteran. According to Kimball, Walt's passing the previous year seemed to have left Ub feeling somewhat nostalgic for those early days. In a rare reflective state, Ub reminisced with Kimball about one of his earliest impressions of Walt at the Pesmin-Rubin Studio in Kansas City. Young Disney was huddled over a drawing board practicing the fine art of signing his name. According to Ub, he knew then and there that Walt Disney (not Walter or W. E. Disney), with enough drive and ego intact, would go on to produce great things.

After Walt's death in 1966, Roy O. Disney put off his own planned retirement to take over the operational duties of the company. In memory and honor of his younger brother, Roy officially named the new park "Walt Disney World."

With improvements in animatronic technology, it had finally become feasible to create Walt Disney's proposed *Hall of Presidents* attraction in its entirety. As Walt had dreamed, the show would be expanded to include every animatronic president from George Washington to then-president Richard Nixon. All of these presidents would move realistically; several would talk. Central to the attraction was the Abraham Lincoln Audio-Animatronic figure that had first appeared at the 1964 World's Fair and Disneyland. For the World's Fair in New York, Ub devised a method of projecting a night sky filled with stars behind the Abraham Lincoln figure and the Capitol dome during Lincoln's speech. As Lincoln finished his speech and sat down, the music rose in volume and the night sky changed to dawn with the stars disappearing and tinted clouds forming in the morning sky. The pink sky became a deeper red and the clouds turned white until the entire background dissolved into the stylistic image of an American flag. The effect for the new attraction in Florida was created with banks of Ub's newly designed ten-by-ten overhead projectors. Color wheels, filters, masks, a control system, and an assortment of other devices produced the dramatic effect.

The second challenge rested with the pre-show film screened prior to the introduction of the presidents on stage. The story of Lincoln's life and his role as the president of the United States is told through the use of large panoramic paintings, each photographed with a specially designed camera and projected with five 70mm projectors on a 200-foot-long screen. The end results are stunning, but the process of getting there was difficult.

A group of accomplished artists from England were commisioned by the studio to produce the original paintings. The challenge for Ub was to figure out how these paintings could be photographed and projected on such an enormous screen. It was an impossible task for one projector to fill the 200-foot-wide screen, so he planned on five projectors to project one fifth of the width of the picture. This in itself was doable, but the real difficulty lay in the method of photography.

A series of still paintings dissolving into one another would be very dull absent the dynamic movement of zooms and pans. A fluid camera that moved around and in on the paintings could work, but Ub questioned how he could do this with a five-camera rig. Ub devised a method that would shoot each camera position separately. Ultimately this idea proved too unwieldy, and he soon abandoned it in favor of another solution. A single, specially designed camera was built to photograph a frame of film that had the same aspect ratio of height to width as that of the 200-foot-wide screen. This special camera would advance a long strip of 35mm film horizontally through the camera; shoot a frame, and then advance again. Each frame showed the entire painting. The film was then rephotographed on an optical printer into five separate films, each representing one fifth of the total screen. When prints from these five films were projected on the screen, the entire image was reproduced with perfect blending between the images. The new camera allowed for the desired movement and brought the otherwise static paintings to life.

To photograph with the new camera, Ub sketched up a tubular-steel overhead gantry to support the camera from above and allow zooming and panning. The studio welding shop completed the system within a couple of weeks. Ub trained Eddie Cook, a longtime camera operator to be in charge of the photography. Tests were completed, and production was just getting underway in summer of 1971 when Ub suddenly was confronted by his most difficult challenge.

Tom Kettering noticed that Ub was having trouble using his left hand. He continually used his right hand to maneuver his left arm up to reach readouts on a tape machine. Ub felt the symptoms of a heart attack. Soon after checking him into St. Joseph's Hospital, doctors performed tests and diagnosed his problem as a severe case of arteriosclerosis. For nearly a week, Ub was under strict supervision of doctors. Visitors frequented him from the studio; he conferred daily with Eddie Cook on the progress of shooting. Ub was frustrated he could not participate in the shooting of the film. Disney president Donn Tatum, came to Ub's bedside to suggest that when he was able to return to the studio, he should work part-time to decrease his stress level. Ub never had the chance.

On the Wednesday morning of July 7, 1971, sons Don, Dave, and wife Mildred were in the waiting room when doctors and nurses rushed to the call of alarm bells. Within minutes the head doctor returned to the waiting room to give the sad news—Ub was gone. When the doctor later handed Mildred a small bag of Ub's personal belongings, including his eyeglasses and watch, Don recalled the empty feeling that this was all that was left of his father who had made such an indelible impression upon the industry. Newspaper obituaries the following day were concise:

*Funeral services for Ub Iwerks, 70, associated with Walt
Disney and Disney Studios 52 years, will be tomorrow in
Burbank's First Presbyterian Church. The longtime friend
and Kansas City school chum of the late Walt Disney
teamed up with Disney in 1919 at Kansas City where the
pair produced advertising and entertainment slides shown at
movie houses. They toyed with animation on the side, then
moved here a short time later to break into animated
cartoons. Iwerks was chief animator on the first Steamboat
Willie cartoon exhibited in 1928. Steamboat Willie later
evolved into Mickey Mouse. Iwerks left the Disney organization in the 30s to form his own studio where he created and
produced several Flip the Frog cartoons. But he returned to
the Burbank studios during World War II and had been chief
technical designer for films, Disneyland and the new Disney
World in Florida. He won Academy Awards in 1965 and
1966 for his technical work. He is survived by his widow,
Mildred, and two sons, Don and Dave, both on the
Disney staff.*

Mildred Iwerks would live for more than twenty years. She died
in 1992.

Ub's true legacy is a passion that has transcended time. His inventions and creations live on today, constantly rediscovered by new
audiences and new generations. Many of the Ub Iwerks films of the
1930s have been labeled cult classics. His technical inventions provided the groundwork for modern digital technology. Almost everywhere one travels around the world, it is almost impossible not to see
the image, in one form or another, of the little mouse Ub once
sketched while hunched over his drawing board in 1928. Ub has been
labeled "a quiet man who left a deep mark on animation," and an
"unsung hero" in the creation of Mickey Mouse. It is true that
without the success of Mickey, things may have turned out very dif-
ferently. The contributions Ub made were never lost on Walt.
Roy E. Disney reflects upon Ub's contributions to the studio:
"He animated Mickey, he is the guy and even Walt I think started

admitting that toward the end—that without Ub, there wouldn't have been a Mickey and a Minnie, and I'm sure a bunch of other characters as well." Although Ub never took credit for the creation of Mickey Mouse and numerous biographies have either eliminated or minimized his contributions through the years, the Walt Disney company in 1989 acknowledged him as the true designer of Mickey Mouse, awarding him the first Disney Legends Award. For many who had followed Ub's career, it was a long-overdue honor.

After taking over projects Ub left behind, it was clear to Don Iwerks that underneath all Ub's complex formulas and ideas lay the real energy and core of Ub's spirit—the unrelenting desire to discover and entertain. "What a fun job it is to make people happy—whether it's the cartoons, the live-action films or the theme parks—it's wonderful to be part of that creation. Ub was a major contributor to some degree of happiness in the world and what he did in conjunction with Walt."

Leonard Maltin summed up their relationship succinctly: "I think they had a great working relationship because they sparked each other—they fed off each other in a very effective way—so that without Ub, Walt probably couldn't have done some of the things he did and without Walt, Ub's inventions wouldn't have been put to such good use."

Another Disney Legend, Ken O'Connor, respected Ub's abilities as something truly special: "Versatility acquainted with genius, Ub was a modern-day Leonardo da Vinci in a modest way. I worked in the studio layout department. We'd always come into horrendous problems; mechanics, camera operations, multiple exposures, distortion, diffusion, confusion. The key to solve it was Ub. He'd never say no. Give him enough money and time and he'd do it. Archimedes said, 'Give me a place to put a fulcrum and a suitable lever and I'll move the world.' That was Ub's idea."

Glossary

Anamorphic lens: A photographic lens used to compress imagery horizontally, creating a wide-screen image. Ub Iwerks designed a special anamorphic lens to photograph *Sleeping Beauty*.

Animation: The process of creating the illusion of movement by projecting a series of static images in succession. Essentially all motion-picture films are "animated," according to this definition.

Circarama (CircleVision): A motion-picture film projected in 360 degrees around the viewer. Ub Iwerks perfected, and was awarded a patent for, the design of a system utilizing multiple cameras oriented vertically, each photographing, by means of a mirror, one segment of the 360-degree view.

Dye-transfer process: The premiere system first developed by Kodak in the 1930s to make color photographic reproductions. Ub Iwerks improved upon the three-color system in the 1940s for the Disney Studio to increase its saturation and contrast range capabilities. The process was used for the production and publicity color photos.

FPS: Frames per second. Modern motion-picture sound film is projected at 24 fps. Early silent film was projected at 16 fps. Rarely does modern animation use a separate image for each frame of film; more often the images are filmed "on twos" (two frames for each image) or more to reduce the number of drawings needed.

Holds: The process an animator uses to exaggerate poses. By shooting multiple frames of the same image, the animator may time his drawings to emphasize a specific silhouette.

Liquid optical printer/wet gate printer: A process developed by Ub Iwerks in which scratches on a film negative were eliminated by rephotographing each film frame submerged in liquid perchloreth-ylene, which has a refractive index such that light scattered by surface scratches is cancelled, thus eliminating the scratches.

Persistence of vision: The process wherein the human eye retains an image for a split second after viewing. This retention in memory creates a false sense of movement that allows the mind to think it is seeing actual movement when it is in fact seeing a succession of still images.

Sodium traveling matte process, also known as the sodium vapor process: The most highly regarded system in the 1960s and 1970s for the production of traveling mattes, developed by Petro Vlahos, Wadsworth E. Pohl, and Ub Iwerks. The benefit of the system in comparison to others is that it produces a traveling matte film in the camera at the same time as it exposes the original color negative. The matte image is identical in size and placement to the color negative image. This system eliminates the need to produce traveling mattes in the post-production process. Instead, the actors are filmed in front of a yellow screen illuminated with sodium vapor lamps, which produce light of an extremely narrow frequency bandwidth. A special prism in the Technicolor camera splits the optical beam in two directions: the majority of the light is passed through the prism to the color negative, while the sodium content of the beam is reflected to the traveling matte film. Thus the illuminated sodium background screen is exposed fully to the matte film, and records the actors in silhouette, while the color negative receives no sodium light and records the actors normally.

Sonovox: A device that generates a sound (for example, a train engine) and routes it through an attachment that is held against the throat. The sound vibrations are transmitted to the larynx where they meld with the natural speaking voice. The result is a train engine sound that speaks actual words.

Traveling matte: The process in which an actor can be photographed in one location (a soundstage) with a background scene photographed at a different location (an exterior site), and both images combine to create one seamless scene. Both photographic elements, foreground and background, are photographed independently and rephotographed together via an optical printer to create the new combination negative. The optical printing process utilizes the foreground matte and the foreground action negative together and is photographed by the optical printer camera. This leaves the background area of the new negative unexposed. The film is rewound in the camera and a second exposure is made with the background and a silhouette matte of the foreground action that prevents further exposure of the foreground areas. Thus the foreground and the background have been rephotographed, creating a new composite negative.

Xerox® process: The process by which animation pencil drawings on paper are reproduced onto clear cels, utilizing the Xerox copier technology, to create a duplicate on celluloid of the artists' original artwork. In the 1960s, Ub Iwerks conceived of a system that would allow a special camera to photograph the artists' original drawings directly onto cels, thus eliminating the hand tracing and inking phases of the animation process. This system is still in wide use today and has reduced animation production costs significantly.

Bibliography

Abrams, Robert E. *Treasures of Disney Animation Art*. New York, 1982.

Adamson, Joe. *The Walter Lantz Story*. New York, 1985.

Adamson, Joe. Interview by Leslie Iwerks, Oct. 19, 1998.

Anderson, Paul. *The Davy Crockett Craze: A Look at the 1950s Phenomenon and Davy Crockett Collectibles*. Hillside, Ill., 1996.

Atencio, Xavier. Interview by John Kenworthy. May 4, 1997.

Bain, D. and B. Harris. *Mickey Mouse: Fifty Happy Years*. New York, 1977.

Barrier, Michael. *Hollywood Cartoons: American Animation in its Golden Age*. New York, 1999.

Barrier, Mike. "An Interview with Carl Stalling." *Funnyworld*, Spring 1971.

Beaudine, Jr., William. Interview by John Kenworthy, Apr. 22, 1997.

Beck, J. and W. Friedwald, *Looney Tunes and Merrie Melodies*. New York, 1989.

Boyd, Jack. Interview by John Kenworthy, Sept. 24, 1997.

Bragdon, Claude. "Mickey Mouse and What He Means." *Scribner's Magazine*, July 1934.

Broughton, Bob. Interview by John Kenworthy, Jan. 29, 1997.

Broughton, Bob. Interview by Leslie Iwerks, Sept. 16, 1998.

Canemaker, John. "Grim Natwick." *Film Comment*, Jan./Feb. 1975.

Ceram, C. W. *Archaeology of the Cinema*. New York, 1965.

Clark, Les. Interview by Don Peri, Aug. 13, 1978.

Cotter, William. *The Television World of Disney*. New York, 1999.

Counts, Kyle. "The Making of Alfred Hitchcock's *The Birds*." *Cinefantastique*, Fall 1980.

Cowles, John. Interview by John Kenworthy, June 1997.

Crafton, Donald. *Before Mickey*. Cambridge, Mass., 1984.

Culhane, John. *Walt Disney's Fantasia*. New York, 1983.

Culhane, Shamus. *Talking Animals and Other People*. New York, 1986.

Cutting, Jack. Interview by Don Peri, Apr. 24, 1979.

Davis, Marc. Interview by Leslie Iwerks, Sept. 17, 1998.

DeSeversky, Major Alexander P. *Victory Through Air Power*. New York, 1942.

Disney, Roy E. Interview by Leslie Iwerks, Oct. 19, 1998.

Disney (Walt) Productions. *Mickey Mouse*. New York, 1978.

Edlund, Richard. Interview by Leslie Iwerks, Sept. 17, 1998.

Ellenshaw, Peter. Interview by John Kenworthy, Aug. 8, 1996.

Ellis, Frieda (Mrs. Izzy). Correspondence with John Kenworthy, 1996.

Eugster, Al. Correspondence with John Kenworthy, 1996.

Feild, Robert. *The Art of Walt Disney*. New York, 1942.

Finch, Christopher. *The Art of Walt Disney*. New York, 1973.

Friedman, Ed. Interview by John Kenworthy, June 15, 1996.

Friedman, Ed. Interview by Leslie Iwerks, 1997.

Gifford, Denis. *British Animated Films, 1895–1985*. Jefferson, N.C., 1987.

Goff, Harper. Interview by Don Peri, Apr. 24, 1979.

Gottfredson, Floyd. Interview by Don Peri, Oct. 1, 1977.

Gottfredson, Floyd (Disney Productions). *Mickey Mouse in Color*. New York, 1988.

Grant, Joe. Interview by John Kenworthy, July 31, 2000.

Greene, K. and R. Greene, *The Man Behind the Magic: The Story of Walt Disney*. New York, 1991.

Gurr, Bob. Interview by John Kenworthy, Apr. 24, 1997.

Hand, David Dodd. *Memoirs*. Cambria, Calif., 1986.

Harman, Hugh. Interview by Don Peri, Oct. 1, 1977.

Hartt, Reg. "Talking with Grim Natwick." *Animania*, #26.

Hauser, Maury. Interview by John Kenworthy, Apr. 23, 1997.

Hedren, Tippi. Interview by Leslie Iwerks, Sept. 24, 1998.

Holliss, R. and B. Sibley. *Walt Disney's Mickey Mouse: His Life and Times*. New York, 1986.

"How an Antitank Gun Works." *Popular Science Monthly*, Oct. 1942.

Huemer, Dick. Interview by Don Peri, March 26, 1976.

Iwerks, Betty. Interview by Leslie Iwerks, July 26, 2000.

Iwerks, Don. Interview by Leslie Iwerks, Sept. 16, 1998.

Iwerks, Don. Interview by Leslie Iwerks, July 25, 2000.

Iwerks, Marvin C. *The Iwerks Family in America, A History and Geneology*, 1998.

Iwerks, Mildred. Interview by Leslie Iwerks, 1987.

Iwerks, Ub. "Movie Cartoons Come to Life." *Popular Mechanics*, Jan. 1942.

Jackson, Kathy Merlock. *Walt Disney: A Bio-bibliography*. Westport, Conn., 1993.

Jackson, Wilfred. Interview by Don Peri, Jan. 12, 1977.

Johnston, Ollie. Interview by John Kenworthy, Feb. 3, 1997.

Jones, Chuck. *Chuck Amuck*. New York, 1989.

Jones, Chuck. *Chuck Reducks*. New York, 1996.

Jones, Chuck. "Diary of a Mad Cel-washer." *Film Comment*, May/June 1976.

Jones, Chuck. Interview by John Kenworthy, Sept. 17, 1996.

Jones, Chuck. Interview by Leslie Iwerks, Sept. 11, 1998.

Kanfer, Stefan. *Serious Business, The Art and Commerce of Animation in America from Betty Boop to Toy Story*. New York, 1997.

Kausler, Mark. Interview by Leslie Iwerks, Sept. 19, 1998.

Kenner, Hugh. *Chuck Jones: A Flurry of Drawings*. Berkeley, Calif., 1994.

Kettering, Tom. Interview by John Kenworthy, Sept. 19, 1996.

Kimball, Ward. Interview by John Kenworthy, June 9, 1996.

Kinney, Jack. *Walt Disney and Assorted Other Characters*. New York, 1988.

Koehler, William. *The Wonderful World of Disney Animals*. New York, 1979.

Lenburg, Jeff. *The Great Cartoon Directors*. New York, 1983.

Lenburg, Jeff. *The Encyclopedia of Animated Cartoons*. New York, 1991.

Lipton, Norman. "Disneyland's Circarama." *Popular Photography*, Dec. 1955.

Lycett, Eustace. Interview by John Kenworthy, Sept. 17, 1996.

Maltin, Leonard. Interview by Leslie Iwerks, Sept. 24, 1998.

Maltin, Leonard. *Leonard Maltin's 1997 Movie and Video Guide*. New York, 1996.

Maltin, Leonard. *Of Mice and Magic*. New York, 1980.

Maltin, Leonard. *The Disney Films*. New York, 1973.

Martin, William. Interview by John Kenworthy, Sept. 28, 1997.

McEvoy, J. P. "McEvoy in Disneyland." *Reader's Digest*, Feb. 1955.

McGhee, Virginia Davis. Interview by Leslie Iwerks, 1998.

Merritt, R. and J. B. Kaufman. *Walt in Wonderland*. Baltimore, Md., 1993.

Merritt, Russell. Interview by Leslie Iwerks, 1998.

Miller, Diane Disney. "My Dad, Walt Disney." *Saturday Evening Post*, Nov. 1956.

Miller, Diane Disney. *The Story of Walt Disney*. New York, 1957.

Mosley, Leonard. *Disney's World*. New York, 1985.

O'Connor, Ken. Interview by Don Peri, June 1977.

O'Connor, Ken. Interview by Leslie Iwerks, Feb. 8, 1994.

Offemann, William. Interview by John Kenworthy, March 18, 1997.

Offemann, Yvonne. Interview by John Kenworthy, March 18, 1997.

Otto, Bob. Interview by John Kenworthy, Jan. 18, 1997.

Pabian, James. *Immigrant's Son.* Huntington, Va., 1992.

Peary, D. and G. Peary. *The American Animated Cartoon.* New York, 1980.

Peck, A. P. "What Makes Fantasia Click?" *Scientific American,* Jan. 1941.

Peet, Bill. *Bill Peet: An Autobiography.* Boston, Mass., 1989.

Richardson, LeRoy. Interview by Leslie Iwerks, 1997.

Richardson, Lloyd. Interview by John Kenworthy, Apr. 24, 1997.

Schickel, Richard. *The Disney Version.* New York, 1968.

Shannon, Leonard. "'Poppins, Revisited." *The Disney Magazine,* Winter 1994.

Sharpsteen, Ben. Interview by Don Peri, Feb. 6, 1974.

Sibley, B. and R. Holliss. *The Disney Studio Story.* New York, 1988.

Smith, David R. "Up to Date in Kansas City" *Funnyworld,* Fall 1978.

Smith, David R. "Ub Iwerks, 1901–1971" *Funnyworld,* 1972.

Smith, David R. Interview by Leslie Iwerks, Sept. 21, 1998.

Solomon, Charles. *The Disney That Never Was.* New York, 1995.

Somerville, Ralph. Interview by John Kenworthy, June 14, 1996.

Sommerfield, Virginia. Interview by John Kenworthy, Aug. 8, 1997.

Taylor, John Russell. *Hitch: The Life and Times of Alfred Hitchcock.* New York, 1978.

"The Big Bad Wolf." *Fortune,* Nov. 1934.

Thomas, Bob. *Building a Company, Roy O. Disney and the Creation of an Entertainment Empire.* New York, 1999.

Thomas, Bob. *The Art of Animation.* New York, 1958.

Thomas, Bob. *Walt Disney: An American Original.* New York, 1976.

Thomas, F. and O. Johnston. *Disney Animation: The Illusion of Life.* New York, 1981.

Thomas, Frank. Interview by John Kenworthy, Jan. 24, 1997.

Thomas, Frank. Interview by Leslie Iwerks, 1997.

Tompson, Ruthie. Interview by Leslie Iwerks, 1993.

Turkisher, Mrs. Arthur. Interview by John Kenworthy, Feb. 18, 1997.

West, Jr., J. G. *The Disney Live Action Productions*. Milton, Wash., 1994.

Whitlock, Albert and June. Correspondence with John Kenworthy, Feb. 1997.

Withers, Jane. Interview by John Kenworthy, Aug. 8, 1996.

Wolf, Berny. Interview by John Kenworthy, Jan. 27, 1997.

Zukor, Lou. Interview by John Kenworthy, June 19, 1996.

Zukor, Maury. Interview by John Kenworthy, Feb. 7, 1997.

For helpful information provided in interviews, E-mail, and correspondence, many thanks to: Peter Adamakos, Joe Adamson, AMPAS, Paul Anderson (Godfather #2), ASIFA, AWN, Mike Barrier, Jerry Beck, Ian Birnie, Nick Bosustow, Dennis Bradley, Mike Broggie, David Butler, Sody Clampett, Donald Crafton, Phyllis Craig, Tom Crone, Suzanne Curasi, Art Davis, Marv Davis, Harvey Deneroff, Disney Archives, Peter Esmonde, Richard Fleischer, June Foray, Van Arsdale France, Eilleen "Dot" Powers George, David Gerstein, Carl Girod, Steve Grossfield, Lou Guarnier, Ted Hakes, Jerry Hathcock, John Hench, Mrs. Rudi Ising, Wendy Jackson, Bill Justice, Mark Kausler, Kristine Krueger, Mark Langer, Richard J. Lesosky, William Littlejohn, Dave Mackey, Leonard Maltin, Antran Manoogian, Mark Mayerson, David Mruz, Stuart Ng, Floyd Norman, Ken O'Connor, Mrs. Ray Patin, Paul Penna, Howard Prouty, Tom Ray, Virgil Ross, Martha Sigall, The Society for Animation Studies, Tom Sito, Mary Kay Speaks, Lawrence Stalling, Steve Stanchfield, the Tashlin family, Sheri Tattenham, Carl Urbano, Clair Weeks, Western District of Missouri Court Proceedings, Kathy White, Fanny Whittaker, Kirk Wise, Steven Worth (Godfather #1), Frank Wylie.

Index

A

Abbingwehr, Ostfriesland, Germany, 1–2
Abbott, L. B., 203
    The Birds, 205–206
ABC television, *Disneyland* television show, 179
Academic sponsorship, educational films, 166
Academy Award nominations
    for *The Birds* for Special Effects, 206
    Mary Poppins, 212
Academy Awards
    for color traveling-matte composite cine-
        matography, 212
    Der Fuehrer's Face, 155
    for improved optical printer for special effects,
        198
    Mary Poppins, 212
    Mickey Mouse, 147
    Seal Island, 169
Acme Tool Company
    impression on Chuck Jones, 112–113
    maintenance on equipment at Iwerks Studio,
        111
"Acting" by Mickey, 55–58
Acting by Ub, *Martha, Just a Plain Old-fashioned
    Name* song reel, 22
Adamson, Joe
    on Iwerks Studio humor, 131
    on loss of challenge in animation, 143–144
    on profits at Iwerks Studio, 135–136
Adult themes and situations, 102
The Adventures of Ichabod and Mr. Toad, 174
Advertisements. *See also* Marketing and promo-
    tion
    help wanted advertisement in *Los Angeles
        Times*, 90
    for Laugh-O-gram Films in *Kansas City Star*,
        18
Advertising. *See also* Kansas City Film Ad
    Service
    animation in, 11, 12
    early work in, 4
Aerial photography, 158, 189
Aesop's Fables cartoons
    Paul Terry, 48
    sound cartoons, 61
    Stalling's defection to, 87
African characters in Iwerks cartoons, 124
Aircraft. *See also* Aviation

identification, 156–157
The Air Race (Spite Flight), 106–108, 158
Aladdin and his Wonderful Lamp, 125
Alfred Hitchcock Presents, Stalling's music, 79
Alfred Hitchcock's Mystery Magazine, 202
Ali Baba, 125
Alice's Wonderland series. *See also* Davis, Virginia;
        Julius
    Alice Cans the Cannibals, 34
    Alice Chops the Suey, 37, 38
    Alice Foils the Pirates, 37
    Alice in the Jungle, 34
    Alice on the Farm, 37
    Alice Picks the Champ, 36–37
    Alice's Brown Derby, 47
    Alice's Day at Sea, 27
    Alice's Egg Plant, 35–36
    Alice's Mysterious Mystery, 39
    Alice Solves the Puzzle, 34
    Alice's Orphan, 38
    Alice's Spanish Guitar, 37
    Alice Stage Struck, 34
    Alice the Jailbird, 33–34
    Alice the Peacemaker, 30, 33
    Alice Wins the Derby, 47
    Dawn O'Day as Alice, 35, 36
    differences from Oswald cartoons, 43
    Disney Brothers' Cartoon Studios, 26
    filming live action scenes, 30
    Margie Gay as Alice, 36
    Lois Hardwicke as Alice, 39–40
    Laugh-O-gram Films, 21–22
    use of mechanical representations, transforma-
        tions, and gags, 47
All Wet, 48
America the Beautiful, 189, 223–224
Amusement parks. *See also* Disneyland theme
        park; Walt Disney World
    Walt's trips with daughters, 178
Anamorphic wide-angle lens, 196
Anchors Aweigh, 162
Anderson, Ken, credits and bylines, 80
Anderson, Paul, *The Crockett Craze*, 184
Anderson, William "Bill," 163
    moving Ub's office, 187
Andrews, Julie
    Academy Award, 212

Mary Poppins, 209–210, 212
Androgynous appearance of female characters, 47
Animals as animation subjects. *See also* Animation cruelty; Detachable appendages; Mechanical representations, transformations, and gags; Pete characters
 cats. *See* Cats as animation subjects
 Fiddlesticks, 92
 fish in *20,000 Leagues Under the Sea,* 180
 frogs as animation subjects, 89. *See also* Flip the Frog
 Gabby Goat, 140
 Mary Poppins, 210
 mice. *See* Mice as animation subjects
 The Opry House, 74
 "Pink Elephants on Parade" sequence in *Dumbo,* 153–154
 Plane Crazy, 57
 rabbits. *See* Bugs Bunny; Oswald the Lucky Rabbit
 spiders, 79
 Steamboat Willie, 69–70
Animated Cartoons: How They are Made, Their Origin and Development (Lutz), 7–8
Animated Picture Corporation, 122
Animation cameras
 purchase by Iwerks Studio, 95
 smoother-operating drive on, 46
Animation combined with live action. *See* Combination of live action with animation
Animation cruelty
 Alice's Orphan, 38
 Plane Crazy, 57
Animation innovations. *see also* Gravity-defying dances; Mechanical representations, transformations, and gags; Perspective; Straight-ahead style of drawing
 constant motion, 30, 37
 deep-focus technique, 149
 distortion effects in *Chinaman's Chance,* 103, 138
 mobile perspective effect, 56
 personality animation, 174
 shortcut style, 33
 time passage transitions, 122–123
 traveling-matte process, 211
 woodblock effect, 74
 Xerographic Developing Apparatus, 194
 xerographic process, application to animation, 192–196
Animation production
 creating realistic movement, 10–11
 differences in Walt's and Ub's methods, 77–78

first exposure to, 6
paper dolls and puppets, use in, 7
Animation techniques. *See also* Animation innovations; Anthropomorphic elements; Mechanical representations, transformations, and gags; Perspective; "Rubber-hose" style of animation; Straight-ahead style of drawing
 anatomy, 68–69
 androgynous appearance of female characters, 47
 cel animation process, 10
 circle as design element, 53–54, 68–69
 "clean up" work by apprentices, 76
 combining live action and animation, 9–10
 cut-and-slash, 8
 cycles, 8, 55
 distorted shadows, 36–37
 extremes, 30, 77. *See also* In-between drawings or "in-betweening"
 gravity-defying dances, 73
 implication of movement, 68
 in-between drawings, 8, 56, 76–77
 internal motivation of characters, 57–58
 lightning-artist technique, 19
 limited animation, 8
 model sheets, 17, 30
 perspective, 97
 pose-to-pose animation, 30
 repeats, 55
 rotoscoping, 10–11
 stop-motion filming, 8–9
 time passage transitions, 122–123
 20,000 Leagues Under the Sea, 180
Animatronics
 Great Moments with Mr. Lincoln, 212
 Hall of Presidents, 225–226
 Mary Poppins, 210
Annakin, Ken, 175
Anthropomorphic elements, 11. *See also* Mechanical representations, transformations, and gags
 Laugh-O-gram Films, 17
 phone in *The Cuckoo Murder Case,* 97
 piano in *The Opry House,* 74
Antique cars, Ub's interest in, 182
Antique guns, Ub's interest in, 114
Arabian Nights Studio, 25
 closed down, 30
Archery, Ub's interest in, 113–114
Architecture of the Middle East in Iwerks Studio cartoons, 125
Arkansas, Ubbe's employment on farm in, 3
Armstrong, Louis, 124
Arteriosclerosis (Ub's), 227

Ashland Grammar School, 3
Astronomy, Ub's interest in, 113
Atencio, Xavier, 210
   Mary Poppins, 212
Audio-Animatronics, 212–213
   combination with film projections, 214–215
Audley, Eleanor, 215
Automatic lamp changer, 223
Automobiles
   antique cars, Ub's interest in, 182
   Astin Martin, 119
   Chrysler Airflow, 119
   Cole Eight roadster, 30
   Jeff Davis' Cadillac, Ubbe drives to California,
     29
   Terraplane automobile, Art Turkisher's, 119
   Walt sells Cabriolet to raise money for
     Steamboat Willie, 67–68
Autumn, 84
Aviation
   The Air Race, 106–107, 158
   model airplanes, 111, 158
   The Ocean Hop, 49, 158
   Plane Crazy, 55, 158
   Ub's interest in, 49
   WEFT (Wings, Engines, Fuselage, Tail) tech-
     nique of aircraft identification, 150–151
   Willie Whopper, 104–106

B

Babbitt, Art, 152
Babe Ruth, cameo appearance in *Play Ball*, 108
Baby Checkers (Gran Pop Monkey), 141
Baby pictures, Laugh-O-gram Films, 18
Backgrounds and settings. *See also* Rural settings
     and backgrounds
   Flip the Frog, 94
   Jack Frost, 132–133
   metamorphosis in *Jack and the Beanstalk*, 123
   moving-perspective street background, 100
   xerographic process, 195
Backup sodium prism, 221–222
Ballard, Lucien, 200
Balloonland, 131–132
Bambi, 155–156
The Band Concert, 93
The Banker's Daughter, 48
Bankruptcy
   Iwwerks-Disney Commercial Artists, 6
   Laugh-O-gram Films, 24
   Pictorial Clubs, 19
The Barn Dance, 68, 73
Bar sheets, 62–63
   horizontal bar technique for recording sound,
     68

Steamboat Willie, 64
Barton, Charles, 207
Basement. *See* Technical workshop at Iwerks
     Studio (basement)
Bathing Time for Baby, 167
Bauman, Charles, formation of Universal Film
     Manufacturing Company, 66
Beaudine, William Jr., 188–189
Beaudine, William Sr., 188
The Beauty Shoppe (Gran Pop Monkey), 141
Bedknobs and Broomsticks, 222
Bedtime Story books (Thornton Burgess),
     47–48
Before Mickey (Donald Crafton), 32
Benchley, Robert, 152
Betty Boop, 96
   animators, 116
   Grim Natwick as creator of, 98
   origin as dog, 123
   similarity to original Willie Whopper, 105
   top animators on Iwerks Studio staff, 110
   voices used in, 124
Bickenbach, Dick, 116
Bicycle (Ub's), 182
Biederman, Dave, 141
Bi-packed prints, 23. *See also* Cinecolor
The Birds, 202–207
Birth of Ubbe Eert Iwwerks, 2
Bjork, Godfrey, 99
Blackboard Review, 143
Black culture, Fleischer Brothers' recognition of,
     124
Blair, Mary, 117
"Blame it on the Samba," 173
Bobby Bumps, 10
Bootleg Pete character, 34
Boots Chemists, 138, 139
Bosko, 124
Boss politics in Kansas City, parodies of, 13–14
Bosustow, Steve, 116, 117
Bouncing balls technique for recording sound,
     68
Bowling, 181
Boyd, Jack, *Mary Poppins*, 211
Boyle, Robert, *The Birds*, 204
BOYS Anti-Tank MK1 Rifle, 156–157
Brave Little Tailor, 18
The Brave Tin Soldier, 126–127
British illustrators, Ub's inspiration from, 141
Broadway Strand Theater, New York, 66–67
Broadway Theater, New York, *Fantasia*, 151
Broggie, Roger, 213
Broughton, Bob
   on *The Birds*, 206
   on color effects work, 171

on combination of live action with animation, 23
on *Duel in the Sun,* 164–165
on tours of process lab, 202
on Ub after Walt's death, 221
on Ub's challenges, 182
on Ub's perfectionism, 167
on Walt's regard for Ub, 200
Brush work, Ub's talent with, 16
Brussels World's Fair, 189
Buffalo, New York, Patrick Powers in, 65–66
Bugs Bunny, 117
   What's Opera, Doc?, 140
"Bumble Boogie," 171–172
Burbank, California, Disney Studio's move to, 149
Burgess, Thornton, *Bedtime Story* books, 47–48
A Busy Day (Gran Pop Monkey), 141
Bylines. *See* Credit and bylines
Byrnes, Gene, 136–137

C

Cady, Harrison, *Bedtime Story* books, 47–48
California
   name change after arrival in, 30
   Roy convincing Walt to move to, 24
   Ub's move to, 29
Calloway, Cab, 124
Camelot, 209
Cameo appearances
   Amelia Earhart in *The Air Race,* 107
   by Ub as animator, 181
   Babe Ruth in *Play Ball,* 108
   Flip the Frog in *Play Ball,* 107
   Mahatma Gandhi, 125
   Mickey Mouse in *Hollywood Party,* 162
   Walt Disney in *The Reluctant Dragon,* 152–153
Cameras. *See also* Animation cameras
   horizontal multiplane camera, Ub builds, 129–130
   nodal-point perspective camera, 196–197
Camera stands
   horizontal multiplane camera, 129–130
   motor problems, 111–112
Cancer, Walt's, 220
Cannon, Johnny, 59, 60
Career and employment (Ub's). *See also* Iwwerks-Disney Commercial Artists
   advertising, 4
   beginnings, 3
   closing of Iwerks Studio, 136
Disney Optical Printing Department head, 160
Disney Studios, 26–84
   first partnership with Walt Disney, 5

first work as commercial artist, 4
as journeyman, 138–144
Kansas City Film Ad Company, 6–16, 24–25
laid off from Pesmen-Rubin, 4
Laugh-O-gram Films, not on original staff, 15
left Kansas City film Ad Service and joined Laugh-O-gram Films, 16
Pesmen-Rubin Commercial Art Studio, 4–5
politics at work, 163, 187
process lab at Disney, 163
production control department at Disney, 148
promotion after heart attack, 187
promotion to head of Film Ad Art department, 25
resignation from Disney Studio, 86–87
resignation from United Film Ad Service, 16
return to Kansas City Film Ad, 24
return to Walt Disney Studio, 145–165
Caricatures
   The Air Race, 107
   ethnic caricatures, 123–124
   first job as commercial artist, 4
Cars. *See* Automobiles
Carter, Al, 5
Cartoon Films, Limited, 138
Cassin, Billie. *See* Crawford, Joan
The Castaway, comic strip based on, 81
Catalog design, first job as commercial artist, 4
Cats as animation subjects, 11. *See also* Detachable appendages; Julius; Krazy Kat cartoons
   Alice the Peacemaker, 30
   in Laugh-O-gram Films, 17
   object of Oswald's affections, 43
   Universal Studios' decision to launch cartoon series, 40
Cauger, A. Vern, 6, 12, 218–219. *See also* Kansas City Film Ad Service
   lack of interest in animated fairy tale, 14
Cel animation process, 10
Celebrity Pictures, distribution of Flip the Frog, 96
Celluloid, problems with density of, 35–36
Cel washers, 91, 114, 116
Challenges for Ub, 143–144
   bowling, 181
   loss of challenge in animation, 143–144, 182
Charles Mintz Studio, defection of staff to, 50
Chas. M. Stebbins Picture Supply Co., Laugh-O-gram Films creditor, 20
Childhood, Iwwerks', 1
"Chim Chim Cheree," Academy Award for, 212
Chinaman's Chance, 103, 124, 138

Chinese men, insensitive treatment of characters
    in cartoons, 124
Chip and Dale, *Working for Peanuts,* 190
Christmas tree, Ub shooting ornaments, 114
Chrysler Airflow, Ub's, 119
Churchill, Winston, *Victory Through Air Power,*
    159
Cinderella, 174
    Laugh-O-gram Films, 18
Cinecolor process, 114, 121
    Jack Frost, 133
Cinemascope process, 185–186
Cinephone sound system, 66
Circarama, 186–187
    award for, 198
    success at Disneyland, 189
    troubleshooting, 199
Circle as design element
    Flip the Frog, 94
    Mickey Mouse, 68–69
    Middle Eastern architecture, 125
    Steamboat Willie, 68–69
    Willie Whopper, 108
CircleVision, 199
    America the Beautiful, 223–224
    film loop cabinets, 218
    Magic of the Rails, 215–216
Clampett, Robert "Bob"
    merchandising for Mickey Mouse, 72
    Porky in Wackyland compared to *Stratos-Fear,*
        109
    relationship with Chuck Jones, 139–140
    on Ub's quitting subcontracting, 140
    at Warner Brothers Studios, 139
Clarabelle Cow, 53
Clara Cleans Her Teeth, 41–42
Clark, Les, 59, 60
    The Skeleton Dance, 76
    Steamboat Willie, 62, 63, 69
    Ub's return to Disney, 149
Clopton, Ben, at Iwerks Studio, 89
Closing of Iwerks Studio, 136
Cochrane, P. D., 42
Cochrane, RH, formation of Universal Film
    Manufacturing Company, 66
Collier's Magazine, Gran Pop Monkey character,
    141
Colony Theater, New York, *Steamboat Willie*
    debut, 70
Color-correction masking process, award for, 198
Color in cartoon films. *See also* Comicolor
    Classic series
Cinecolor, 114
    Fiddlesticks, 92–94
    Jack Frost, 133

Mickey Mouse's shorts, 93
    paint formulas, development of, 48–49
    palette of colors developed for Cinecolor, 114
    technical innovations, 91–92
    three-color Technicolor process (process #4),
        91, 92, 121
    two-color Technicolor process (process #3),
        92
    xerographic process, limitations of, 195
Color Rhapsodies series, 141
    Blackboard Review, 143
    The Frog Pond, 143
    Gorilla Hunt, 143
    The Horse on the Merry Go Round, 141
    Merry Mannequins, 141
    Midnight Frolics, 143
    Skeleton Frolic, 141
    Wise Owl, 143
Color separation process, 176
Color still prints, 163–164
Color technology
    blending of incongruities, 170–171
    color-correction masking process, 198
    color separation process, 176
    paint formulas, development of, 48–49
    still prints, 163–164
    True-Life Adventures, 170–171
Columbia cartoons, 141, 143
Combination of live action with animation,
    9–10, 22, 23, 150. *See also Alice's
    Wonderland* series
    The Air Race, 107
    Bedknobs and Broomsticks, 222–223
    Clara Cleans Her Teeth, 41–42
    criticism from Charlie Mintz, 39
    explanation of technique, 32–33
    Fantasia, 150–151
    Fleischer Brothers. *See Out of the Inkwell*
        cartoons
    jump-cuts, 34, 184
    Mary Poppins, 210, 211
    Saludos Amigos, 159
    Sodium matte process, 183
    The Three Caballeros, 160–162
Comicolor Classic series, 121–122
    Aladdin and his Wonderful Lamp, 125
    Ali Baba, 125
    Don Quixote, 130
    The Headless Horseman, 130
    Jack and the Beanstalk, 122
    Jack Frost, 132–133
    Little Black Sambo, 124
    The Little Red Hen, 123
    Mary's Little Lamb, 125
    Oliver Twist, 136

Sinbad the Sailor, 125
Summertime, 133–134
The Thousand and One Nights, 125
The Valiant Tailor, 18, 130
Comic-strip conventions in Laugh-O-gram
    Films, 17
Comic strips
    Mickey Mouse, 81
    Reglar Fellars, 136–137
    Toonerville Trolley, 45–46
    Van Boring, 116
Commandeering of Disney Studios by U.S.
    armed services, 154
Commercial films, mass production at Disney
    Studio, 166
Commercial work-for-hire. *See* Work-for-hire
Composite imaging, 183
The Concert Feature. See Fantasia
Constant motion in animation, 30, 37
Continuity in films, color blending, 170–171
Cook, Eddie, 227
Cook, Jimmy, 114
Coon, Carleton, 20–21
Coon-Sanders Original Nighthawks Band,
    20–21
Copying. *See also* Xerographic process for anima-
    tion
    use in animation, 17
Corcoran, Kevin "Moochie," 198
Corporate sponsorship, commercial films, 166
Costs of animation production, 192
    cel washing, 91
    CPF (cost-per-foot), 166
A Course in Motion Picture Photography, 7
Cowles, John, investment in Laugh-O-gram
    Films, 15
Cowles, Minnie, 15
    naming Minnie Mouse, 54
CPF (cost-per-foot), 166
Crafton, Donald, *Before Mickey,* 32
Craig, Phyllis, 193
Crawford, Joan, 13
Creative freedom for Ub
    decision to leave Walt Disney Studio, 85
    Silly Symphonies, 81–82
Credit and bylines
    after return to Disney Studio, 156
    animation, 48
    Mickey Mouse, 79–81, 224, 228–229
    Mickey Mouse comic strip, 81
    Plane Crazy, 57
    Porky Pig projects, 139–140
    The Reluctant Dragon, 152–153
    Walt's views on, 80
    writing, 48

Criterion Theater, Los Angeles, premiere of
    Trolley Troubles, 45–46
The Crockett Craze (Anderson), 184
Crossbow, Ub's interest in, 114
Crown Theater, Pasadena, 169
Cruelty. *See* Animation cruelty
The Cuckoo Murder Case, 97
Culhane, Jimmie, 116
    on Berny Wolf's arrival, 110
    The Brave Tin Soldier, 127
    joins Iwerks Studio, 98
    on learning from Ub, 101
    The Little Red Hen, 123
    on Offemann, 99
    on sensuality of Iwerks Studio characters, 102
    on Ub building horizontal multiplane camera,
        130
    on Ub's work in the basement, 129
    unionization of animators, 128–129
Culhane, Jimmie "Shamus," at Disney, 146
Current events as inspiration for Ub, 96
Cursing in Iwerks Studio cartoons, 97
Cut-and-slash techniques, 8
Cycles technique, 8

D

"The Dancing Man," 213
Dan Patch (racehorse), 173–174
Darby O'Gill and the Little People, 196–197
Dark humor. *See* Animation cruelty
Davis, Jeff, 26–27
    Ubbe drives car to California, 29
Davis, Marc
    Cinderella, 174
    on impact of xerographic process, 195
    on Ub's return to Disney, 150
Davis, Virginia ("Ginny")
    on filming, 30
    last of Alice series, 35
    move to California, 26–27
    original hiring for *Alice's Wonderland,*
        22
Davy Crockett, King of the Wild Frontier feature
    film, 184
"Davy Crockett, King of the Wild Frontier" tele-
    vision series, 184
Davy Crockett and the River Pirates, 185
Davy Jones Locker, 114
The Dawn of Better Living, 167
Deaths
    Eert Ubben Iwwerks, 134
    Mildred's, 228
    Ub's, 227
    Walt's, 220
Decorah, Iowa, Eert Ubbén Iwwerks moves to, 2

Deep-focus technique, 148–149
Defections
    completion of last Oswald cartoon, 59
    from Disney to Charles Mintz Studio, 50
    from Disney to Ub Iwerks Studio, 85–88
    from Fleischer Brothers to Iwerks Studio,
        110
    from Max Fleischer to Iwerks Studio, 98
    secrecy surrounding Mickey Mouse's develop-
        ment, 55, 56
    Ub's, 85–88
Denison, E. J., 60
Density of celluloid, problems with, 35–36
Dental hygiene films
    in *Clara Cleans her Teeth,* 41–42
    Tommy Tucker's Tooth, 20
Depression. *See* Great Depression
Der Fuehrer's Face, 155
Descha's Tryst with the Moon (Laugh-O-gram
    Films Lafflet), 19
De Seversky, Alexander P., 158
Detachable appendages
    Julius, 47
    in Laugh-O-gram Films, 17
    Mickey Mouse, 58
    Oswald the Lucky Rabbit, 42, 46–47, 47
Deus ex machina device, 37
Dial M for Murder, 190
Dinner Time (Van Beuren), 65
Dinning Sisters, 173
Disney, Diane, 209
Disney, Edna (née Edna Francis)
    marriage to Roy Disney, 43
    secretly working on Mickey Mouse, 56
Disney, Lillian (née Lillian Bounds)
    marriage to Walt Disney, 43
    naming Mickey, 54
    secretly working on Mickey Mouse, 56
    Steamboat Willie dry run, 64
Disney, Roy. *See also* Walt Disney Studio
    bowling with Ub, 181
    convincing Walt to move to California, 24
    on cost of Cinephone process, 66
    Disneyland television show, negotiating deal
        for, 179
    learns of Ub's resignation, 86
    marriage to Edna Francis, 43
    on Mickey's personality, 58
    negotiating agreement with government, 155
    postponement of retirement after Walt's death,
        225
    proposal from MGM to use Donald Duck,
        162
    recruiting Grim Natwick, 98
    on relationship between Ub and Walt, 221

    selection of site for Florida theme park, 216
    settlement of strike, 159
    suggesting studio name change, 80
    telegrams Walt about Ub's resignation, 86–87
    on Ub's removal of scratches on film,
        169–170
    on Ub's resignation, 88–89
    on Ub's return to Disney, 146
    on Walt's reaction to educational films,
        167–168
Disney, Roy E.
    on cost of Cinephone process, 66
    on relationship between Ub and Disney family,
        221
    secretly working on Mickey Mouse, 56
    on Ub's contributions to the studio, 228–229
Disney, Walt. *See also* Iwwerks-Disney
        Commercial Artists; Laugh-O-gram Films;
        Walt Disney Studio; Walt Disney Television
    acting out cartoon stories, 59, 60
    amusement parks, trips with daughters, 178
    animating no longer, 30
    animation in advertising, 11
    arguments with Carl Stalling over scores,
        74–75
    bankruptcy, 6, 24
    beginning of friendship with Ubbe, 4, 9, 14,
        225
    cameo appearance in *The Reluctant Dragon,*
        152–153
    correspondence
        asking Ubbe to come to California, 25, 26,
            28–29
        with Charlie Mintz, 27
        with Charlie Mintz regarding *Alice Cans the
            Cannibals,* 34
        regarding Alice series, 39
        regarding Oswald the Lucky Rabbit, 39
        to Dr. McCrum regarding Ubbe's arrival in
            California, 30
        invitation to Ubbe to come to California,
            25, 26
        Margaret J. Winkler, 23, 26
        use of *nigger* in letter to Ub, 124
    criticism of Ub, 82–84
    "Daddy's day," 178
    death, 220
    distribution for Mickey Mouse, 60
    on educational films, 167–168
    enthusiasm and optimism, 24
        after losing Oswald, 53
        financing sound recordings, 67–68
        soundtracks, 64
    fatherhood, 178
    financial troubles, 19–20, 23–24

first on-screen appearance, 12
first partnership with, 5
foreign trip, 159
hired as coworker, 4
hired at Kansas City Slide Company, 6
idea for animated fairy tale, 14
interest in industrial automation techniques,
    78
Latin and South American trip, 159
learns of Ub's resignation, 86–87
lung cancer, 220
marriage to Lillian Bounds, 43
mass production at Disney Studio, 166
mice, fondness for, 54
Midwestern background and humor, 37
Mortimer (mouse friend), 54
move to California, 24
naïveté, 4, 24
    defection of staff to Charles Mintz Studio,
        50–51
negotiating agreement with government, 155
resignation from United Film Ad Service,
    incorporated Laugh-O-gram Films, 15
sells Cabriolet to raise money for Steamboat
    Willie, 67–68
sequels, aversion to, 185
shared enthusiasm for and fascination with
    technology, 9
signature, 4, 80–81, 225
song reels, 21–22
sound in cartoons, foresight, 60
strike at Disney Studio, 152
"sugar-coated educational stuff," 168
taking credit for others' work, 46, 81, 83–84
on technical imperfections, 171
tinkering with Ub's work, 77–78
on Ub's personnel abilities, 118
Ub's relationship with, 229
    Academy Award congratulations, 147
    beginnings of friendship, 4, 9, 14, 225
    criticism of Ub, 82–84
    defection of Ub, 85–89
    fame's effect on, 80
    frustrations by Ub with Walt's tinkering,
        77–78
    growing tensions, 78, 81–84, 85
    interactions with Ub and Roy, 32
    maturing roles, 49–50
    mutual respect, 200–201
    return to Disney Studio, 147–150
    strength of, 219
    Walt's regard for Ub, 200
views on credits and bylines, 80
xerographic process, skepticism for, 194–195
Disney Brothers' Cartoon Studios. See Walt

Disney Studio
The Disney Films (Maltin), 154, 161
Disneyland television show, 179, 183–184
Disneyland theme park
    continued growth, 216
    creation of, 178–179
    development of new attractions for, 214
    film projectors used at, 216–217
    Great Moments with Mr. Lincoln, 214
    "It's a Small World," 117
    360-degree films, 186
Disney Legends Award, 229
Disney magazine, 210
Disney Studios. See Walt Disney Studio
DisneyWorld. See Walt Disney World
Distasteful scenes. See also Animation cruelty;
        Racial prejudice and racially insensitive
        works
    homosexual characters, 125
    narcotics in Chinaman's Chance, 103
    Poor Papa (Oswald series), 44
    Room Runners' risqué gags, 102
    self-censorship at Walt Disney Studio, 97
    St. Peter in The Air Race, 107
Distortion effects
    in Chinaman's Chance, 103, 138
    See How They Won, 138–139
    shadows, 36–37
Distribution. See also Mintz, Charles
    for Comicolor Classics, 122
    European distribution of Disney films, profits
        from, 175
    for Mickey Mouse, 60
Donald Duck
    "Blame it on the Samba," 173
    Clarence Nash as, 123
    Der Fuehrer's Face, 155
    The New Spirit, 147
    proposal from MGM for Anchors Aweigh, 162
    The Three Caballeros, 160–162
    Working for Peanuts, 190
Don Quixote, 130
"Das Doppelte Lottchen," 199–200
Double exposing split-screen technique, 200
Double-headed optical printer (Optical Printer
        #2), 160, 198
    award for, 198
    The Three Caballeros, 160–162
Double-printing, combination technique, 33
Driscoll, Bobby, 175
Dry runs. See Test screenings
Dueling scenes, 37
Duel in the Sun, process work on, 164–165
Dumaurier, Daphne, 202
Dumbo, 153

release, 154
Dunn, Linwood
   The Birds, 203
   King Kong, 159–160
E. I. DuPont de Nemours (Du Pont Chemical
   Company)
   celluloid density, 36
   as Laugh-O-gram Films creditor, 20
Duraflex, use in Audio-Animatronics, 213, 214
Durante, Jimmy, 162
Duvall, Earl, 116

E

Earhart, Amelia, 106, 107
Earle, Eyvind, 196
Eastman Kodak company. *See* Kodak
Ebsen, Buddy, 213
Edison Phonograph Company, 65–66
Edlund, Richard, 197
   on *Mary Poppins,* 211
Edouarde, Carl, 66–67, 68
Education (Ub's), 2–3, 6–8
   reading, 7–8
   stop-motion filming, learning, 8
   studying others' work, 9
Educational films, 190
   mass production at Disney Studio, 166
Education for Death, 155
Effects. *See* Special effects
Effects Department, Disney's, 197
Electricity for lights needed for nodal-point
   perspective camera, 197
Electronic candles, 216
Electrostatic process (copying), 193
Elephants. *See Dumbo*
Ellenshaw, Peter, 175, 207
   Davy Crockett and the River Pirates, 185
   "Davy Crockett" series, 184, 185
   influence on Ub's painting, 188
   move to the United States, 176
   A Tour of the West, 186–187
Elmer Fudd, *What's Opera, Doc?,* 140
Emmy Awards, "Operation Undersea," 184
Employment (Ub's). *See* Career and employment
The End of the Perfect Day, song reel for, 21
England, production of films in, 175
Englander, Otto, 116
   The Brave Tin Soldier, 126–127
   The Little Red Hen, 123
Enthusiasm and optimism, 14, 219, 229. *See
   also* Morale at Iwerks Studio
   challenges, 143, 181
   at Iwerks Studio, 136
   Laugh-O-gram Films, 19–20, 24
   mealtimes, 167

single-minded focus on work, 187
soundtracks, 64
at time of *Steamboat Willie,* 71
Walt after Laugh-O-gram Films bankruptcy,
   24
EPCOT (Experimental Prototype Community
   Of Tomorrow), 216
Escapist films, 154
Esthetic Camping (Laugh-O-gram Films Lafflet), 19
Ethnic caricatures, 123–124. *See also* Racial
   prejudice and racially insensitive works
Eugster, Al, 116
   The Brave Tin Soldier, 127
   cigars, 126
   at Disney, 146
   joins Iwerks Studio, 98
   The Little Red Hen, 123
   on loss of challenge for Ub, 182
   on quality, 133
Evolution of animation, 16–17
Exaggerated character action in Laugh-O-gram
   Films, 17
Exhibitor's Herald, review of *Steamboat Willie,* 70
Exhibitors Herald-World, announcement of frog
   character, 90
Experimental Prototype Community Of
   Tomorrow (EPCOT), 216
Extremes. *See also* In-between drawings or "in-
   betweening"; Pose-to-pose animation
   animation technique, 30, 77

F

Fairbanks, Douglas Sr.
   The Gaucho, 60
   as inspiration, 36–37, 54–55
   as role model for Mickey Mouse, 54–55, 57,
   60
   taking Mickey Mouse cartoons to Polynesia,
   72
Fairy tale, decision to create animated, 14
Fairy-tale series, Laugh-O-gram Films, 16, 18
Fame. *see* Credit and bylines
Family background (Ub's), 1–2
Fantasia, 148, 150, 151
Fantasound multispeaker sound system,
   150–152
Farmer, Wesley, 114
Farranger, Ray, 118
Father (Ub's). *See* Iwwerks, Eert Ubbén
"Feed the Birds" sequence, *Mary Poppins,* 212
Feld, Milton, 12
Feline characters. *See* Cats as animation subjects
Felix the Cat cartoons, 11
Female characters, androgynous appearance of,
   47

Fennel, Paul, Cartoon Films, Limited, 138
Fiddlesticks, 92, 93
Fiddlin' Around, similarities with *Fiddlesticks*, 93
Fields, W. C., 96
Film. *See also* Cameras; Stop-motion filming
   early animated advertisements, 12
   introduction by father to, 2–3
Film Ad Company. *See* Kansas City Film Ad
   Service
Film Booking Offices (FBO), 66
Film Daily
   Laugh-O-gram Films creditor, 20
   review of *Steamboat Willie*, 72
   review of *Trolley Troubles*, 45–46
Film editing, three-editing-machine, 207
Film loop cabinets, 217–218
Film projectors used at Disneyland, 216–217
Film speed and sound in cartoon films, 63
Financial problems. *See also* Bankruptcy
   at Iwerks Studio, 136
Fires at Iwerks Studio, 118–119
Firestone, 167
Fleischer, Dave, 10
Fleischer, Max, 10, 96. *See also* Betty Boop
   defections to Iwerks Studio, 98
Fleischer, Richard, 180
Fleischer Brothers, 10–11, 22. *See also* Betty
      Boop; *Out of the Inkwell* cartoons
   defections to Iwerks Studio, 98
   moving holds, 77
   recognition of black culture, 124
   rotoscoping technique, 10–11
   sound cartoons, 61
Flip the Frog, 90–104
   cameo appearance in *Play Ball*, 108
   Chinaman's Chance, 103, 124, 138
   competition from the Mouse, 104
   The Cuckoo Murder Case, 97
   development of, 94, 99–100, 102, 103
   distribution by MGM, 96
   Fiddlesticks, 92
   Flip's Lunch Room, 125
   The Milkman, 100
   naming, 90
   Phoney Express, 101
   Puddle Pranks, 94
   Room Runners, 102
   scenes from to *Alice's Orphan*, 38
   Soda Squirt, 115
   voice, 94
   What a Life!, 100
Florida, new theme park site, 216
Food Will Win the War, 155
Four Methods of Flush Riveting, 147
The Four Musicians of Bremen, Laugh-O-gram

Films, 16, 18
Fowler, Admiral Joe, 216
Fox Movietone system, 65
Frames per second (fps), 63
Frank Newman Theater chain, 12
Fred Waring and his Pennsylvanians, 172
Freeport, Illinois, immigration to United States
   by Eert Ubbén Iwwerks, 2
Freleng, Friz
   The Banker's Daughter, 48
   hired at Disney Studios, 44
   Oswald the Lucky Rabbit, 46–47
   at Warner Brothers Studios, 139
Friedman, Ed
   on closing of Iwerks Studio, 136
   on Offemann, 99
   on practical jokes, 118
   on working at Iwerks Studio, 120
The Frog Pond, 143
Frogs as animation subjects, 89. *See also* Flip
   the Frog
Frozen assets, European, 175–176
Full-length feature cartoons, manpower needed
   for production of, 145
Funeral notice (Ub's), 228

G

Gabby Goat, 140
Gags and puns. *See also* Mechanical representa-
      tions, transformations, and gags; Pranks
      and practical jokes
   The Air Race, 106–107
   Bedknobs and Broomsticks, 222–223
   eccentricity at Iwerks Studio, 131
Gran Pop Monkey, 141
   risqué, 102
   sound and sound effects, 74, 94
   visual puns, 34
   Viva Willie, 111
The Gallopin' Gaucho, 60
   musical score, 65
   similarity of *Viva Willie*, 111
   soundtrack for, 65, 68
Gandhi, Mahatma, cameo appearance, 125
Garrity, Bill, 148
The Gaucho (Douglas Fairbanks), 60
Gay, Margie (as Alice), 36
General Motors, 167
George, Eileen "Dot," joins Iwerks Studio, 95
Germany, family history in, 1–2
Gertie the Dinosaur, 9–10
Giegerich, Charlie, 90
Gifford, Frances, 153
Gillett, Burt, 82–83
   loyalty to Disney Studio, 88

Gillis, Willie, 213
Gilson, Merle, 118
    at Iwerks Studio, 89
Glenn, Glen, 116
Goff, Harper, test screening of *Seal Island,* 169
Goldenson, Leonard, 179
Golf in Slow Motion (Laugh-O-gram Films
        Lafflet), 19
Goliath II, 194
Good neighbor policy, 159
Good Scouts, 115
Goof Troop (Walt Disney Television), 35
The Goofy Movie (Walt Disney Television), 35
Gorilla Hunt, 143
Gottfredson, Floyd, 81
    loyalty to Disney Studio, 88
    near defection to Ub Iwerks Studio, 85–86,
        88
Government training films and inspirational car-
        toons, 155
Grandchildren (Ub's), more time spent with, 224
Grandparents (Ub's), 1–2
Gran Pop Monkey character, 141
Gravity-defying dances
    Flip the Frog, 92–93
    Mickey Mouse, 73
Great Depression, 85
    profits at Iwerks Studio, 136
    What a Life!, 100
Great Guns, 47
The Great Locomotive Chase, 185
Great Moments with Mr. Lincoln, 212–214
Green, Bert, 7
Grieg, Edvard, 75
Grierson, John, 156
Guns and gunsmithing, Ub's interest in, 114,
        156

H
Half-siblings (Ub's), 2
Hall of Presidents, 213, 225–226
Hamilton, Rollin "Ham"
    at Iwerks Studio, 89
    at Ub Iwerks Studio, 85
Handpainted mattes, 175
Hanna-Barbera, migration of staff from Iwerks
        Studio, 116–117
Hannah, Jack, 190
Happy Days, 136–137
Happy Harmonies series (MGM), 122
Hardaway, Bugs, 117
    joins Iwerks Studio, 95
    Phoney Express, 101
Hardaway, Hazel, recognized Ub's heart attack,
        187

Hardwicke, Lois (as Alice), 39–40
Harman, Hugh
    Arabian Nights, 25
    Bosko, 124
    at Disney Brothers', 30
    hiring at MGM, 122
    at Laugh-O-gram Films, 15
    mice sketches, 54
    mouse character in Oswald cartoons, 48
    Ub's return to Disney, 146
Hathcock, Jerry, Cartoon Films, Limited, 138
Haunted Mansion attraction, 214–215
The Headless Horseman, 130
Heart attack (Ub's), 187
Heart problems (Ub's)
    arteriosclerosis, 227
    heart attack, 187
Hedren, Tippi, *The Birds,* 203–205
Heineger, Ernst, 215–216
Heineger, Jeanne, 216
Hell's Bells, 79, 202
Hell's Fire, 114, 115
Help wanted advertisement in *Los Angeles Times,*
        90
Hench, John, 64
Hepburn, Audrey, 209
Herbert T. Kalmus Gold Medal, Society of
        Motion Picture and Television Engineers
        (SMPTE), 198
High school (Ub's), 3
Hill, Howard, 113
"His Master's Voice," 65–66
Hispanic characters, insensitive treatment in car-
        toons, 125
Hitchcock, Alfred, 162, 190, 202
    gift to Ub, 206–207
Hoag, Bob, *The Birds,* 203
Hobbies (Ub's). *See* Interests and hobbies
Hollywood Party, cameo appearance by Mickey
        Mouse, 162
Homes (Ub's)
    2008 Chelsea Avenue, Kansas City, 25
    Dixie Canyon, Sherman Oaks, 135
    Mary Ellen Avenue, Van Nuys, 182
    Murietta Avenue, Sherman Oaks, 206
    rental after arriving in California, 30
Homosexual characters, 125
Horace Horsecollar, 53
Horizontal bar technique for recording sound, 68
Horizontal multiplane camera, Ub builds,
        129–130
The Horse on the Merry Go Round, 141
Horseshoe matches at Iwerks Studio, 95–96
Horsley, David, formation of Universal Film
        Manufacturing Company, 66

Hot Dog, 59
Howard, Cal, 116, 140
How Motion Pictures Are Made, 7
How to Draw for the Movies (McCrory), 7
Hurd, Earl, 10

I

Illinois, immigration to United States by Eert
    Ubbén Iwwerks, 2
Immigration to United States by Eert Ubbén
    Iwwerks, 2
Impatience with staff (Ub's), 167
In-between drawings or "in-betweening," 8, 56,
    76–77. See also Extremes; Pose-to-pose
    animation
Independence for Ub, 84, 85–104
Industrial films, mass production at Disney
    Studio, 166–167
Innocence. See also Disney, Walt (naïveté)
    Dumbo, 154
Innovations. See Animation innovations;
    Technical innovations
Insects as animation subjects, 79, 172
Inspiration
    after landing MGM contract, 96
    from British illustrators, 141
    for new cartoon character, 53
    The Skeleton Dance, 75
Inspirational cartoons, government, 155
Instructional films, 156
    government, 147, 155–157
Insultin' the Sultan, 125
Integration of live action and animation. See
    Combination of live action with animation
Intercollegiate Press, Laugh-O-gram Films credi-
    tor, 20
Interests and hobbies (Ub's). See also
    Automobiles; Aviation
    antique cars, Ub's interest in, 182
    archery, 113–114
    astronomy, 113
    bicycle, 182
    bowling, 181
    crossbow, 114
    games of skill, 113
    guns, 114, 156
    gunsmithing, 156
    horseshoes, 95–96
    marksmanship, 114
    mechanical design, 142
    model airplanes, 111, 158
    motorcycles, 182
    painting, 188
    photography, 135, 188
    sailing, 142–143

Interruptions (for Ub), 201–202
Inventions, Eert Ubbén Iwwerks and, 2–3
Iowa, Eert Ubbén Iwwerks moves to, 2
Ising, Rudolph ("Rudy")
    Arabian Nights, 25
    Bosko, 124
    on choice of rural settings and backgrounds,
        38
    at Disney Brothers', 30
    explanation of combination technique, 32–33
    hiring at MGM, 122
    at Laugh-O-gram Films, 15, 16, 19
Isis Theater, Kansas City, 21
Isle of Naboombu sequence, Bedknobs and
    Broomsticks, 222
Isolationist stories
    Balloonland, 131–132
    Jack Frost, 132
"It's a Small World" at Disneyland, 117
Iwerks, Dave
    model airplanes with Ub, 111
    more time spent with, 224
    Ub's death, 227
    working at Disney's Special Effects Division,
        179
Iwerks, Don
    as baby, 55
    on father's lack of patience, 198–199
    on grandfather, 134
    on grandmother, 134–135
    hands used as models for Lincoln
        animatronics, 213
    meals with father, 167
    model airplanes with Ub, 111
    more time spent with, 224
    as toddler, 100
    on Ub as father, 135
    on Ub returning to Disney Studio, 147
    on Ub's antique gun interests, 114
    on Ub's archery interests, 113
    Ub's death, 227
    on Ub's reaction to Walt's death, 220
    Ub's relationship and involvement with,
        179–180
    on Ub's spirit, 229
    on Ub's value of time, 182
    working at Disney's Process Lab, 179
    work on America the Beautiful, 189
Iwerks, Mildred (née Mildred Sarah Henderson)
    courtship and marriage, 44
    creativity, 188
    death of, 228
    family stress, 55
    gardening, 188
    gift sent from Alfred Hitchcock, 206

meeting, 43
more time spent with, 224
Steamboat Willie dry run, 63–64
Ub's death, 227
on Ub's relationship with Walt, 83
Ub's return to Disney, 147
on Ub's sailboat, 143
Iwerks, Ub, name change after arrival in
California, 30
Iwerks Studio. *See* Ub Iwerks Studio
Iwwerks, Carolyn (née Carolyn Lehman Miller),
2
Iwwerks, Deborah (née Deborah Mayo Pierce), 2
Iwwerks, Deborah Mae, 2
Iwwerks, Eert Ubben, 2
Iwwerks, Eert Ubbén, 1–2
death, 134
desertion of Laura May and Ubbe, 3
divorces, 2
immigration to United States, 1
marriages, 2
vocation and occupations, 2–3
Iwwerks, Grietjke, 1
Iwwerks, Laura May (née Laura May Wagner), 2
desertion by Eert Iwwerks, 3
embitterment about Eert Iwwerks, 134
move to new home in California, 29
move to new home in Kansas City with Ubbe,
25
move to rest home, 135
Parkinson's disease, 134
reaction to Ub's marriage, 55
suicide attempt, 55
support of, 3, 5, 15
Walt moves in with, 23–24
Iwwerks, Lillian Pierce, 2
Iwwerks, Maike, 1–2
Iwwerks, Ubbe Eert
birth of, 2
name change to Ub Iwerks, 30
Iwwerks, Ubbe Reemt, 1–2
Iwwerks-Disney Commercial Artists, 5
bankruptcy, 6
first paying client, 5
Restaurant News (newspaper), 5

J

J. R. Bray Studio, 10
Jack and the Beanstalk
Comicolor Classic version, 122
Laugh-O-gram Films version, 16, 18
Jack Frost, 132–133
Jackson, Wilfred
loyalty to Disney Studio, 88
new at Disney Studio, 59

Steamboat Willie, 62–63, 64, 69
Jack the Giant Killer, Laugh-O-gram Films, 18
Jazz music, 20, 124
The Jazz Singer, 60
Jelly Roll Morton music, 115
Jenkins Music Company, Kansas City, 20
Jerry the Mouse, 162
Johnny Tremain, 188–189
Johnson, Robert, 119
Johnson and Johnson, 167
Johnston, Ollie
The Jungle Book, 196
Mary Poppins, 211
on Mickey's character, 57, 58
on Ub's animation, 77
on Ub's return to Disney, 150
on Xerographic process, 194
Joke films. *See* Laugh-O-gram Films
Jokes. *See* Gags and puns; Pranks and practical
jokes
"Jolly Holiday" sequence, *Mary Poppins,* 210,
211, 222
Jolson, Al, 61
Jones, Chuck, 116
Acme Tool Company's impression on,
112–113
courtship and marriage to Dorothy Webster,
112
fired from Iwerks Studio, 98
hired at Iwerks Studio, 91
hired at Iwerks Studio (second time), 112
on inking, 192–193
relationship with Bob Clampett, 139–140
on Ub's aerial photography, 158
on Ub's influence, 113
on Ub's technical experimentation, 131
on Walt's and Ub's work, 78–79
at Warner Brothers Studios, 139
What's Opera, Doc?, 140
Jones, Jennifer, 164–165
Julius (*Alice's Wonderland* series), 33, 34
animation cruelty, 38
constant movement of, 37
dueling scenes, 37
gags, 34
mechanical transformations and gags, 37
Jump-cuts, 34, 184
The Jungle Book, 196
Justice, Bill, 190
Mary Poppins, 210, 211, 212
Juvenile characters in Iwerks Studio works,
100

K

Kahl, Milt, *Mary Poppins,* 211

Kansas City, Missouri
 Eert Ubbén Iwwerks moves to, 2
 moving from, 29
 parodied in "Laugh-O-grams," 12–14
 police department, parody of, 14
 political parodies, 13–14
 progress in, 3
 return after farm job, 3–4
 Swope Park, 3, 18–19
Kansas City Film Ad Company. *See* Kansas City
  Film Ad Service
Kansas City Film Ad Service, 218–219
 Friz Freleng hired by Disney Studios, 44
 hiring by, 6
 work at, 6–15
Kansas City Slide Company. *See* Kansas City
  Film Ad Service
"Kansas City Spring Clean Up" (Laugh-O-
  gram), 14
Kansas City Star newspaper, 14
 advertisement for Laugh-O-gram Films, 18
 job advertisement in, 6
 and WDAF radio, 21
Karnival Kid, 221
Kastner, Erich, 199–200
Kaufman, J. B., *Walt in Wonderland,* 30, 36–37,
  47
Kausler, Mark, 68
 on closing of Iwerks Studio, 136
 on relationship between Ub and Walt, 219
 on Ub and Flip the Frog, 224–225
 on Ub leaving, 93
 on Ub's frustrations, 77–78
 on Ub's straight-ahead drawing, 77
Keaton, Buster, 62
Kettering, Tom, 227
Kilmer, Joyce, 172
Kimball, Ward, 156–157
 3D cartoon, 190
 Bedknobs and Broomsticks, 222
 Cinderella, 174
 Mary Poppins, 211
 trip to Expo '67 with Ub, 225
King Features Syndicate, Mickey mouse comic
  strip, 81
King Kong, 159–160
A Kiss in the Dark (Victor Herbert), song reel
  for, 21
Kloepper, Adolph, at Laugh-O-gram Films, 15,
  20
Knickerbocker pants (knickers), 36
Kodak
 dye-transfer process, 163–164
 16mm Cine Kodak Special cameras,
  186

Ko-ko the Clown, *Out of the Inkwell* (Fleischer
  Brothers), 10–11
Kopietz, Fred, 90, 116
Krazy Kat cartoons, 11, 141
 Ignatz the mouse, 53

L

Labor organization. *See* Organized labor
Laemmle, Carl
 formation of Universal Film Manufacturing
  Company, 66
 hiring Walter Lantz for Oswald cartoons,
  50–51
 Oswald character idea, 40, 42
 predictions on synchronized sound, 60–61
 taking Oswald from Mintz, 141
Lafflets, 19
Lankershim Lanes, North Hollywood, 181
Lansbury, Angela, 222
Lantz, Walter, 50–51
 on sound in cartoons, 73
 use of black jazz music, 124
Larson, Eric, *Mary Poppins,* 211
Laugh-O-gram Films. *See also Alice's Wonderland*
 baby pictures, 18
 bankruptcy, 24
 equipment purchased by Arabian Nights, 25
 financial troubles, 19–20, 23–24
 incorporated, 15
 lightning-artist technique, 19
 purchase of used Universal camera, 18
 reverse filming, 19
 Ub joins, 16
Leather Workers Journal, 5
Leave it to John, 139
Lessing, Roy and Gunther, 86
LeSueur, Lucille. *See* Crawford, Joan
Lettering
 first job as commercial artist, 4
 at Laugh-O-gram Films, 16
Lighting
 Great Moments with Mr. Lincoln, 214
 for nodal-point perspective camera, 197
The Light in the Forest, 185
Lightning-artist technique
 Alice the Peacemaker, 33
 creation of, 12
 at Laugh-O-gram Films, 19
Limbs (animated characters'). *See* Detachable
  appendages
Limited animation technique, 8
Lincoln, Abraham, 212
 Hall of Presidents, 213, 225–226
Lindbergh, Charles, 55, 57
Linearity of xerographic process cartoons,

196
Liquid optical printer, creation of, 170
Little Black Sambo, 124
Little Orphan Willie, scenes from to *Alice's Orphan*, 38
The Little Red Hen, 123
Little Red Riding Hood, Laugh-O-gram Films, 16
"Little Toot," 172
Live action. *See* Combination of live action with animation
Live action films, Disney Studio's switch to, 173–174
Lloyd, Harold, *Luke's Trolley Troubles*, 45
Looney Tunes, similarity of titles to Willie Whopper, 105
Los Angeles Times, help wanted advertisement in, 90
"Lost on a Desert Island" (comic strip), 81
Lounsbery, John, *Mary Poppins*, 211
Love, Ed, 128
Lowerre, Jimmy, 8
Lucerne, Switzerland, 215–216
Luke's Trolley Troubles (Harold Lloyd), 45
Lung cancer, Walt's, 220
Lutz, Edwin G., 7–8, 30
Luz, Dora, 160–161
Lycett, Eustace, 187
Lyon, Red, at Laugh-O-gram Films, 15

M

Mace, Leslie, as salesman at Laugh-O-gram Films, 15, 16
MacQueen, Scott, discovery of newsreel sequence from *Up in Arms*, 162
Magic of the Rails, 215–216
Maltin, Leonard
    on *Cinderella*, 174
    identification of newsreel sequence from *Up in Arms*, 162
    introduction by, vi–vii
    Of Mice and Magic, 109, 141
    on *Narrow Margin*, 180
    on *The Office Boy*, 102–103
    on the Pink Elephants' sequence, 154
    on relationship between Ub and Walt, 229
    on *So Dear to My Heart*, 173–174
    on *The Three Caballeros*, 161
    Video and Movie Guide (Maltin), 180
Mandatory overtime, union-busting, 129
Mandatory weekend shifts in animation, 127–128
March of the Dwarfs (Grieg), 75
Marcus, Mike, 56
Marketing and promotion. *See also* Merchandising

Disneyland television show, 183–184
    high-quality color still prints, 163–164
    lack of skill by Ub, 92
    with Margie Gay as Alice, 36
    Oswald the Lucky Rabbit, 50
    20,000 Leagues Under the Sea, 183–184
    Walt as focal point for, 80
Marksmanship, Ub's interest in, 114
Martha, Just a Plain Old-fashioned Name (Joe Sanders composition), song reel for, 21, 22
Marx Brothers, 96
Mary Poppins, 209–210
Mary's Little Lamb, 125
Mature cartoons, creation at Iwerks Studio, 111
Maxwell, Carman "Max"
    Arabian Nights, 25
    at Laugh-O-gram Films, 15
McCay, Winsor, *Gertie the Dinosaur*, 9–10
McCrory, John Robert, *How to Draw for the Movies*, 7
McCrum, Thomas
    correspondence, 30
    Tommy Tucker's Tooth, 20, 41–42
    The Mechanical Cow, 47
Mechanical design, Ub's fascination with, 142
Mechanical representations, transformations, and gags, 37. *See also* Detachable appendages
    The Air Race, 106–107
    Alice comedies, 47
    Gran Pop Monkey, 141
    Laugh-O-grams, 12
The Mechanical Cow, 47
    Stop That Tank: The BOYS Anti-Tank Rifle, 156–157
Meeker cartoon animals, 53
Melody, 190
Melody Time, 171–172
Merchandising
    Davy Crockett, 184, 189
    Mickey Mouse, 72
Merritt, Russell
    on Disney's move to California, 24
    Walt in Wonderland, 30, 36–37, 47
Merry Mannequins, 141
Messmer, Otto, 11
Metamorphosis. *See also* Anthropomorphic elements
    backgrounds in *Jack and the Beanstalk*, 123
    The Three Caballeros, 161
Metro-Goldwyn-Mayer. *See* MGM
Metzinger, Margaret, 43
MGM
    cartoon films, 96
    Comicolor Classic Series, disinterest in, 121–122

distribution of Flip the Frog, 96
Donald Duck, proposal for use of, 162
and Flip the Frog, 94
glossiness, 96, 97
Happy Harmonies, 122
prospects of distribution by, 85
Mice, Walt's fondness for, 54
Mice as animation subjects. *See also* Mickey
    Mouse; Minnie Mouse
first ideas for Disney Studios, 53
in Flip the Frog cartoon, 93
Jerry the Mouse, 162
Krazy Kat cartoons, Ignatz the mouse, 53
Oswald cartoons, 48
Mickey Mouse
Academy Award for, 147
The Band Concert, 93
The Barn Dance, 68, 73
becoming civilized, 82–83
cameo in *Hollywood Party,* 162
The Castaway, 81
character development, 54–55, 57
creation of Minnie, 54
cruel streak, 58
development of appearance, 60
eyes, 60
The Gallopin' Gaucho, 60, 111
head and ears, 69
impersonation of Paderewski, 74
merchandise, 72
naming, 54
The New York Times Magazine on, 72
The Opry House, 73–74
original ideas, 53–54
personality, 58
Plane Crazy, 55, 158
popularity, 72, 79
The Runaway Brain, 35
shoes, 60
Steamboat Willie, 62
tail, 58
Mickey Mouse Club, 72–73
television show, 207
Mickey Mouse Park, plans for, 178
Middle Eastern characters, insensitive treatment
    in cartoons, 125
Midnight Frolics, 143
Midwestern background and humor, 37, 43
    So Dear to My Heart, 173–174
The Milkman, 100
Mills, Hayley, 198, 199–200
Milotte, Alfred and Elma, 168–169
Minnie Mouse
creation of, 54
The Gallopin' Gaucho, 60

Mintz, Charles. *see also* Charles Mintz Studio
Color Rhapsodies, 141
contract with Virginia Davis, 35
criticism of Alice series, 33, 38–39
criticism of *Poor Papa,* 44–45
on Julius, 33, 39
marriage to Margaret Winkler, 27
planning for Oswald the Rabbit, 39
renegotiation of Oswald contract, 50
signing contract with Universal, 42
Universal Studios' decision to launch cartoon
    series, 40
Miranda, Aurora, 160–161
Mission Control at Disneyland, 217
Missouri. *See* Kansas City, Missouri
Mobile perspective effect, 56
Model airplanes, Ub's interest in, 111, 158
Model sheets, use of, 17, 30
Montreal Expo '67, 225
Moon Cabriolet roadster, Walt's, 67–68
Moore, Fred, 156–157
Morale at Iwerks Studio, 128
Ofemann's effect on, 99
Morganthau, Henry, 147
Mortimer (Walt's mouse friend), 54
Moser Studio, 7
Mother (Ub's). *See* Iwwerks, Laura May
Motion in animation. *See also* Gravity-defying
    dances
constant, 30, 37
implication of, 69
straight-ahead drawing, 77
Motion Picture Magazine, 7
Motion Picture News
Laugh-O-gram Films creditor, 20
review of on *Great Guns,* 48
Motion Picture Research Council, 183
Motivation, Mickey's character, 57–58
Motivation, Ub's lack of enthusiasm, 82
Motorcycles, Ub's interest in, 25, 182
Motor drive for stop-motion filming, 8–9
Mouse characters. *See* Mice as animation
    subjects
Move
of Disney Studio, 149
of Iwerks Studio, 141
Movement in animation. *See* Motion in
animation
"Movie Cartoons Come to Life" (*Popular
    Mechanics* magazine), 150
Movie theater organists, 21
Moving Picture World
review of *Alice Cans the Cannibals,* 34
review of *Great Guns,* 48
Multifocused, multiplane camera, 149

Multiphonic sound, 151
Multiplane camera technology, 129–130, 150
   vertical multiplane camera, 148–149
Munchausen, Baron von, 105
Music and musical arrangements. *See also*
     Soundtracks; Stalling, Carl
   "Bumble Boogie," 171–172
   jazz music, 20
   recording sessions in New York for *Steamboat*
     Willie, 65, 67–70
   Sherman Brothers, *Mary Poppins*, 210, 212
   Song-O-Reel (song reels), 21–22
Mustache-growing contest, 36
Muybridge, Eadward, 7
My Fair Lady, 209
Mysteries of the Deep, 169–170

N

Naïveté (Walt's). *See* Disney, Walt
Name change after arrival in California, 30
Naming
   Flip the Frog, 90
   Mickey Mouse, 54
   Minnie Mouse, 54
   Walt Disney World, 226
Narcotics in *Chinaman's Chance*, 103
Narrow Margin, 180
Nash, Clarence "Ducky," 123
National film Board of Canada, 156–157
Nature films, 168–171
Natwick, Grim, 91, 116. *See also* Willie
     Whopper
   Cartoon Films, Limited, 138
   development of Flip the Frog, 103
   at Disney, 146
   distortion effects, 103
   fresh style of, 100
   impact on Iwerks Studio, 99
   increased responsibilities at Iwerks Studio,
     118
   Jack and the Beanstalk, 123
   Jack Frost, 132
   joins Iwerks Studio, 98
   relationship with Ub, 100–101
   supervisory role at Iwerks Studio, 101
   unionization of animators, 128–129
The Navigator (Buster, Keaton), 62
Nelson, William Rockhill, 14
Newman Theater. *See also* Laugh-O-gram Films
   animated ads for, 11
News events coverage, Laugh-O-gram Films, 18
The New Spirit, 147
Newsreel filming, Laugh-O-gram Films, 18
Newton, Robert, 175
New York

Pat Powers introduces Walt to, 66
sound recording studios, 65
The New Yorker, on *The Three Caballeros*,
   161–162
The New York Times
   Laugh-O-gram Films creditor, 20
   review of *Steamboat Willie*, 70, 72
New York World's Fair, 212
"Nine Old Men," 58, 149
   Mary Poppins, 211
   1941 (Spielberg's), 154
Nitrate cels, 118
Noise in the workplace, Ub's dislike of, 119,
   201
Nolan, William C. (Bill), 11, 55–56
Northeast High School, 3
Nudity
   Jack Frost, 132
   Room Runners, 102
Nugent, Elliott, 162

O

Obituary (Ub's), 228
The Ocean Hop, 49, 106, 158
O'Connor, Ken, 153
   on Ub's genius, 182–183, 229
O'Day, Dawn (as Alice), 35, 36
Offemann, Emile, 98–99, 117
   increased responsibilities, 129
   overruled by Ub, 117
   work conditions, effect on, 127–128
The Office Boy, 102
Of Mice and Magic (Maltin), 109
Oh Teacher, 46
Old Mill Carbon and Ribbon Co., Laugh-O-
   gram Films creditor, 20
Oliver Twist, 136
On Borrowed Time (Watkin), 176
100 Men and a Girl, 151
101 Dalmatians, xerographic process, 195, 196
One-Eyed Pete character, 34
One-person process for stop-motion filming, 8–9
"Operation Undersea," 184
Opium in *Chinaman's Chance*, 103
The Opry House, 73–74
Optical effects
   Cinderella, 174
   20,000 Leagues Under the Sea, 180
Optical Printer #2. *See* Double-headed optical
   printer (Optical Printer #2)
Organized labor
   Disney strike, 151
   unionization of animators, 128–129
Orlando, Florida, selection of site for theme
   park, 216

Orphan boy character in Flip the Frog cartoons, 100
Ostfriesland, Germany, 1–2
Oswald the Lucky Rabbit cartoons, 41–53
  All Wet, 48
  The Banker's Daughter, 48
  completion of last, 59
  differences from Alice comedies, 43
  Great Guns, 47
  Hot Dog, 59
  The Mechanical Cow, 47
  metamorphosis of character, 46
  The Ocean Hop, 49, 106, 158
  Oh Teacher, 46
  Poor Papa, 44
  renegotiation of contract, 50–51
  taken away from Mintz, 141
  Trolley Troubles, 45–46
  Ubbe's Beach Story, 48
Otto, Bob, 170
  nodal-point perspective camera, 196
Out of the Inkwell cartoons (Fleischer Brothers), 10–11, 22

P

Pabian, Jim
  hired at Iwerks Studio, 90–91
  on learning from Ub, 101
Pacific Title and Art Studio, The Silent Flyer, 41
Paderewski, Mickey's impersonation of, 74
Paint formulas, development of, 48–49
Painting
  Eert Ubbén Iwwerks and, 2–3
  Ub's interest in, 188
Paper dolls, use in animation, 7
The Parent Trap, 199–200
Paris, World's Fair in, 186
Parker, Fess, 184–185
Passion. See Enthusiasm and optimism
Patents
  Xerographic Developing Apparatus, 194
  Xerographic Fusing Apparatus, 193
Patience, Ub's lack of, 198–199
Patin, Ray, 145
Pearl Harbor, attack on, 154
Pearl Jam, influence of Stalling's music on, 117
Peck, Gregory, 164
Peet, Bill, 194
Peg Leg Pete
  The Banker's Daughter, 48
  The Ocean Hop, 49
Peg registration, 8
Pellet gun received by Ub in Christmas gift exchange, 114

Pendergast, James, 13–14
  death of Eert Iwwerks, 134
Penguins, Mary Poppins, 210
Penner, Joe, 125
Perchlorethylene, in wet-gate technique, 169–170
Perfectionism, Walt's sense for technical imperfections, 171
Perfectionism (Ub's), 101, 167
  photography, 135
  production control department at Disney, 148
Personality animation, 58, 174
Personnel issues, Ub's handling of, 117–118
Perspective in animation
  The Cuckoo Murder Case, 97
  Good Scouts, 115
  mobile perspective effect, 56
  moving-perspective street background, 100
  Plane Crazy, 56
  single-vanishing-point effect, 97
  three-dimensional perspective rendering, 56
Perspective in film
  forced perspective effects, 196
  nodal-point perspective camera, 196
Perspective runs, 8
Pesmen, Louis, 4
Pesmen-Rubin Commercial Art Studio, 4–5, 225
Pete characters
  Alice comedies, 34
  The Banker's Daughter, 48
  Great Guns, 48
Peg Leg Pete, 48, 49
  Steamboat Willie, 68, 70
Pete the policebear, 48
Petticoat Lane animated advertisements, 13
Pfeiffer, Walt
  father of, 5
  at Laugh-O-gram Films, 15
Phone in The Cuckoo Murder Case, 97
Phoney Express, 101
Phonographic system inventions, Eert Ubbén Iwwerks and, 2–3
Photochemical mattes, 211
Photoelectric control system in Audio-Animatronics, 213
Photographic process, composite of matte and live-action elements, 175–176
Photography. See also Kodak
  anamorphic wide-angle lens, 196
  animation camera, smoother-operating drive on, 46
  Circarama, 186–187
  darkroom in Ub's garage, 135
  Don Iwerks interest in, 179
  Eert Ubbén Iwwerks and, 2–3

Kodak dye-transfer process, 163–164
trips with Mildred after heart attack, 188
Piano in *The Opry House,* 74
Pictorial Clubs
    attachment of Lafflets in reels shipped to, 19
    bankruptcy, 19
    distribution of Laugh-O-gram Films fairy-tale
        series, 16
Pincushion Man, *Balloonland,* 131–132
"Pink Elephants on Parade" sequence in *Dumbo,*
    153–154
Pinocchio, 145
A Pirate for a Day (Laugh-O-gram Films
    Lafflet), 19
Pirates of the Caribbean ride at Disneyland, 216
Plane Crazy, 55–58, 158
    comic strip based on, 81
    completion in record time, 56–57
    inspiration for, 55
    musical score, 65
    quantity of drawings, 55–56
    similarity of *The Air Race,* 107
    soundtrack for, 65, 68
Play Ball, 108
Pohl, Wadsworth E., 211
    Mary Poppins, 212
Police department, parodied in "Laugh-O-
    grams," 14
Political issues, parodied in "Laugh-O-grams,"
    13–14
Politics at work
    with Bill Anderson, 163, 187
    at Warner Brothers Studios, 139–140
Pollyanna, 198
Poor Papa, 44
"Poppins Revisited," *Disney* magazine, 210
Popularity of Mickey Mouse, 72, 79
Popular Mechanics magazine, 150
Popular Science magazine, 156–157
Porky in Wackyland, comparison to *Stratos-Fear,*
    109
Porky Pig
    dislike by Ub, 140
    Porky and Gabby, 140
    Porky in Wackyland, 109
    Porky's Superservice, 140
    projects subcontracted to Ub, 139
Porter, Eleanor, 198
Pose-to-pose animation. *See also* In-between
        drawings or "in-betweening"
    animation techniques, 30
    Walt's preference for, 77–78
Post-synchronization of soundtracks
    The Barn Dance, 73
    Steamboat Willie, 65, 67–70

Pothole problems in Kansas City parodied in
    "Laugh-O-grams," 12–13
Pour Vous (magazine), 79–80
Powers, Patrick A., 65–66
    behind Ub's defection, 85–89
    Celebrity Pictures, 96
    criticism of *The Brave Tin Soldier,* 127
    criticism of *The Skeleton Dance,* 127
    fronting capital, 95
    profits on Iwerks Studio, 136
    recruiting more staff for Iwerks Studio, 98
    secretly lures Ub away from Disney, 85
    on *The Skeleton Dance,* 78
    uses Ub to leverage deal with Walt, 87
Pranks and practical jokes
    archery gag, 113
    date with Margaret Metzinger, 43
    at Iwerks Studio, 118, 128
Prequel to *Davy Crockett: King of the Wild
        Frontier,* 185
Pressures on Ub
    family. *See* Iwwerks, Laura May (née Laura
        May Wagner)
    from Walt, 81–83
Presynchronized music, 73
Printer #2. *See* Double-headed optical printer
        (Optical Printer #2)
Printing
    bi-packing, 23
    color still prints, 163–164
    Disney Optical Printing Department, 160
    double headed printer. *See* Double-headed
        optical printer (Optical Printer #2)
    double-printing, 33
    liquid optical printer, creation of, 170
    refining skills, 25
    Triple-Head Optical Printer (#10), 198
Process Lab at Disney
    Don Iwerks working in, 179
    Ub's move to, 163
Process photography, 182–183
Production control department at Disney, Ub's
    work in, 148
Profits
    CPF (cost-per-foot), 166
    distribution of European distribution of
        Disney films, 175
    at Iwerks Studio, 135–136
PROJECT FLORIDA, 216. *See also* Walt
    Disney World
Projection equipment at theme parks, 223
    film loop cabinets, 217–218
Promotion by studios. *See* Marketing and promo-
    tion
Prop effects, 210

Publicity. *See* Marketing and promotion
Public transportation system, parodied in
   "Laugh-O-grams," 12–13
Puppets, use in animation, 7
Puss in Boots, Laugh-O-gram Films, 18

R

Rabbits as animation subjects. *See* Bugs Bunny;
   Oswald the Lucky Rabbit
Racial prejudice and racially insensitive works,
   124
   Chinaman's Chance, 103
Radio station WDAF, 21
Ragtime musicians, 20
Rain effects, 150
   Bambi, 155–156
   "Little Toot," 172
Rank Organization, 183
Ray Patin Animation training school, 145
RCA Photophone, 65
Reading and research, 7–8, 182
   inspiration for *The Skeleton Dance,* 75–76
Recording devices. *See also* Sound techniques;
   Sound technology; Soundtracks
   Eert Ubbén Iwwerks and, 2–3
   Iwerks Studio, 95
Recording sessions in New York for *Steamboat
   Willie,* 65, 67–70
Record number of drawings on *Plane Crazy,*
   55–56
Red Line train tracks, studio's proximity to, 95
Reglar Fellars comic strip, 136–137
Relationships (Ub's)
   with family after heart attack, 187–188
   with father, 134
   with mother. *See* Iwwerks, Laura May (née
      Laura May Wagner)
   with sons, 135, 179–180
   with Walt. *See* Disney, Walt
The Reluctant Dragon, 152–153
Reopening of Iwerks Studio, 138
Rescued (Laugh-O-gram Films Lafflet), 19
Research. *See* Reading and research
Resignation from Disney Studio (Ub's), 86–87
Respect for Ub, from colleagues, 189
Restaurant News (newspaper), 5
Reuben's Big Day (Laugh-O-gram Films Lafflet),
   19
Reusing scenes from other movies, 194
Reverse filming and printing
   at Laugh-O-gram Films, 19
   Mary Poppins, 210, 212
Reverse images, 206
Reversing cycles in animation, 17
Reviews

Film Daily on *Steamboat Willie,* 72
Film Daily on *Trolley Troubles,* 45–46
Motion Picture News on *Great Guns,* 48
Moving Picture World on *Alice Cans the
   Cannibals,* 34
Moving Picture World on *Great Guns,* 48
The New York Times on *Steamboat Willie,* 70,
   72
   on *The Skeleton Dance,* 78
Variety on *Steamboat Willie,* 72
Reynolds, Aletha, at Laugh-O-gram Films, 15
Richardson, Leroy
   basement projects, 130
   creation of model airplanes for *Victory Through
      Air Power,* 158
   Don Iwerks working for, 179
   help in building crossbow, 114
   helping Ub with archery gag, 113
   helps Ub build sailboat, 143
   joins Iwerks Studio, 111–112
Risqué gags, 102
RKO
   absorption of Film Booking Offices (FBO),
      66
   Seal Island, 169
Robin Hood, distorted shadow device, 36–37
Robot animals. *See* Mechanical representations,
   transformations, and gags
Rob Roy, The Highland Rogue, 175, 176
Rockefeller, Nelson, 159
Rogers, Wathel, 210
   Audio-Animatronics, 213
Romance, Oswald cartoons, 43
Roosevelt, Franklin, *Victory Through Air Power,*
   159
Rotoscoping technique, 10–11
   Iwerks Studio, 133
Rowlandson (English cartoonist), 75–76
Roxy Theater, New York City, *Trolley Troubles,*
   45–46
"Rubber-hose" style of animation. *See also*
   Oswald the Lucky Rabbit cartoons
   Columbia cartoons, 143
   The Runaway Brain, 35
Rural settings and backgrounds, 37–38. *See also*
   Oswald the Lucky Rabbit cartoons

S

Sabotage (Hitchcock), 162, 202
Sailboat, Ub builds, 143
Sailing, Ub's interest in, 142–143
St. Joseph's Hospital, Walt's admission to, 220
St. Peter in *The Air Race,* 107
Salaries in animation positions, 127
Saludos Amigos, 159, 160

Sanders, Joe L., 20–21
Schlesinger, Leon
  politics at Warner Brothers Studios, 139–140
  promotion of Bob Clampett, 140
  subcontracting with Disney Studio, 41
Schooling, 3
Schutte Lumber, Laugh-O-gram Films creditor, 20
Scotland, Arkansas, Ub's employment on farm in, 3
Scratches on film, 169–170, 217
Seal Island, 168–169
Sears, Ted, 116
Secrecy around Mickey Mouse, 55, 56, 59
See How They Won, 138–139
Sense of humor. *See also* Animation cruelty;
      Gags and puns; Midwestern background
      and humor; Pranks and practical jokes
  eccentricity at Iwerks Studio, 131
Sequels
  Davy Crockett: King of the Wild Frontier, 185
  Saludos Amigos, 160–161
  See How They Won, 139
  Tommy Tucker's Tooth, 41–42
  Walt's aversion to, 185
Settings. *See* Backgrounds and settings
Seven Dwarfs. *See also Snow White and the
      Seven Dwarfs*
  The Winged Scourge, 147
Sewell, Hazel, secretly working on Mickey
      Mouse, 56
Sewell, Marjorie, in *Clara Cleans her Teeth*,
      41–42
Sexual content in cartoons. *See also* Betty Boop
  Room Runners, 102
Shannon, Leonard, 210
Sharpsteen, Ben
  bringing Ub back to Disney, 160
  called by Ub about instruction, 146
  Cinderella, 174
  nature films, 168–169
  on Ub's opinions of 16mm film blown up to
      35mm, 168
  Ub's return to Disney, 147
Sherman Brothers, *Mary Poppins*, 210, 212
Shortcut style, *Alice the Peacemaker*, 33
Short subjects. *See also Alice's Wonderland* series
  comedic films. *See* Lafflets; Laugh-O-gram
      Films
  Song-O-Reel (song reels), 21–22
  testing new technology, 194
  Tommy Tucker's Tooth, 20
Siblings, 2
Signature logo, 80–81
The Silent Flyer (Pacific Title and Art Studio), 41

Silly Symphonies, 74–76
  Autumn, 84
  creative freedom for Ub, 81–82
  Hell's Bells, 79, 202
  "Mickey Mouse Presents . . .", 79
  The Skeleton Dance, 75–78
  Summer, 82–83, 89–90
  Who Killed Cock Robin?, 162, 202
Sinbad the Sailor, 125
Single-vanishing-point effect, 97
16mm Cine Kodak Special cameras, 186
16mm film blown up to 35mm, 168–169
The Skeleton Dance, 75–78
  Pat Power's criticism of, 127
Skeleton Frolic, 141
Sleeping Beauty, 196
Smith, Dave
  on Ub's preference for quiet, 201
  on Ub's resignation, 88
Smith, Ethel, "Blame it on the Samba," 173
Smith, Win, 81
Snappy characters. *See* Oswald the Lucky Rabbit
Snow White and the Seven Dwarfs, 145
  opening similar to Comicolor Classic series,
      121
Soap-bubble effect in *Cinderella*, 174
Society of Motion Picture and Television
      Engineers (SMPTE), Herbert T. Kalmus
      Gold Medal, 198
Sociological approach of Iwerks Studio,
      131–132
Soda Squirt, 115
So Dear to My Heart, 173–174, 213
Sodium prism system, 183, 204
  backup prism, 221–222
  Bedknobs and Broomsticks, 222
Sodium screen process
  Mary Poppins, 211–212
  The Parent Trap, 200
Sodium Traveling Matte Process, 183
  Mary Poppins, 211, 212
Somerville, Ralph, 117
  on stop-motion animation, 130–131
Sommerfield, Virginia, 167, 181, 202
Song-O-Reel (song reels), 21–22
Sonovox, 150, 153
Sound department at Disney Studio, 153
Sound in cartoon films
  beginnings, 60–62
  Fantasound multispeaker sound system,
      150–152
  and film speed, 63
  Steamboat Willie, 61–62, 66–71
Sound recording studios, New York, 65
Sound techniques. *See also* Soundtracks

bar sheets, 62–63
bouncing balls technique for recording sound, 68
horizontal bar technique for recording sound, 73
phonograph recordings, 61
Sonovox, 150
Sound technology, 153
  Fantasound multispeaker sound system, 150–152
  multiphonic sound, 151
  stereophonic sound, 151, 152
  three-dimensional sound, 151
Soundtracks
  Cinephone sound system, 66
  Good Scouts, 115
  multiphonic sound, 151
  post-synchronization of, 65, 67–70, 73
  Vitaphone, 61
Space-age influence, *Stratos-Fear,* 108–109
Special effects. *See also* Rain effects; Sound technology
  Audio-Animatronics, 212–214
  The Birds, 202–207
  Cinderella, 174
  Davy Crockett and the River Pirates, 185
  distortion effects, 103, 138
  forced perspective effects, 196
  Johnny Tremain, 188–189
  King Kong, 159–160
  live action films effects teams, 175
  Mary Poppins, 210
  Melody Time, 172
  soap-bubble effect, 174
  storm effects, 188–189
Spence, Irv, 124
Spiders as animation subjects, 79
Spielberg, Steven, 154
Spite Flight (The Air Race), 106–108, 158
Split-screen technique, double exposing, 200
"Spoonful of Sugar" scene, *Mary Poppins,* 210, 211–212
Stalling, Carl
  arguments with Walt over scores, 73–74
  defection from Disney, 87
  Flip the Frog, 94–95
  The Gallopin' Gaucho, 65, 68
  joins Iwerks Studio, 94
  move to Warner Brothers, 117
  Plane Crazy, 65, 68
  presynchronized music, 73
  sabbatical from Iwerks Studio, 98, 132
  seasons subset to Silly Symphonies, 82–83
  Silly Symphonies, 74–79
  song reels, 21–22

Steamboat Willie, 64
Three Little Pigs, 98
  at Warner Brothers Studios, 139
Stanislavskian animation, 57–58
A Star Pitcher (Laugh-O-gram Films Lafflet), 19
"Steamboat Bill" (song), 63, 68
Steamboat Bill, Jr. (Buster, Keaton), 62
Steamboat Willie, 61–64, 66–71
  debut, 70
  dry run, 63
  recording sessions in New York, 65, 67–70
  reviews, 70, 72
  Walt sells Cabriolet to raise money for, 67–68
Stereophonic sound, 151
Stevenson, Robert Louis, 175
Stock market crash, 85
Stokowski, Leopold, 150–151
Stone mills for grinding paint pigment, purchase of, 48–49
Stop-motion animation
  Mary Poppins, 210, 212
  multiplane camera, 130
Stop-motion filming
  composite of matte and live-action elements, 175–176
  learning, 8, 25
  motor drive for, 8–9
  one-person process for, 8–9
  two-person process for, 8–9
Stop That Tank: The BOYS Anti-Tank Rifle, 156–157
Storm effects, 188–189
Storybook opening, Comicolor Classic series, 121
The Story of Robin Hood, 175
Straight-ahead style of drawing, 30, 56, 77
  The Skeleton Dance, 76
Stratos-Fear, 108–109
  telescope in, 113
Strike at Disney Studio, 151
"Sugar-coated educational stuff," 168
Sullivan, Pat, 11
Summer, 82–83, 89–90
  comparison, 172
Summertime, Comicolor Classic series, 133–134
Support of mother, 3, 5
  absence from original staff of Laugh-O-gram Films, 15
  move to California, 29
  move to rest home, 135
Surrealistic imagery, 108. *See also The Skeleton Dance*
  Balloonland, 131–132
Swanson, W. H., formation of Universal Film Manufacturing Company, 66

Swiss Federal Railway, 215
Switzerland, Mildred and Ub's trips to, 216
Swope Park, Kansas City, 3, 18–19
   Martha, Just a Plain Old-fashioned Name song
     reel, 21, 22
The Sword and the Rose, 175
The Sword in the Stone, 196
Symbolism in Iwerks Studio works, 131–132
Synchronized sound, 62–63
   Laemmle's predictions, 60

T

Tague, Lorey, at Laugh-O-gram Films, 15
Talking pictures. *See* Sound in cartoon films
Tashlin, Frank "Tish-Tash," 116
Tatum, Donn, 227
Teaching animation (Ub), 145, 146
Teaching medium, cartoons as, 156
Tebb, Mary, 117
Technical aspects of animation
   accuracy, 101
   distortion effects, 103, 138
   Ub's chance to explore, 105
Technical aspects of film, Ub's immersion in,
   111
Technical innovations. *See also* Color technology;
   Combination of live action with animation;
   Lightning-artist technique; Sound in car-
   toon films
   aerial photography, 158
   animation camera, smoother-operating drive
     on, 46
   Audio-Animatronics, 212–213
   automatic lamp changer, 223
   award for, 198
   bouncing balls technique for recording sound,
     68
   camera stand motor problems, 111–112
   celluloid density, 36
   Circarama, 186–187
   CircleVision, 199
   color-correction masking process, 198
   color in cartoons, 91–92
   color separation process, 176
   development of photographic processes, 135
   Disneyland theme park, 179
   distortion lens, 103, 138
   double exposing split-screen technique, 200
   double-headed optical printer (Optical Printer
     #2), 198
   electronic candles, 216
   film loop cabinets, 217–218
   horizontal bar technique for recording sound,
     68
   motor drive for stop-motion filming, 8–9

   multiphonic sound, 151
   multiplane camera, 130
   nodal-point perspective camera, 197
   paint formulas, 48–49
   palette of colors developed for Cinecolor, 114
   projection equipment at parks, 223
   scratches on film, removal of, 169–170
   stop-motion animation, 130
   three-editing-machine, 207
   traveling-matte process, 211
   Ub's focus on, 95
   wet-gate, 169–170
   Wright, Gilbert, 153
   Xerographic Developing Apparatus, 194
   xerographic process, application to animation,
     192–196
Technical workshop at Iwerks Studio (basement),
   101, 129–130
Technicolor
   exclusive agreement for three-color
     Technicolor process, 91, 121
   three-color Technicolor process, 91, 92, 121
   two-color Technicolor process (process #3), 92
Technicolor camera fitted with sodium prism, 183
Technological interests. *See also* Aviation;
   Mechanical representations, transforma-
   tions, and gags
   enthusiasm for and fascination with, 9
   Fantasound multispeaker sound system,
     150–152
   introduction to, 2–3
   Iwerks Studio purchases best production
     equipment possible, 95
Telescope in *Stratos-Fear,* 113
Television. *See* Walt Disney Television
Temple, Shirley, visit to Iwerks Studio, 115–116
Termite Terrace at Warner Brothers Studios, 139
Terraplane automobile, Turkisher's, 119
"Terraplane Blues," 119
Terry, Paul, *Aesop's Fables* cartoons, 48
Test screenings
   Seal Island, 169
   Steamboat Willie, 63
Thomas, Bob, *Walt Disney: An American
   Original,* 80
Thomas, Frank, 58
   Mary Poppins, 211
The Thousand and One Nights, 125
300 game in bowling (Ub), 181
360-degree film. *See also* Circarama;
   CircleVision debut, 186
The Three Caballeros, 160–162
Three-color Technicolor process (process #4),
   91, 92, 121
Three-dimensional (3D) films, 189–190

Three-dimensional perspective rendering, 56
Three-dimensional sound, 151
Three Little Pigs, 98, 132
Time transitions, 122–123
Timing sheets, 200
Titles, title cards and animation
    Martha, Just a Plain Old-fashioned Name song
      reel, 22
    Plane Crazy, 57
    The Silent Flyer, 41
    Willie Whopper, similarity to Looney Tunes,
      105
Toby Tyler, or Ten Weeks in the Circus, 207
Tommy Tucker's Tooth, 20
    sequel to, 41
Tomorrowland attractions at Disneyland, 217, 218
Tompson, Ruthie, 31–32, 148
Toombs, Leota, 215
Toonerville Trolley comic strip, similarity of
    Trolley Troubles, 45–46
A Tour of the West, 186–187
The Toy Parade, 130–131
Tracing, use in animation, 17, 30
    combination technique, 32–33
Training films. *See* Instructional films
Traveling matte composite cinematography
    Academy Award for, 212
    Mary Poppins, 211, 212
Travers, P. L., 209
Treasure Island, 175, 176
"Trees," 172
Triple-head Optical Printer (#10), 198
Trip to the Moon ride at Disneyland, 217, 218
Trolley Troubles, 45–46, 46–47
Troubleshooting and problem solving
    Toby Tyler, or Ten Weeks in the Circus, 207
    "Ub gags," 166–167
True-Life Adventures series
    color technology, 170–171
    creation of, 169–170
Tuberculosis, Roy Disney, 24
Turkisher, Art
    The Brave Tin Soldier, 127
    joins Iwerks Studio, 98
Terraplane automobile, 119
20,000 Leagues Under the Sea, 180
    publicity, 183–184
Two-color processes
    Cinecolor, 114
Technicolor process #3, 92
Two-person process for stop-motion filming, 8–9

U

Ubbe's Beach Story, 48
"Ub gags," 166–167

Ub Iwerks Studio, 86–146
    beginnings of, 85–89
    MGM contract, 96
    new studio space on Santa Monica Boulevard,
      Beverly Hills, 95
Union activity. *See* Organized labor
Union Bank Note Company of Kansas City,
    Ub's employment with, 3
Union-busting, 129
United Film Ad Service. *See* Kansas City Film
    Ad Service
Unity of design, Ub's sensitivity to, 69
Universal pictures. *See also* Oswald the Lucky
    Rabbit
    renegotiation of Oswald contract, 50
    taking Oswald from Mintz, 141
Up in Arms, 162
U.S. military
    commandeering of Disney Studios, 154
    film projectors, 217
U.S. Travel Service, 223–224

V

The Valiant Tailor, 18, 130
Valley Advertiser newspaper, 300 game in bowling
    (Ub), 181
Van Beuren's cartoons, 65. *See also Aesop's*
    Fables cartoons
Van Boring comic strips, 116
Van Dyke, Dick, 210
Van Roenkel, Sam, 50–51
Variety, review of *Steamboat Willie,* 72
Vertical multiplane camera, 148–149
Victor's "His Master's Voice," 66
Victory Through Air Power (De Seversky), 158
Video and Movie Guide (Maltin), 180
Vidor, King, process work for, 164–165
Violence in animation. *See* Animation cruelty
Vitaphone, 61
Viva Willie, 111
Vlahos, Pietro "Peter," 211
    Mary Poppins, 212
Vogan Candy, Oswald chocolate frappe bar, 50
Von Sternberg, Josef, 96

W

Walker, Card, 216
Wallace, Oliver, *Cinderella,* 174
Walliman, Otto, at Laugh-O-gram Films, 15
Walt Disney: An American Original (Thomas),
    80
Walt Disney Studio. *See also Alice's Wonderland*
    series; Oswald the Lucky Rabbit
    agreement releasing Ub from contract, 86
    Cinephone process, agreement for, 66

defection of staff to Charles Mintz Studio, 50

establishment of Disney Brothers' Cartoon Studios, 26

hiring of Friz Freleng, 44

migration of staff from Iwerks Studio, 116–117

name change to, 80

Optical Printing Department, 160

renegotiation of Oswald contract, 50

self-censorship, 97

signature logo, 80–81

Stalling's sabbatical from Iwerks Studio, 98

three-color Technicolor process, 91, 92, 121

Ub's return, 145–165

Walt Disney Television
 Goof Troop, 35
 The Goofy Movie, 35

Walt Disney World, 216
 Hall of Presidents, 225–226
 naming, 226
 PROJECT FLORIDA, 216

War cartoons, 155

Warner Brothers Studios
 cartoon films, 96
 Leon Schlesinger at, 41
 migration of staff from Iwerks Studio, 116–117
 politics at, 139–140
 subcontracting with Ub, 139

Watkin, Lawrence E., 89, 176
 on mutual respect between Ub and Walt, 201
 on relationship between Ub and Walt, 219

The Way Outs, 141

WDAF (radio station), 21

Webster, Dorothy
 courtship and marriage to Chuck Jones, 112
 increased responsibilities, 129
 joins Iwerks Studio, 95

WED Enterprises, 214–215

Weekend shifts in animation, 127–128

WEFT (Wings, Engines, Fuselage, Tail) technique of aircraft identification, 150–151

Wehe, Ed, 43

West, Mae, 96

Westinghouse Electric Company, 167

Westward Ho, the Wagons, 185

Wet Gate, invention of, 169–170

What a Life!, 100

What's Opera, Doc?, 140

Whitlock, Albert, 203

Who Killed Cock Robin?, 162, 202

"Who's Afraid of the Big, Bad Wolf?", 98

Wide-angle lens, anamorphic, 196

Wide-screen format, 196

Willie Whopper, 104–115
 The Air Race, 106–108, 158
 development of character, 108
 Good Scouts, 115
 Hell's Fire, 114, 115
 Insultin' the Sultan, 125
 Jane Withers, 109–110
 Play Ball, 108
 Spite Flight (The Air Race), 106–108, 158
 Stratos-Fear, 108–109
 Viva Willie, 111
 vocal characterization, 109–110

The Winged Scourge, 147

Winkler, George, 50

Winkler, Margaret J.
 Alice's Wonderland, 23, 26
 interest in feline character, 33
 marriage to Charlie Mintz, 27

Winkler Productions, signing contract with Universal, 42

The Wise Little Hen, 123

Wise Owl, 143

Withers, Jane
 Jack Frost, 132
 with Shirley Temple, 115–116
 Willie Whopper, 109–110, 115

Wolf, Berny, 116–117
 at Disney, 146
 Jack and the Beanstalk, 123
 Jack Frost, 132
 joins Iwerks Studio, 110

Wood, Lawson, 141

Woodblock effect, 74

The Woodland Potter (Laugh-O-gram Films Lafflet), 19

Work conditions in animation, 127–128

Work-for-hire
 Disney Studio, 41, 166–167
 Iwerks Studio, 138
 Laugh-O-gram Films, 18, 20

Work hours in animation, 127–128

Working conditions, noise, 119, 201

Working for Peanuts, 190

World's Fairs
 Brussels, 189
 Montreal Expo, 225
 New York, 212
 Paris, 186

Wright, Gilbert, 153

Writing story lines (Ub's), All Wet, 48

X

Xerographic Developing Apparatus, patent for, 194

Xerographic process for animation, 192–196

award for, 198
Bedknobs and Broomsticks, 223
Xerox Corporation
    patent assignment for Xerographic Fusing
        Apparatus, 194
    Ub's visit to, 192

Z

Zamora, Rudy, 125
    joins Iwerks Studio, 95
Zukor, Lou, 128
Zukor, Maury, 128